How to Survive Without a Salary

HOW TO SURVIVE WITHOUT A SALARY

BY CHARLES LONG

W

Warwick Publishing Group
Toronto   Los Angeles

© 1993 Charles Long (Revised Edition)

Published by the Warwick Publishing Group
Warwick Publishing Inc., 24 Mercer Street, Toronto, Ontario M5V 1H3
Warwick Publishing Inc., 1300 N. Alexandria, Los Angeles, California 90027

Artwork: Brenda Comeau-Watson
Cartoons: Canada Wide Feature Services Limited, Toronto

ISBN 1-895629-02-0

Distributed in the United States and Canada by:
Firefly Books
250 Sparks Avenue
Willowdale, Ontario M2H 2S4

Ninth Printing 1995

Printed and bound in Canada by Webcom

CONTENTS

Chapter Six: The Second-Hand Market 118

Chapter Seven: Auction Buying 140

Chapter Eight: Alternatives to Buying 160

Chapter Nine: Cheap Tips 181

Chapter Ten: Caesar's Due 195

Chapter Eleven: What Do You Do for a Living?
(and other difficult questions) 218

Preface to Previous Edition

Since the first publication of this book, in 1981, the economy has flip-flopped through a bewildering maze of changes. Inflation hit record heights early in the decade, fell in '83, rose steadily and now, in 1991, is falling again. Housing prices led the inflation roller coaster and interest rates followed. Stock markets soared in the mid-eighties and crashed in '88. Employment blossomed in some sectors and died in others, as employers reacted to recession and new world trade arrangements.

At the moment, the economy appears to be biting its nails, relieved at current low interest rates but worried about what might happen next. Whether we're poised at the brink of recovery or the brink of collapse is for soothsayers and politicians to argue about. All you and I can see for sure is that things will continue to change. There will be winners and losers as the economic maelstrom whirls on. And there will be a few of us — conservers — who steer around the whirlpool for quieter waters.

The question is whether — with the mainstream economy biting its nails — the conserver should now rethink the economic survival tactics that worked well enough ten years ago? Does the past decade have any new lessons for conservers? Will the decade to come bring any new dangers?

The one certainty, past and future, is change. Inflation rates, interest rates, and the rest will continue to rise and fall like the seasons. Forecasts of economic recovery or catastrophe speak to the size and frequency of those swings, not to any new economic state, permanent and unchangeable. There will be fat times and lean times. Those who survive the lean times best will be those who learn to prepare themselves in the fat times.

The original version of "Getting Ready" (Chapter 4) was prepared with a particular type of reader in mind — someone earning an ordinary income and getting ready to voluntarily do without. The tactics, however, are as valid for economic cycles as they are for personal cycles: getting free of unproductive debts, assembling the means for greater self-sufficiency, taking control of needs and learning to satisfy them in less costly ways. Whether you aim at a more independent lifestyle as a matter of personal choice, or as a possible necessity that looms with the next economic cycle, the means of preparing yourself remain the same.

Boom or bust, the pillar of most financial lives is debt. The line between good debts and bad debts may shift a little as interest rates shift, but the distinction between the two remains the same. A good debt is one that earns a profit — at least enough profit to pay the cost of the debt. A bad debt is borrowing for consumption. A good debt is an investment. A bad debt is a ball and chain that can turn life into a struggle, even for those who have big salaries.

Over the past ten years, in good times and bad, I have heard hundreds of ordinary people talk about their financial lives. With few exceptions, the first concern expressed is debt: how to get out of debt, or — for those who have been there — how good it feels to break the charge card habit and leave the shackles of consumer debt behind. The cost of consumer debt has dimensions that go beyond the shifting calculation of current rates. Consumer debt carries a psychological cost that remains high, no matter how low the interest rate might fall.

When interest rates fall, however, the good debts get even better. Investing in a house, for example, becomes much more attractive when mortgage rates fall. Low interest rates also affect the decision to rent things or buy them, shifting the balance in favour of buying. The same calculations and comparisons apply; it is just that the results are a little different in different economic times.

Of all the drifts that have been reshaping the larger economy over the past decade, none has been more dramatic than the changing nature of employment. Two trends are manifest. The first — the one that causes all the public anguish — is the overall level of unemployment, seemingly stuck at record levels even when other signs point to recovery. The second trend, individual obsolescence, is the more private anguish of having skills that are no longer needed in the marketplace.

One by one, or in the statistical aggregate, workers by now must realize that the North American economy is no longer a bustling assembly line. The factories have moved abroad to exploit lower wages and standards. At home, only one worker out of six still makes things. The other five process data, fry hamburgers, answer the phone, teach others, cut hair and sell things. Like it or not, this is no longer a manufacturing economy. This is an economy that processes information and provides services. Politicians can blame the high dollar, low productivity, free trade or each other. But there is no way to get the factory economy back without lowering wages and standards to Third World conditions. There is nothing inherently wrong with a service and information economy. Critics may argue that there are too many rotten, low-paying jobs in the service sector, but there were a lot of rotten, low-paying jobs in the old factory economy, too. What's hardest to swallow in the new job market is the fact that it changes so much faster than the old diploma-to-pension career at the nearest factory. The information sector changes as the technology changes, and the service sector changes as the population shifts. Either way, workers have to learn new skills or move much more often than they used to. And those who can't keep up swell the unemployment numbers. The forty-year career is dead. We can no longer expect to learn a job at twenty and retire from it at sixty.

And yet, just when job and skill mobility has become essential, the knee-jerk reaction is to cling even more tightly to the security of what we have in mind. *If I leave this job I may never find another/ better to hoard my seniority/ or push for import quotas on the competition and try to hang on until 65.*

Ironically, the prospect of unemployment seems to threaten even those who would like to be independent of regular employment. When other workers are fighting to hang onto any job, they confide, what prospects remain for earning a living without a regular job? Doesn't casual income (Chapter 5) dry up in times of high unemployment? And, worse, will it be possible to re-enter a regular job if I can't manage to make it on my own?

Happily, the conserver tactic of taking no more than we need from the wage economy works as well in hard times as it did when regular jobs were easier to find. Here's why:

First, workers are not the only ones to feel insecure in the midst of the job revolution. The employer, too, is faced with the need to re-tool, re-train and re-organize to keep up in a rapidly changing world. Obsolete skills are a burden for the employer just as they are a handicap for the employee. "Contracting out" has become a fact of life in the work place as employers attempt to meet their needs with workers who will not expect to hang around for forty years. The result? . . . . more and more opportunities for small-scale, short-term, freelance, casual work in the economy.

Secondly, a straight-line career is a cumbersome thing, hard to steer and slow to adjust to the rapid changes assaulting the job market. In contrast, those who take a more casual approach to income might have half a dozen irons in the fire at any one time. Much of that activity will be at the lower end of the pay scale, at the "apprentice" level, where learning on the job is acceptable. And the casual earner, unlike the careerist, remains flexible enough to chase any new opportunity that presents itself, and to abandon any course that threatens to become obsolete.

As I wrote in 1981, the key to security is not in holding on more tightly, or in trying to earn even more, but in learning to spend less. The fewer our material needs, the easier they are to satisfy. The further we live from the consumer economy, the less we have to worry about the vagaries of those economic cycles. Security doesn't come from having more but from needing less. The principle stands. When unemployment threatens, the conserver — who doesn't need the job — is secure. The consumer, in contrast, has to hang on for dear life and pray the job doesn't move to Mexico. The conserver is in control. The consumer is not.

A revised edition is rather like a second marriage. You are allowed to correct the mistakes you made the first time around, to say the things you wish you had said before. And sometimes, like this time, the world has changed in the meantime. The changes needed to bring this text up to date were surprisingly easy. We changed the inflation figures and some of the prices to reflect the current economic realities, we updated the tax and pension information, and we re-worked many of the examples. Although some of the numbers changed the conclusions were remarkably consistent. A conserver strategy is as sound today as it was ten years ago. For those who know how, life can get better even as times get tougher.

Finally, take some comfort from the fact that amidst all the bad news of the past decade, the good news is that the world has changed its opinion of conservers. You no longer have to hide this book from your respectable friends. When we first set out to reduce our needs, our friends and neighbors called us tightwads. When the me-first generation was at the height of the boom, buying BMW's on credit, we drove an old truck for cash and were called eccentrics. Now, just recently, somebody told me that ours was an "environmentally responsible lifestyle" and the whole world would soon have to learn to reduce, re-use and recycle. And all along I thought I was getting the furniture second-hand and ignoring auto fashion merely because I didn't want to work in somebody else's office for the rest of my life.

So there you have it. In a decade we've gone from being cheapskates, to eccentrics, to environmentalists, without changing one damned thing. Except, perhaps, our little bit of the world.

1

What's the Catch?

When I tell people that we live quite comfortably without a salary, the usual response is incredulity. "What's the catch?" friends ask, as they survey the standard array of children, pets, and balky appliances that signal a rather ordinary middle-class household.

The disbelievers might be more accepting if they found us living in the back seat of a '59 Ford, or subsisting on day-old bread and dandelion salad. An aristocratic sabre scar or ticket stubs from Bogota, left lying casually about, might lend other kinds of credence to our mysterious lifestyle.

The truth is more prosaic. There are no magic formulae or secret sugar daddies to milk. What we do have is a lifestyle - carefully planned and slowly built - that reduces our needs for cash to a level that we can easily meet with casual income.

In truth, there really is no catch. There are only many small steps taken over the years. While none of those steps, in themselves, are unique, the cumulative effect has been a dramatic change in the way we behave as consumers. Though our material lives are far from spartan, the way we define and satisfy our needs set us apart from the average North American consumer. WE ARE CONSERVERS.

Living without a salary is really a rather ordinary way to live. It may seem extraordinary to those whose norm is a forty-hour week, a boss, a mortgage, and a regular paycheck, but millions of very normal North Americans live without salaries. Businessmen, farmers, professionals, and entrepeneurs of every stripe live without a salary. This book is not for them.

This book is about the *Conserver Lifestyle*. Living without a salary is incidental, an end point, an objective for some, but by no means the answer for every harried middle-class consumer.

For many - worried about inflation, interest rates and energy costs - the conserver lifestyle is no more than a means of coping better with what they already have. The same techniques that have allowed us to live without a salary, have been just as useful to others in altering their economic lives so they can afford to buy a home, go back to school, or take a year or two to travel the world. This book is for them.

Businessmen, farmers, rock stars and others who have forsaken the forty-hour week, succeed or fail by their ability to apply a fairly standard set of techniques and rules for profitable enterprise. These include the saleability of the product, overhead, capital formation, cost controls and cash flow. The techniques and principles required for business success differ only in scale from the rules that should govern an ordinary household economy. For the conserver household, there is one more critical difference - *costs are more important than earnings*. Whether we speak of initial costs, maintenance costs, replacement costs, or whatever, there is nearly always more advantage in reducing costs than in increasing earnings. That is not always the case in modern business.

The corporate attitude to costs has a lot to do with the enormous scale and bureaucratization of business, with the separation between ownership and management. For the professional manager, size carries more prestige, and more salary, than any other index of performance. One of the more simplistic assumptions of economic analysis is that, in a capitalist economy, individual businesses will act to maximize the rate of return on investment(profit). In theory, controlling costs is just as important to that end as increasing sales. But ask a bottling executive if he would rather run the neighborhood soft drink plant returning a healthy 20%, or be president of Coca Cola with profits of 10%, or zero%. I'll wager he would rather run Coca Cola at a loss than manage a small town plant at any level of profit. Just as the aspiring rock star would rather be a bankrupt Beatle than work the beer halls for a steady $50,000 a year.

Of course modern business has an interest in profits, but the managers and bureaucrats that run them also have a stake in size and prestige that undercuts the profit motive and tends to make costs a less than equal partner in the planning equation. It amounts to keeping up with the Joneses on a giant scale. Like the suburbanite, proud of owning the most expensive car on the block, the modern businessman has more at the bottom line than the rate of return on investment.

That's not to say that growth for its own sake is necessarily bad for business. It would be akin to arguing that minimalist art is superior to Flemish realism. *It's really a matter of choice.* No less so in the household economy. Whether you want the biggest car on the block, the most efficient car, or the most efficient way of getting from A to B (even if it means taking the bus), it's really a matter of choice.

The point is that the conserver household can use techniques for decision making that are very similar to those used by business. The tools are no less valid if the motives and objectives are different. If the objective is to survive without a salary, or merely to put some fat back into the household budget, then the question of controlling costs is paramount. If the objective is growth, then the revenue side needs greater effort, and damn the costs.

The Joneses and the bureaucracies, government or corporate, have traditionally taken the "bigger is better" route, and damn the costs. *Conservers look at what it costs to be bigger, what it costs to consume more, and even what it costs to make a bigger income.*

Why make the distinction, though? Aren't income and outgo, costs and revenue, merely different sides of the very same coin? In the purest form of analysis, and if all costs are considered, income and expense are plus and minus of equal units. In theory. In practice it just ain't so.

A PENNY SAVED

I hate to argue with Ben Franklin, but in the twentieth century a penny saved is not a penny earned. Sorry, Ben, but a penny saved is a hell of a lot more than a penny earned today. Consider the simple example of a $1000 purchase: a holiday, a little furniture, or a replacement for the worn out fridge. Nothing unusual or extravagant, but it's more than the paycheque will cover. So put it on the charge card, right? If you pay it off in a year, at current retail credit rates, that new fridge will end up costing you $1185. Now, if you are in the 35% income tax bracket, you'll have to earn $1823

11

to buy that $1000 item. We could add the costs of earning the $1823, a portion of commuting costs, payroll deductions, union dues, and so on, but let's keep it simple this time and call it $1823.

Meanwhile, the cost conscious conserver found a quality used fridge or a "no name" holiday resort for half the price the Joneses paid. They pay cash (which is one of the reasons they got a better deal, but more on that later) and, to be fair, we'll add the foregone interest they might have earned by charging the item and leaving their cash in the bank. So the fridge, or whatever, will cost them $500 plus $35 in lost interest for a total of $535. If they are in the same 35% tax bracket, they'll have had to earn $823 to buy the item...which the Joneses had to earn $1823 in order to buy. A difference of $1000! So in this case, $500 saved is $1000 earned.

Moreover, if the conservers are really conscientious, they've either put those unused earnings to work in investments, or they've been able to cut back on their income from employment. If the unused earnings are invested, the difference between the conservers and the Joneses gets bigger by the rate of return on investment. Even by using a savings account at 6%, the conservers will double their advantage over the Joneses after 12 years. If they take the alternate route and cut back on earnings, rather than invest the unused earnings, they will drop into a lower tax bracket and will likely reduce at least some of the costs of working cited above. In either case, the difference in necessary earnings will almost certainly be greater than the basic $1000 calculated, and the difference will continue to grow over the years. And remember we started by saving only $500 on a very ordinary purchase.

What's the catch? There is none. There is only a change in emphasis. Having grown up in a era of cheap energy, stable prices and material expectations limited only by personal ambition, we of the post-depression generation were taught that the only route to satisfaction and success was to continually increase our earnings and consumption. The world has changed. The "Club of Rome", inflation, taxation, and some pretty basic arithmetic all tell us that today there is more to be gained, more easily, by reducing costs than by increasing income.

This book, then, is about two things: *saving money and earning casual income.* Of the two, saving money is by far the more important. In the first place, as we've seen, a penny saved is worth at least two or three earned. And secondly, North Americans - particularly those of this generation - know a great deal less about saving money than they do about earning it. It's part of the tradition. The only people who watched their pennies were those who had to. There's more pejorative venom in the word "cheap" than in the word "extravagant". A spendthrift can be admired, a miser cannot. We not only have a lot to learn about thrift, we must also be convinced that it's socially acceptable.

A PENNY EARNED

What about the other side, though? If we're all so inept at spending money and so adept at earning it, why waste words on casual income? I'll elaborate later but let me admit, at this point, to a minor case of semantic chicanery: *surviving without a salary is not the same as surviving without money.* Life without a salary is possible, socially acceptable, and can be accomplished with a surprising degree of comfort and satisfaction. Living without money can be none of these. In the sixties there was a popular myth among the granola set that anyone could take a roll of plastic sheeting and a Swiss army knife and go to live in the woods and cohabit with mother nature. Like the lilies of the field, they withered in the fall and are now selling insurance in the suburbs. It takes very little money to live, but it does take some.

If there is any apology due for including a section on income, it's to those readers, probably a majority, who have no desire or intention of leaving their careers. Their interests, quite legitimately, lie in making better use of what they already earn: to buy a home, to travel, or just to cope with rising prices. For them the making of casual income is probably superfluous. Their regular income, wisely spent, will likely stretch to cover all their needs.

For those who are serious about an alternate lifestyle without a regular job, it is virtually impossible to escape the need for some regular source of cash. However, earning casual income is at once more difficult and more simple than most careerists imagine. The difficult part was described by Will Rogers when he said, "There's nothing dumber than an educated man, once you get him off the thing he's educated in". We've swallowed our own propaganda about specialization of skills to the point where many otherwise intelligent people doubt their ability to take on the simplest task without a degree, a night course, or a learned consultant to unveil the mumbo-jumbo and nonexistant mysteries. That's the difficult part, convincing highly trained people that they have other saleable skills and personal assets besides *the thing they're educated in.*

The easy part of generating casual income lies in the enormous range of possibilities that exist for casual employment, part-time self employment, and simple fortuitous enterprise. There's a market for just about anything you feel like doing. But there is a catch; the more highly organized your enterprise gets, or more profitable, the faster the market contracts. There is wider scope for tiny business than for bigger business.

It's the casual nickel and dime stuff, the once-a-week-if-I-feel-like-it jobs that are easiest to start and stop, and that provide the freedom only dreamed about by desk bound nine-to-fivers. You may never get rich being a dilettante in the market place, but most of the time it feels like being rich. If your needs are simple, it can be more than enough.

CAN ANYBODY DO IT?

How easy is it? Can anyone survive without a salary? When visitors ask me those questions, I assume they are really asking "could *I* do it?", and I tailor the answer to the questioner. I used to think that just about everyone could, provided they were prepared to work hard and prepare themselves thoroughly. The human race, after all, is a good deal older than the forty-hour week and superannuated security. The humblest citizen of ancient Rome took far more holidays than the cushiest union contract in today's industrial world can provide, but then they didn't have automobiles and color TV's to support. Poor, hungry, illiterate peasants in the harshest parts of today's third world, build and occupy homes of their own, an impossible dream for many young middle class families awash in North American affluence. But those peasant homes don't have the requisite plumbing and wall-to-wall carpets that dissatisfied North Americans expect.

It was, I have often thought, entirely a matter of making the choices. Conscious choices, deliberately calculated, like the economists' models we studied in school; so many guns or so much butter. Each of us could choose...two hour's leisure or the electric knife, a bigger car or another bedroom, a condominium in Florida or an earlier retirement in the back yard. Every choice, every wish, was theoretically possible as long as the equation balanced. If there could be a sacrifice of equivalent value in another part of our lives, any goal could be achieved, any dream come true. My mother told me if I practiced hard enough and long enough I might some day play second base for the Cincinnati Reds. Being twelve, I chose to spend the requisite hours talking to girls instead; but, as far as I was concerned at the time, it was a deliberate and calculated choice. There were risks involved in either course; I might spend the hours practicing baseball and still not find the talent to get off the bench of the farm league duffers, but then there was an equal chance I could spend all that time with the girls and not get to second base with any of them either.

How real is that freedom, though? Can we still make choices about our lives or are there more illusions of freedom than practical opportunities? I can't put the question any more graphically than the lady who told me recently that all she wanted out of life was a vegetable garden and the time to work at her pottery. She was a career administrator, stuck in a middle-aged rut. "Is it all just a romantic dream?" she asked, with a poignant touch of quiet desperation. For her, I'm sure, the will and resources to realize her dreams are there. The hardest part will be climbing out of the rut itself. She will probably find life on the "outside" suprisingly easy. The question, though, is central to everyone making such a decision. *Is freedom from the nine-to-five just a romantic dream?*

I answered the lady somewhat equivocally by saying that it depended mostly on her own attitudes and expectations. A bucolic life of crafts and garden was remote from her own experience, and yet something she valued highly. In that sense it was romantic. But that didn't make it unattainable or unrealistic. If she had the skills and resources, or was willing to sacrifice more time to get them, then the dream was certainly obtainable. The critical question was whether she could make the dream work in real life, and moreover, find the satisfaction in it that she was looking for. If the dream was all sunshine and flowers, would the rainy days and inevitable weeds spoil it for her? Could her amateur artist's ego stand up to a few initial rebuffs in the marketplace? Would her will power and sense of humour be able to survive the compromises, disappointments, and setbacks that distinguish real life from dreams? In the end we agreed that, yes, it was a romantic dream, but that didn't mean that - with a few warts and weeds - it couldn't also become a reality. It really depended what she was made of.

The ways in which dreams come true or crash on the rocky shoals of reality are as timeless as the dreams themselves.

Harrowsmith magazine ran a feature not long ago which asked the question 'Why Homesteaders Fail'. The case histories of unreal expectations, inevitable disappointments and occasional success made a remarkable parallel with the first homesteaders who settled Upper Canada 150 years before. Susanna Moodie and Catherine Parr Traill were sisters who settled in an area north of Peterborough, Ontario in the 1830's. Their backgrounds were the same of course; English gentility, more or less forced by financial circumstances to try a new life in the colonies. They were neighbors in the new land. Both women faced similar hardships; the bitter cold, unaccustomed labors, crude facilities, and unfamiliar social mores. The list will be familiar to any modern "back to the lander". They both had dreams. They dreamed of land and vast estates and an escape from the strictures of an empty purse in a genteel hand. And there were warts such as dishonest land agents, uncooperative neighbors, sickness, and even a rebellion that drew the men into the militia and left the women to cope alone.

The problems and circumstances are well known to the most casual reader of history. Especially instructive in this case, however, are the attitudes of these two women and the effect that had on the success of each in adapting to her new circumstances.

Susanna Moodie pined always for English comforts. She was resourceful enough to make coffee from dandelions, and hardworking enough when necessity demanded it, but the hardships engendered more bitterness than cheerful accomodation. In the end she wrote: "If these sketches should prove the means of deterring one family from sinking their property, and shipwrecking all their hopes, by going to reside in the backwoods of Canada, I shall consider myself amply repaid for revealing the secrets of the prison house, and feel that I have not toiled and suffered in the wilderness in vain."

Her younger sister, Mrs. Traill, faced the same hardships with a more cheerful determination. Obstacles, to her, were challenges, not defeats, and she adapted and thrived until she died at the age of 97, a mother of nine, a respected botanist, and widely published author. In her introduction to "The Canadian Settler's Guide" she wrote: "In Canada persevering energy and industry, with sobriety, will overcome all obstacles, and in time will place the very poorest family in a position of substantial comfort...To the indolent or to the intemperate man Canada offers no such promise...He has not the elements of success within him. Canada is not the land for the idle sensualist. He must forsake the error of his ways at once, or he will sink into ruin here as he would have done had he stayed in the old country." The warning could have been aimed at her sister. It applies as well to today's refugees from urban pressure. Some will make it and there are some who won't. And to bring this ramble back to the original question, it's not always a matter of choice. Some, in Mrs. Traill's words, just don't have the elements of success within them.

Nor is it always talent, spiritual or temporal, barring the way to personal choices. I, for example, am already too old to ever make it in the major leagues...even if I never talk to a girl again. And the only time I ever tried to chew tobacco I threw up. It's a dream that I'm no longer free to choose. *The fact is, there are many people who will never be able to survive without a salary.*

Happily, there are many half-way measures on the way to a conserver lifestyle that provide the advantages without the risks of actually telling the boss what you think of him. In other words, not everyone is able or willing to declare economic independence, but everyone can apply at least some of its lessons to get more out of the money they work so hard to earn.

Nor should the city dweller feel that he has to move to the country to gain his independence. Life in the country, indeed, has many advantages. Food, housing, heat and many other necessities can be obtained more cheaply or even free in the countryside. But the urbanite has access to cheaper electricity, telephones, transportation, entertainment and cultural facilities. *This is not a back to the land book.*

What does it really take, though, to go all the way to economic self-sufficiency? How difficult is it? It's pointless, of course, to talk about dollars and cents. That depends on how elaborate your needs are. If you're hooked on T-bones, Gucci's, and Club Med holidays you may never be able to kiss your paycheck goodbye.

As a starting point, I suggest that most people who are serious about surviving sans salary should begin with the acceptance of four basic premises:

1. The key is to control expenditures.

2. No matter how low your cost of living, you will require some form of income.

3. Some time will be required to prepare yourself. Lifestyle changes don't happen overnight like a New Year's resolution.

4. Welfare, charity, or indulgent rich uncles may help some people survive without jobs, but they are still forms of dependence. Some people need them, just as some people will always need careers. But this book is about independence and self-sufficiency, not swapping one form of servility for another. Ask those who have to survive on welfare. Most would find more satisfaction in the meanest of jobs.

By now it should be clear that I don't have any magic formulae for retirement to easy street. If you're looking for miracles buy a lottery ticket. Reality takes a lot more hard work and preparation. *But it can be done.* And it can be enormously satisfying. If you are prepared to work at it, and if you can manage some self-confidence, flexibility, patience, and a touch of self-indulgence, then you're already equipped with most of what it takes to escape from any rut.

HARD WORK

Leaving the drudgery of nine-to-five means less work and more leisure, right? Wrong! If you believe in the dynamics of capitalism it won't take much to convince you that most people are already working at the most highly remunerative task they can do. Or, if you believe in the Peter Principle, you will know that most workers are already employed at the most highly paid job they can't do. In either case, be aware that the job you've been doing for the last ten or thirty years probably returns more dollars and cents per hour of your time than you'll be worth at just about anything else.

Let me illustrate with hypothetical neighbors, a plumber and a gardener. The plumber, who usually gets $120 a day for his skills, decides that food is getting too expensive. So during a twenty week growing season, he spends one day a week tending a big backyard garden. He keeps careful records and by October figures he has produced fruits and vegetables that would have cost $1000 at the supermarket. He's thrilled...until his wife points out that if he had spent his days off plumbing instead of fooling around in the back yard, he could have earned $2400! He would have to work more than twice as hard at gardening than he ever did at plumbing in order to come out even on an hourly basis.

His neighbor is a gardener who makes a mere $40 a day at his trade. When his plumbing springs a leak he panics at the potential expense and decides to do it himself. After three days of shopping for supplies, dismantling the pipes, consulting the do-it-yourself manual, and putting it back together twice, he proudly shows the finished work to his neighbor. "That's a terrific job", says the professional plumber, "you probably saved yourself a sixty dollar service call." Of course he could have made twice that much by spending the three days gardening.

Obviously, the example is oversimplified. By the time the plumber paid taxes, union dues, transportation expenses, and wrote off a few unpaid bills, his $2400 for plumbing on his days off would have shrunk considerably. And the next time the gardener's pipes begin to leak he'll doubtless know how to do it faster and with fewer mistakes.

Nor does this example explore the non-monetary considerations. The plumber's homegrown veggies will taste better to him than anything he could buy at the supermarket. When the gardener's toilet erupts some Sunday (like toothaches, these things never happen during office hours) he may rue the time and work involved, but if he can do it himself at least he won't lose a night's sleep over what the bill might be.

Finally, most humans are far too complex and clever to be satisfied with the exercise of a single task, a single skill, or a single career - to the exclusion of everything else. Few plumbers could stand to spend every waking hour at the trade, no matter how much we offered to pay them. It's no less true for brain surgeons, civil servants or gardeners. Economists tell us that workers, like nations, can maximize their incomes by specializing in the things they do best, and buying or trading with other specialists to obtain their other needs. But common sense tells us that for sanity's sake, if not for profit, it behooves us to perform other, less highly paid tasks as well. Even economists shave themselves, drive their own cars, and some even mow their own lawns. In theory they should hire others to perform those tasks and spend their time instead doing whatever it is that economists do.

In practice, everyone performs some unprofitable tasks. To the extent we spend our valuable time on work that someone else could do faster or cheaper, then we're earning less than our maximum income potential or working harder than we must to obtain the same result. This is true for the economist who mows his lawn or the administrator who would rather make pottery. Those who are planning early retirement, a year or two off, or just cutting back on overtime will almost certainly have to spend less or work even harder at something else to maintain the regular income.

That's the bad news. The good news is that it doesn't have to feel like work. Spending that hour in a backyard garden can be a pleasure, even if it is an inefficient way for a plumber to spend his time. Likewise, if he'd spent his whole week gardening, the forty-first hour in the garden would certainly revert to "work".

The good news is that many of us happily choose to work twice as hard at the things we enjoy as we do at the things that pay the most. Paul Gauguin was a successful stockbroker in Paris. When he chucked it all to paint in Tahiti he took a drastic cut in the hourly returns for his time. From comfortable urban affluence, he was reduced to cadging credit from the island's Chinese grocer. From the economist's point of view it was a hard way to make a living. But Gauguin didn't seem to mind, and the world is certainly a richer place for his colors than it ever was for his stockbroking.

Make no mistake about it, though, surviving outside the normal economic modes of a nine-to-five career takes a load of hard work. You may enjoy it more, you may consider it more worthwhile, but don't expect the world to make you richer for your greater efforts, and don't expect to have forty extra hours of free time on your hands.

Cincinnatus was ploughing his fields when he was called to Rome to become dictator of all the empire. When the campaign was won he resigned his lofty post and went happily back to his ploughing. His accountant was no doubt aghast at his folly, and we can only speculate on the entreaties of his advisors: "just hang on one more year as dictator and you can buy the biggest farm in the Roman Empire; you've got a career ahead of you here, don't throw it all away on a whim; you're a good emperor, farmers are a dime a dozen; maybe it's just the male menopause, take a holiday and then decide." But Cincinnatus went back to the farm, the

Senate found another Caesar, and the Romans honored him above other, more ambitious leaders. For all that honor and satisfaction, though, the fact remains that ploughing is harder work for the money than being emperor.

Whatever your job, if your needs are as great as your paycheque, giving it up will likely mean working harder, not less.

CONFIDENCE

Alternative lifestyles, like everything else, are only possible if you believe they're possible. Surviving without a salary means a lot of doing without, doing it yourself, or doing something else for money. All that *doing* means that much of the time you'll be doing things you've never done before. And there won't be time or money to take a night course in it or hire someone else who has done it before. At times the only resource you'll have is yourself, and if you don't believe that's enough, it won't be.

It's here that modern, Western man is at his greatest disadvantage. We've spent generations listening to economists preach specialization. In a sense they were right. Western capitalist society is a showcase of material well-being. Our psyches may not be in such great shape, but we're up to our Vic Tannied tushies in all the things that other people can make for us. Most of us, in turn, have been trained to make or do just one thing for the rest of the economy. We do it extremely well, but by and large that's all we do.

It's the poor people from places where the goodies are not so abundant who have been led, by necessity, to learn and retain a wider variety of survival skills. Peasant farmers can build a house, repair a plough, butcher meat, make a cart, select and store the seed, and so on. Our modern farmers pay specialists to do all those things. Primitive tribeswomen learn to grow food, preserve it and prepare it. They deliver babies, make cloth, tan hides and pull teeth...without a degree in any of those things. Highly organized western man can doubtless do all of those tasks to a higher standard. Perhaps we can do them more efficiently. But, individually, most of us would find more than a few of those simple everyday tasks overwhelming. Don't believe me? Give your wife a cotton plant and tell her you need a shirt. Better still - try it yourself.

Walk into MacDonalds with a live cow and a bushel of wheat and ask them to whip up some hamburgers. Every last kid behind the counter would know that the flesh of the cow has to be cut and minced, and that the wheat must be ground, risen and baked, but I'll bet that not one of them would have the confidence to try it. That's what we have packing houses, butchers, millers and bakers for. The processes are complex, skilled and highly regulated. Or is it just that we've organized the processes into such highly specialized tasks that we've lost touch with the real and basic simplicity of the thing?

I once corresponded with a highly educated man, a psychologist, an academic. He told me that he had a piece of property covered with beautiful stone, and that he wanted to build a stone house. He enjoyed working with his hands, but wanted experts to build the house because the skills, he thought, were beyond his capacity. Design stress, load factors, bearing walls and whatchamacallits were highly technical engineering problems. He was a simple Phd. I advised him to try it anyway, just for fun and the pleasure of working with stone. I tried to assure him that stone walls stayed up because the law of gravity kept them there, not because a computer model pronounced them sound. He demurred and went to Mexico instead. He returned with his enthusiasm for stone renewed. "Illiterate, untrained peasants are building stone walls everywhere," he wrote. "Maybe it's simpler than I thought!"

The psychologist might have understood had I reminded him that salesmen, seducers, and mothers of little children have practiced psychology since long before there was a word for it. His Phd is merely for understanding what they have done intuitively, and perhaps for explaining it or practicing it in a slightly more sophisticated way. But that doesn't mean that the seducer needs a diploma on the wall to influence another's behavior; and mothers don't need a Phd to offer lollipops at the proper time; and psychologists don't need engineering tables to put one stone on top another and call the result a wall. Any peasant can build a wall. All the engineer can do is explain why it did, or did not, fall. I hope someday he finds the confidence to put one stone atop another and trust that it will stay there; or have the courage to try again if, by some mystery, it falls.

If confidence is essential for the do-it-yourselfer, it's downright critical when it comes to doing-it-for-money. Most of us are mildly schizophrenic about our skills. There are one or two things for which we have a license or a union card (our standard vocation), and then there are other things at which we may be equally skilled but have only practiced for our own amusement (our avocations). We charge as much as the market will bear for our vocational skills, and still feel underpaid. But we give away the product of our avocations almost apologetically. At our daughter's birthday party, a little friend arrived with a beautiful hand made present - an intricately braided belt. Her mother was embarrassed. "I'm terribly sorry," she explained, "but there just wasn't time to get to the store." Without reservation, it was the nicest present at the party.

I have often suggested to people that they could supplement their incomes by selling crafts or hobby skills. The usual reaction is modest demurral: "Oh, I'm not good enough for that"; or "anybody can do this...why would they pay for it?"; or "I'm no good at selling things." And yet they may work at jobs which almost anybody could do, and sell their services there with great effectiveness. They believe in their jobs, but they don't accept their avocations with the same degree of confidence. It's too enjoyable to be work, and it (the hobby) is too easy to have value in the marketplace; but, most of all, is it good enough to be worth money to other people?

In many cases avocations may not be worth a whit in the marketplace. *But there is only one way to find out. Without the confidence to try...and try again...you had better have an income that doesn't need to be supplemented.*

FLEXIBILITY

If there is a single thread that runs through most efforts to reduce the need for cash, it is flexibility. An adaptable, inventive approach to life and its problems allows us to substitute cheaper resources for dearer ones, and find simpler answers and less expensive sources to satisfy needs. It's the ability to solve problems, often in unconventional ways.

Our chickens had a problem one year with foxes. Depredations on the flock were even more severe than those threatened by the lady of the house every time she found them pecking in the spinach patch. It became imperative to fence them in, or fence the foxes and the mistress out. The universal solution is chicken wire. Fencing a yard thirty feet square takes a small fortune just for the mesh, however. Appalled at the expense, we began to look for alternatives. A board fence was functional, but the cheapest lumber around at the time was random, rough-sawn cedar picked up at the mill for thirty cents a board foot - or $180 for a fence five feet high. In the end, for a mere $20, the saw mill delivered an enormous load of slab waste. From it we selected the requisite 600 board feet of solid lumber (good on three sides, bark on the fourth) and cut the rest into three full cords of firewood. The fence is more durable than the mesh at a fraction of the price, and the free firewood will boil maple sap for the next few years. We boil sap in a large, stainless-steel pan that a sharp-eyed friend salvaged from the garbage of a company that saw the expensive pan only as a used "hot oil bath". The fire is built in an arch of discarded chimney brick, and the heavy pan slides neatly back and forth in a steel frame that someone threw away as a bed.

More on such substitutions later. For now I only want to illustrate that the most common solution to any problem is often the most expensive one as well. The commercial economy provides a ready answer to meet any need. The economy expects you to go out and buy the patent answers to your problems. You, on the other hand, have to be flexible enough to dodge through and around that network of ready-made solutions if you want to keep your money for more important things. *A wise consumer learns where he can buy the cheapest chicken wire or get the best deal on a syrup evaporator. The conserver goes one step farther and learns to do without, adapt alternatives, or invent his own solutions.*

Not that long ago, and even today in some parts of the country, mention of this kind of flexibility as a separate quality would have seemed redundant. It was a way of life. Stale bread became bird food and turkey stuffing. If you didn't have a cellar shelf, a packing crate would do as well. Our short, sweet taste of material abundance seems to have spoiled all that. Today we throw the stale bread away and drive to the store for commercial bird feed and pre-packaged stuffing mix. When's the last time you saw a kid on a cart built from a crate and a mismatched set of lawnmower wheels?

The "good old days" weren't all that terrific, but people did have the personal qualities to cope with the difficulties. One of those qualities was a healthy skepticism towards the marketplace. Few of our mothers could have been hoodwinked into believing that packaged breadcrumbs were any better than the ones from the bottom of the drawer. The idea of selling freezers to eskimos used to be a joke. Now supermarkets sell pre-packaged ice cubes in the depths of the winter and it doesn't even raise a chuckle.

If the doomsayers are right and we do have hard times ahead again, we may all be forced by circumstance to forgo our extravagances. We may all have to revert to solving needs with what we have around us instead of running to the marketplace to apply the balms that advertisers say we need. I hope that we can regain the flexibility that requires.

Some of us, though, are choosing *hard times* now; tightening belts to buy a house, paint nudes in Tahiti, or just take a year off to write the novel. For us, choosing alternatives and adapting them to needs is not like the grim regimen of real poverty. It's a challenge, a game of Monopoly between us and the commercial lords of Boardwalk and Parkplace. We're looking for shortcuts around the high rent district for reasons of our own. In one sense that makes it harder. If we were really poor we would not have any choice. We would be excluded from the fat and baubles of the marketplace automatically, without the option of dropping back in from time to time. Having the high-priced options all around us makes it even more difficult to find and adapt to cheaper alternatives. It's easier to think of the ready solutions dangled before us by advertisers and accepted so unquestionly by our peers. It's harder to see choices that would be obvious to a poor man or a poor society.

We once had a small city garden that the neighborhood children treated as a roadway, a shortcut from the alley on which it bordered to the busy street in front of the house. Nothing grew but the gum wrappers and litter of the junior parade. We tried everything; earnest pleas, threats of mayhem, laying in wait with the garden hose. We even tried partial surrender - a flagstone path so the little lemmings could keep the short cut but stay off the blankety-blank plants. They trampled everything but the path. We put up a wire fence - they climbed it. We put up a board fence -they vaulted it. Fellow sufferers across the alley escalated their defenses to a high, chain-link fence with steel posts set in concrete. That seemed to work, and I was almost tempted to raid the savings and buy the deluxe solution myself. With that in mind, we renewed our interest in the garden and brought in a big juicy truckload of rotten, wet manure. Took it right up the alley and dumped it over the board fence in a long, waist-high pile at the edge of the would be garden. Bright and early in the morning the thunder of little sneakers came pounding up the alley, vaulted the fence, and planted themselves up to the knees in what only they could describe so colorfully...at full volume. By the end of the summer, the expensive fence across the alley was breached once more, and our fertile little patch was still untrodden. That was a cheap alternative that we stumbled onto, so to speak, rather than chose. Nevertheless, it taught me a lesson about inventive solutions that neither I nor those kids will ever forget.

We don't often see the corporate world being that flexible, but one classic example comes to mind. My first year as an undergraduate saw the completion of an extensive campus rebuilding program. After several years of mud and disruption, the college finished in grand style with a lavish icing of outdoor lights, lush sod, and winding concrete paths. Within a year there were muddy ruts and impromptu paths all over the sod, and the concrete walks were hardly touched. The landscapers tore up the useless paving, resodded the entire area, and waited. Two months later they came back. This time they paved only the functional paths the students were making across the lawns from building to building. Planning is important, but being flexible enough to recognize and accept the shortcuts pays as much in the long run.

PATIENCE

Not everybody can live without a regular paycheck. Even fewer can afford to walk away from a job when the mood first strikes them. Unless you're the only heir of an ailing Granny, there's comfort in knowing your lifestyle is pretty well self-sufficient *before* you ask the boss where he keeps his brains. Patience. Self-sufficiency takes some preparation.

Patience is also a virtue when it comes to the somewhat erratic shopping habits that are part of living on less. As you'll see in Chapter Three, regular weekly shopping - buying as the need arises - is the working man's way to spend his pay. Rich folks and conservers buy things only when the price is right. You can buy in bulk, ahead of time, or at sales, in anticipation of a need. More often, the need arises first. Then you put it off and put it off until the whatsits are being sold at half-price for clearance, or you happen to find one on the rummage table. My wife accuses me of elevating lowly procrastination to economic theory, but from whatever vice it springs, biding your time is the essential part of bargain hunting.

A TOUCH OF SELF INDULGENCE

Having listed *hard work, confidence, flexibility and patience* as the essential personal qualities it takes to survive sans salary, I've already scared off the vicarious Walter Mitty's of the would-be drop-out set. Lest serious readers start to worry that this is becoming the Dale Carnegie course for abstemious lifestyles and voluntary underachievers, let me add that luxury, too, has an important place in the conserver household.

Real poverty is not a laughing matter. It's destructive, depressing and self-perpetuating. It's an economic state. It's also a state of mind. It's not the same as living cheaply.

Our little family lives quite happily and comfortably on a great deal less cash than the same sized family would get on welfare. We aren't poor. We don't feel poor and we don't live poorly. We have few of the material things that really poor people around us take for granted. No cable TV, instant foods, or fashionable clothes. Even if we wanted to, we couldn't afford to smoke. On the other hand, we enjoy drinking wine with meals, eat the finest of foods, and travel abroad more frequently than most. They are modest indulgences, but in our lifestyle they are vital.

The problem is that penny pinching gets to be a habit. Fortunately, we enjoy the simple life and have never felt deprived for want of snowmobiles, fitted carpets and expensive toys. There are times, though, when I must admit that we are sorely tempted to blow the budget. There are times when the rusty old Ford balks and we think how nice it would be to push it over a cliff and buy a zippy new sedan that always starts. There are times when winter begins to drag and we feel a little envy for folks who can book the first available flight for Nassau and to hell with waiting for the charter deal. Oh yes, there are times. But almost always the old habits prevail, and we keep our spending to careful limits.

It's times like that when we need a pressure valve. Without some release, the constant discipline on money matters would begin to feel rigid and mean - more like a dreary trap than a means of freedom and independence. In a word, we would feel poor.

That's when we throw another log on the grate, open a bottle of the best wild grape, and sit down to a juicy roast of loin or brace of squab. Candle light, a little music and a crackling fire. By the end of the evening we're back to feeling grateful that the clunky old Ford can be patched again and there's at least another week of skiing left before the sap begins to run. By the end of such an evening we can feel richer than any Vanderbilt cruising Bermuda in the Bentley.

It seems to work with the children too. My daughter would like to wear the brand name jeans her classmates sport, but knows that most of them could not afford the trips to London or Andros that she has enjoyed. The boy of the family wants the $80 skates that seem to be *de rigeur* on the hockey rinks, but visiting friends envy his tree house and handy swimming hole. As long as they have a few juvenile "luxuries" to compensate for the sacrifices, they will never feel poor. Of course, if they really had their way I'd go back to work and buy them *all* the things they think they need. Fortunately, for me, they haven't discovered democracy yet.

I wouldn't advocate that anybody blow the budget on the whim of luxury. Our own little indulgences are, after all, mostly free. Giving yourself the afternoon off to sit in the shade with a glass of grape tended only by Pan is hardly going to break the bank; but it *feels* so damned good that you can't possibly miss the double breasted suit and three-martini lunch that you can no longer afford.

CHOICES

What, then, is the catch? The qualities I've described above could be a prescription for success in any endeavor. *There is no catch.* It's as straightforward as becoming Minister of Finance, President of Coca Cola, or the best darn second baseman in Cincinnati. There's no easy formula for the good life outside the confines of regular employment...just as there's no easy formula for success within that world. It boils down to what's within you, and also what choices you make. How much money you spend, and how and where you earn it are the choices.

I suspect that the reason a life like ours arouses incredulity is that many people are so accustomed to letting society and the advertisers make the important choices for them that they no longer see them as choices. The greatest joy I find in teaching people how to retire is the dawning of awareness on ordinary faces as they begin to see choices that they never realized were theirs - even if the choices are little ones, mundane ones, nickels and dimes. A young man marvelled as he realized that being a one car family instead of a two car family would make them richer by $4000 a year. He was an educated man. He had simply never added up the cost and made a conscious choice before. A lady who needed cutlery found it at a tiny fraction of what she otherwise would have paid at the department store. A tight household budget expanded before her eyes as she began to see the unadvertised alternatives. A hobbyist who spends hundreds every year on cameras and equipment chose to keep his interest up, but suddenly saw it as an investment that could bring profits as well as expenses. *Choices.* Choices that most of us have and few of us realize. Choices that not everyone would wish to make, but choices that should at least be consciously considered and not made simply because that's the way the Joneses do it.

Individuals have different needs, different assets, and different skills. If they then behave in a common way, that really is too bad. Thoreau said he was not out of step with other men, he simply heard the beat of a different drummer. I trust that those independent souls, sufficiently attuned to different drummers that they would contemplate breaking the nine-to-five norm, will understand when I say that the techniques and sources discussed in this book are not meant to be applied in every situation, like a recipe. It is, rather, a menu from which the reader might pick and choose ideas suitable for his own needs or useful to his own ambitions.

That's enough of generalizations for now, however. Surviving without a salary raises some practical problems which must be solved. The following chapters raise those problems and suggest some practical approaches to solving them. That's what we're here for, so let's begin...

2

Assessing Yourself (Making a Budget)

Surviving without a salary is by and large a financial endeavour. Oh, there are countless physical problems, aesthetic rewards, and maybe even some spiritual moments, but at the end of every month it's clear that the essence of the exercise - the foundation - is finance. You either have it or you don't, and the beauty of the sunset, for all its incalculable value, won't begin to pay the utility bills.

The starting point for every financial plan is a budget. The declaration of financial independence is no different. And ironically, making plans to live on less requires a more carefully wrought budget than the big-money plans of the rich. High finance can afford to be sloppy. The less you have, the more carefully you have to count it.

I have to admit right here that, essential or not, making a budget is a dreadful bore. It really isn't fair. One of the fundamental reasons we left careers was a yawning indifference to money and the things it buys. Our ambitions had nothing to do with dollars. This then is the drop-out's catch 22. Those who like money enough to spend their time earning it don't need to bother with budgets and the like. On the other hand, those of us so indifferent to money that we leave our jobs must spend a great deal more time planning our more miniscule financial affairs. *Boring!* But you can't have your dessert until you eat your spinach, so let's get budgets out of the way first and save the good stuff until later.

WHAT'S A BUDGET?

A budget is an estimate of income and expenses. A financial plan of what you'll have and what you'll need in the coming year. If you work at a regular job, the income side of the estimates will be a piece of cake. The expenditure side will take a little more effort. For most of us mortals, trying to remember where our money went last year is tough enough to do in any useful detail. To figure out where it's going *next year* means an evening of sweat and guess and at least one spat with your mate. It's particularly hard on reformed smokers. Chew an eraser and persevere. Next year you'll be glad you did.

It's next year that the other role of budgeting comes into the fore. If a budget were only an estimate of what will happen to the family finances in the year to come, it would have no more value than any other type of forecast. Tarot cards or the bumps on your head might tell you as much about what the future holds. Knowing your economic future might cure a few sleepless nights (or create a few), but it won't help you do anything about it unless you also use the budget as a control mechanism.

WHY BOTHER?

Most of the time I can assess my economic health by counting the change in my pocket, and I automatically know the answer to any question beginning with "Do you think we can afford...?". Yes, a budget is a big pain in the old wazoo, but it really is worth the effort...for three big reasons:

First of all, a budget helps to identify and solve problems before they happen. It's no guarantee against unexpected bills and other nasty surprises, but it does give you a way to make provision ahead of time for things that might go wrong. Even when things go right, most of us have times of the year when cash gets short and other times when it looks as if there's some fat in the wallet. If we're lucky, the fat and the lean balance out over the year and we come out even at the end. Without a budget, it gets harder to predict and recognize those times. One month we end up with a few extra bucks and feel flush enough to blow it on a big night out. Then next month the kids are due at the dentist and we wonder if we'll have to put the family jewel in hock. A budget can tell you ahead of time that the kids will be due at the dentist, the front tires are getting smooth, and the washing machine is ten years old and likely to start spitting out of unplanned orifices. If your budget is good enough to predict such problems, you'll still have surprises, but more and more of them will be nice surprises. Like, "Gee, no cavities this time!"; and when you've budgeted for the dentist's trip to Disneyland such announcements fall like manna on your ears. Or, "Gee, junior put his bubblegum in the wash and now the machine doesn't leak anymore!"

Secondly, a good budget is a valuable tool in making specific decisions or choices. Any dunce can look at the balance in his check book and decide whether or not he can afford a new suit. That simple approach, however doesn't tell him that having a suit means not having the ski weekend or the extra insulation in the attic he was hoping to have "when he could afford it". Viewed one at a time, such choices are evaluated only on their own merits and the day-to-day state of the pocketbook. A budget exercise sets up a whole year's array of choices in a single *shopping list* and decisions are made with all the alternatives in mind at once.

Once the budget is done for the year, subsequent decisions are easy. "Can we afford it?" isn't guesswork anymore. The extra money is there (and shows) or it isn't, and some other specific expense has to be cut to make room for the new need.

Finally, a budget is important for the sense of security it provides. It's easy to get depressed these days. Soaring inflation, runaway deficits, dwindling oil reserves, sassy kids and cancer. Nothing's as safe as it used to be. There are people who make a living, for God's sake, telling us how terrible things are. When the price of gas goes up for the third time in a week, when you can't remember which kind of 'illions the newscaster used to describe the national debt or Exxon's profits, when sucking your thumb seems like the most rational response to more bad news, then there's some comfort in pulling out the family budget and convincing yourself that, yes, you really can make it through another year. It might not be getting any easier, but knowing what's ahead, in dollars and cents, is more comforting than wondering and waiting for the worst. It's not the answer to the world's problems, but it beats the heck out of sucking your thumb.

GETTING STARTED

If you've never done a budget before, the place to start is in last year's records. Pull out all the check stubs, credit card receipts, tax forms or other records that you can find. Then get a long piece of paper, and down the left hand side list all the things you spent your money on. Group them, where possible, in broader categories. Across the top write: *week - month - year - special -total.* The result will look something like the format of the sample expense record (figure 1).

The categories for your expenses will have to be tailor made. If, for example, you live in an apartment, "housing" might include only rent, utilities, and cleaning supplies.

Now, start adding up the receipts and bits of paper you've saved. Check the dates to get some idea of how complete they are, then do some guessing to fill in the gaps. For example, if you usually gas up the car once a week but have only 40 receipts instead of 52, figure out how much the average fill-up costs were, multiply that by the 52 weeks.

1. 40 receipts total $600
2. Average fill-up is $15 ($600 ÷ 40)
3. Total gas expense for year is $780 ($15 × 52)

The idea is to come as close as possible to what was actually spent. If you've saved every receipt from every expenditure then it's a simple job of adding up all the numbers. But if you're that fastidious then you are probably an accountant and you can skip this chapter. We mortals will have some gaps to fill in.

The biggest gaps will be from the smallest expenditures, the day-to-day cash from the pocket outlays. Each of these pocket money expenses is too small to bother recording, but the overall total can be a surprisingly large hunk of money. To get a handle on it try carrying a pocket notebook for a week. Jot down the small change as you spend it. Bus fare, coffee break, newspaper, lunch, a haircut, parking meters, and so on. A week's sample times 52 will give you a good idea of what goes in a year. Be fair though! For accuracy's sake, don't cut back just because you're keeping track.

FILLING IN THE NUMBERS

As you arrive at reliable totals in each category, put them on the chart. Record the usual weekly or monthly amount in the columns, and an annual total on the right.

The "special" column is for expenses that you don't expect to have on a regular basis: an addition on the house, another car, that broken tooth, or the furnace that finally had to be replaced. If it's not something that happens every year, stick it into "special". That's for last year's expenses. Forecasting special expenses for next year's budget gets a little stickier, but last year you *know* what was spent. Put it in.

The usual procedure is to enter the total for any purchase. Many items are not paid for in the same year they're bought, however. Cars are often bought on time payment. Houses almost always are. How you record such payments is largely a matter of what's convenient and comprehensible to you. For instance, it usually makes more sense to record monthly mortgage payments than to carry a "special" $100,000 purchase of a house over 25 years of annual budgets. If you bought a car last year, you may find it convenient to enter the down payment in the "special" column, and the installments in the "monthly" column.

Do it in a way that's easy for you, but be aware of two common mistakes. First, don't double count. If you enter the full purchase price of an item, don't then keep entering monthly payments as well. Second, don't lose track of *what* you're buying by burying a lot of big or regular items in a general category like "credit card account" or "bank loan payments". One lady I know was not concerned that her credit card account ran over $4000 a year., In doing her very first budget exercise, she was horrified to learn that nearly all of that went on clothes. She decided to take up sewing. Be specific!

"What's this $1200 miscellaneous expense?"

CHECK

Now that you're satisfied you have accounted for last year's expenses, and that you have recorded them in reasonable order, here is a crude but simple way to check:

- Add up all the expenses actually paid last year (that's the bottom of the right-hand column).
- Add anything you might have saved (the amount by which bank accounts increased over the year...if the balance is smaller than it was a year ago, you have a negative savings - subtract the difference).
- Add all the income taxes, pension plans, unemployment and other payroll decuctions that did not appear as expenses on

your chart (you'll find these listed on your tax form).

✓ Compare the total of the three above with your total income (also shown on the tax form).

If the two totals match, you're either an accountant or you cheated. Skip the rest of the chapter.

If income is smaller than savings and expenses, then you've probably made a mistake. Check your figures. You may have double counted a credit purchase, or listed the full value of something for which you've only made partial payment.

Chances are, however, that the total income figure will be larger than the grand total of all expenses and savings. That almost certainly means you've overlooked some expenses. Not to worry. That's why accountants invented the word *miscellaneous*. Call the discrepancy "miscellaneous expenses" and enter it on your chart. Obviously, the smaller the amount in the "miscellaneous" line the more accurate are your accounts. For most of us, though, budgets are guides - not obsessions. *Close is good enough.*

Now look again at the sample expense record (figure 1). If it seems extravagant to you, that's because I've tried to include as many different circumstances as possible. The method is more important than the numbers, however. Notice, in particular, the quick check at the end and the calculation of miscellaneous expenses.

At this point, many first-time budget makers go into a swoon as they see just how much cash is slipping away in dribs and drabs. The big items, like rent or mortgage or the grocery bill, are familiar enough. The surprise comes with realizing how fast the less visible expenses can add up to big ones; running the car, or bits and pieces for the house. That is the main reason it's so useful to break the records down into as much detail as possible. You might have more to learn by looking at your little expenses than at the big ones.

When you're satisfied that the chart you've developed is reasonably accurate and organized in a way that will be easy enough to maintain, then you're ready to tackle the real budget - *the estimate of next year's expenses.*

THE YEAR AHEAD

Using the same categories developed for the record of last year's expenses, estimate what will happen to each item in the coming year. Account for any changes in circumstances. If the mortgage is up for renewal, recalculate it (or ask the bank to recalculate it) at current interest rates. If you'll have the car or another debt paid off during the coming year, don't multiply payments by the full twelve months to get the total - extend it only until it would be paid off. If you're planning a holiday, put it in. If you've sworn off booze, take it out of the budget.

The "special" expenses warrant some special mention here. The problem is that they don't always fit so neatly into a one year budget. There are several ways to account for them. The choice is yours. For guidance, consider three basic alternatives for budgeting a common purchase, like a car:

Method 1. This is for people who save their money until they have the cash to buy big items. The purchase can be budgeted as a one-shot expense in the year they plan the purchase. That's simple enough to enter in the budget, but difficulties can arise with major items. The problem is that expenses coast along at a steady level, and then in one year they zoom up to cover the big purchase. That's fine if the bank balance is big enough to handle it, but if it's a strain on the reserves then this lump-sum approach has to be planned for or spread out a little.

Method 2. Another way to plan for the replacement of high-cost items like the car is to link a savings plan to the depreciation, or "wearing out", of the old one. Cars depreciate at different rates depending on the model, driving habits, and other factors. You can get an idea of how the value of your own car is depreciating by asking the dealer to quote used prices for your vehicle at different ages (these are sometimes called *blue book* values). Let's assume the value of your car is dropping at an average of 30% per year. You've just paid $8000 for it, so after the first year it's worth only $5600 as a used car. It has lost 30% or $2400 of its value. So the transportation budget includes an expense of $2400 for "car depreciation". The $2400 isn't spent, though; it's put in the bank or in an investment to await the day you'll eventually need it to replace the car. The next year it depreciates another 30%, and the budget includes a depreciation expense of $1680 under transportation ($5600 x 30% = $1680).

After five years, you're ready to trade in the old heap. Your depreciation table has marked its residual value down to $1345 and you've put $6655 away in the bank to replace it. The dealer consults his blue book and offers a trade-in of $1300. Actually he offers $700, but he'll settle for $1300 in the end if that's what the book says it's worth. The trade-in value, plus the saved "depreciation expenses", gives you the $8000 you need to replace the old clunker with a new clunker. Yes, yes, I know...I forgot inflation. The old clunkers might have cost $8000, but the new ones are several thousand more. True, but meanwhile your replacement fund has been building up over the last five years in investments that pay interest. So the replacement fund has been inflating too, as has the resale value of the used clunker. Although depreciated to $1345 on the books, inflation will have increased its dollar value, too. With a bit of luck you'll come out even.

Method 3. In principle, from a budget point of view, borrowing to pay for expensive items is very similar to saving for them, as in method 2. The cost is spread out over several years. The major difference, of course, is that the bank does it for you and you're paying interest rather than earning it. You've borrowed the money to buy the clunker and are paying it off in installments. Each payment provides the bank its interest and a little something to reduce the balance owed until the whole thing is paid. Your transportation budget will include all the monthly payments for the year. Rather than showing a single lump-sum purchase, the budget will show the expense of being spread out evenly over the life of the loan.

How you record these expenses in the family budget is up to you. You'll likely have a mixture of several different methods, depending on the nature of the item and your resources at the time. The cost of your house may appear as a regular debt (mortgage payments), the car as a replacement fund, and that big holiday as a lump-sum "special" expense. Mostly you'll want to avoid losing sight of the big costs that may be creeping up without notice in the budget. You may, for example, be cruising along on $1000 a year for transportation. The budget balances with plenty left over, so you decide to raid the savings and buy a bigger house. Then the

Item	Week	Month	Year	Special	Total
Food: weekly groceries	50				2600
office lunches	10				500
coffee breaks	2				125
eating out		30			360
freezer beef			300		300
Total Food					**3885**
Housing: mortgage payments		300			3600
property taxes			1200		1200
repairs				120	120
heat			600		600
electricity		20			240
water and sewage			35		35
insurance			300		300
maintenance		30			360
other				1150	1150
Total Housing					**7605**
Transportation: gas	15				780
down payment for car				500	500
car payments		200(4)			800
insurance			300		300
maintenance			250		250
new battery				60	60
plane fare				200	200
bus fare		5(40)			200
Total Transportation					**3090**
Clothing: Father			400		400
Mother			400		400
Junior			250		250
Miss			250		250
Total Clothing					**1300**
Health: insurance			800		800
drugs		10			120
dental			150		150
broken tooth				200	200
Total Health					**1270**
Other: telephone		10			120
cable TV		10			120
furniture			500		500
new fridge				1000	1000
drapes				150	150
charity			200		200
entertainment		20			240
anniversary party				60	60
liquor		15			180
subscriptions	2		20		124
club dues	1				52
life insurance			400		400
retirement plan			2000		2000
gifts			400		400
Total Other					**5546**
Preliminary Total					**$22,696**
Miscellaneous Expenses					*

Check

Preliminary total	$22,696
Add: payroll deductions	
income tax	8,000
unemployment insurance	240
recreation fund	75
pension fund (private and government)	700
Add: income tax paid at end of year (subtract if refund)	52
savings (subtract if balance dropped)	700
Total	31,063
Actual Total Earnings	35,000
Difference	3,937

*In this example, actual income excedes all outlays and savings by $3,937. That amount was spent but not recorded. It would now be entered on the chart under 'miscellaneous expenses'.

following year the car needs replacing and suddenly the transportation expenses jump to $7000 or $8000 for a new car - more than the resources can stand. A budget like that isn't of much use for planning. Pick the budgeting method that's most convenient, but don't double count and don't lost sight of the big expenses that might not happen every year.

MAKING GUESSES

When you've accounted for all the things that you know will happen in the coming year, make some guesses as to what other changes are likely to occur. It's a pretty safe bet, for instance, that the prices will be going up. Take a stab at predicting price increases by category. If the cost of living has been bumping up at a steady 10% per year, that can be a general guide. But everything doesn't go up at the average rate. The mortgage payments are usually fixed for a period of time and may not be due to go up at all for the next few budgets. Gas and heating oil will almost certainly be going up at a faster rate than the average cost of living increase. Add 15-20% to them. Food and clothing usually move up more slowly. But don't worry about being too scientific, this is the place for some common sense guessing. Economists try to be scientific about such predictions and they are about as accurate as the weatherman. Don't waste your time being fussy...you're going to be wrong regardless. Close is good enough.

You will be able to correct your guess work at the end of the year. After living with a budget for a year, compare the amounts actually spent with those predicted. Were the differences due to inflation? Changed circumstances - your mother-in-law moved in? Changed needs - you grew a garden, took up smoking? After a few years of trial and error, estimating gets a lot more accurate.

THE INCOME SIDE

When all the costs are more or less projected, amended, and inflated for the year ahead, it's almost time to sneak a peek at the balance. Unless you're a politician hooked on deficit spending, you'll want to see if the income will cover the outgo.

The budget, of course, is concerned with *next* year's income, so start with your basic salary. Add any upcoming raises, bonuses, or overtime pay that you can confidently predict.

Income can be expressed in either gross or net terms, whichever may be more useful for you. Net income, or take-home pay, is easier. The comparison between household expenses and net income can be simple and direct. The net income approach does, however, ignore all of those big payroll deductions, such as pension, unemployment and medical insurance, as well as income tax.

If you want to look at *all* of your expenses in the budget, use the gross income figure, and remember to include taxes and all the other deductions as "expenses". Tax credits, of course, are counted as income and are identified on your tax return.

If you do it right, the result will be the same for either the gross or net approach. What you gain by putting in the larger figure for gross income, you must also lose by counting payroll deductions as expenses. It sounds like a shell game with algebra...now you see it, now you don't. But seeing the extra income and expense, however fleeting, is a useful part of making money decisions, and that, after all, is what budgets are all about. This in fact is what led our own family to early retirement. By budgeting with the gross income method, we saw that our biggest expense was income tax. *It was clear then and there that the most effective eay to cut the cost of living was to cut down on our taxable incomes!*

SO WHAT IF IT DOESN'T BALANCE?

Now compare the income figure with the total of estimated expenses. Remember to include the "miscellaneous" figure in the expense estimates. If income equals expenses, *you've been cheating.* That comes later. At this point there's bound to be a difference. Let's start with the good news and assume that the difference is positive - that income will be greater than expenses. We'll call the difference *savings,* knowing very well that it may not end up in the bank or mattress. It's an advantage that only exists on paper.

This is at once the most difficult and most enjoyable part of budgeting. So far the expenses are mostly straight projections of last year's performance. The savings give you some extra choices. Now's the time to make a list of all those things you've talked about doing *if and when.* It's time to make choices. The choices have to have costs attached, and if you're normal, the "wish list" will cost a great deal more in total than the size of the savings will allow.

Budget balancing is a matter of deciding what is most important to you. You may even decide that the best thing to do with the savings is to save them. Whether it's another expense, true savings, or investment of another sort, when the decisions have been made on disposal of the surplus - list the new costs on the chart. Now it should "balance". That is, the total expenses plus savings should equal the income.

Balancing the budget isn't quite as much fun when the difference is negative. That is, when the first summing-up shows that expenses projected for the coming year will be greater than the estimated income. The process, however, is the same. Expenses have to be reviewed and decisions have to be made about the relative importance of each expense; what can be eliminated, what can be reduced, until you cut down to match the total income.

Obviously some expenses, the mortgage payments for instance, cannot be arbitrarily reduced. Others can only be eliminated by increasing other expenses. Cutting out the freezer beef, for example, will likely mean the grocery bill will go up. It might not go up by the same amount, particularly if you swich to cheaper cuts or substitute more vegetables for meat, but do recognize that some reductions will have offsetting costs in other areas.

When expenses have been trimmed to match the income figure, then the budget is said to be in balance. It should resemble, in form at least, the sample budget (figure 2). Notice the similarities between the "budget" format and the "sample expense record" in figure 1. The "special" items have all changed. Most of the regular expenses have been inflated. The important difference, however, is in what happens to the totals. When we recorded actual expenses, the difference between income and outgo was used to calculate "miscellaneous expenses". In contrast, the budget exercise (figure 2) already has a figure for "miscellaneous". Now the gap between income and expenses has to be accomodated by changing the estimates. In the example, freezer beef, carpets, and furniture were chopped so the amended total expenses would match the total income of $37,240.

Direct Expenses	Week	Month	Year	Special	Total
Food: groceries	54				2808
office lunches	11				550
coffee breaks	2				135
eating out		33			396
cheaper meat					179
Total Food					**4068**
Housing: mortgage payments		300			3600
property taxes		1260			1260
repairs				130	130
heat			720		720
electricity		22			264
water and sewage			38		38
insurance			300		300
maintenance		33			396
Total Housing					**6708**
Transportation: car payments		200			2400
insurance			300		300
gas	18				936
maintenance			280		280
tires (2)				80	80
trip to Florida				1500	1500
bus fare	5				220
Total Transportation					**5716**
Clothing: Father			432		432
Mother			432		432
Junior			270		270
Miss			270		270
Total Clothing					**1404**
Health: insurance			920		920
drugs		11			132
dental			175		175
Total Health					**1227**
Other: telephone		11			132
cable TV		11			132
new TV				300	300
charity			200		200
entertainment		22			264
liquor		20			240
subscriptions	2		22		126
club dues	1				52
life insurance			400		400
retirement plan			2000		2000
gifts			420		420
Total Other					**4266**
Miscellaneous Expenses ($3937 last year, plus 10%)					4331
Indirect Expenses: income tax					
unemployment deduction					
recreation fund					
pension fund					
Total Indirect Expenses					9520
Total Expenses					37,240

Income			
Basic Salary	($2850 per month)	$34,200	
Raise due Sept 1st	(10% for 4 months)	1,140	
Christmas bonus	(December 15th)	1,000	
Sell boat	(May)	900	
Total Gross Income		**$37,240**	

Comparing the two final totals, we see that the estimated expenses will exceed income by $1095. Rather than borrow to cover the deficit, our sample family amended the budget by eliminating the carpets and furniture, and by replacing the freezer beef with cheaper cuts. The amended totals match at $37,240; and the budget is thereby balanced.

NOW WHAT?

Now that you've got a budget, what in the heck do you do with the thing? Actually, the most important purpose has probably already been served. If you've worked your way right through the exercise, you now at least know where all that money goes. It's amazing how many people haven't the vaguest notion of how it disappears so quickly.

The budget is a marvellous means of self-assessment. Knowing exactly where the money goes is the most graphic way to determine: whether your spending choices have been good ones; where and by how much your needs can be trimmed to meet your means; and whether, at this rate, you can survive on your salary? *Can you hope to survive without your salary?*

The budget is also a planning tool. By setting out ahead of time what you'll need and what you'll have, there is time to make the adjustments, think out problems and look for the best solutions...not necessarily the quickest ones. A large part of this planning function is what businessmen refer to as *cash flow* considerations. In a nut shell, that means it's not enough to have it, you must have when you need it. Look at the sample budget again. The Jones' funds are in balance for the year. But that holiday trip in February is going to take $1500 that they won't have to spare until they sell the boat in May. They have a cash flow problem. Better to plan around that now than to realize it in February when it's too late to get the deposit back or switch to a summer holiday.

If you were setting up a business budget you would probably want a more careful cash flow plan - dating expenses and receipts and plotting them over the year to see that there was always enough to cover the bills. For most family budgets, though, it is enough to check the big items or special expenses and see *when* they will occur. Christmas gifts, for example, are in November and December. By then you will have set aside the required amount automatically from paychecks through the year...not by joining a club or opening a special account, but by showing it in the budget, spending only what you've budgeted for, and leaving any surplus to accumulate. That *surplus* has been budgeted for gifts. By the end of the year the entire amount will have accumulated in your account.

BUDGETS HAVE THEIR DRAWBACKS TOO

For those of us who get squinty-eyed and cranky at the very thought of spending an evening with pages of little numbers, a budget isn't something we do unless we have to. Let's face it, budgeting is right down there with income tax and thank you letters on the long list of things we would rather put off until tommorrow. That's why I hesitate to even whisper the fact that budgets do have some shortcomings. If the fact that they are boring is reason enough to put them off, will genuine drawbacks, however small, drop them off the end of your priority list along with losing weight and writing to Great Aunt Bessie. If that's the case, please keep in mind all the positive things that budgets do before you read - and then forget about - the shortcomings.

A budget is a deliberate, self-imposed constraint. To the extent that it limits our frivolous or more negative impulses it serves us well. Being human, though, we do have the occasional positive impulse as well. Constructive urges may not strike as often, but it would be a pity if we let a budget, or any other arbitrary discipline, constrain us from virtue as well as from vice.

How, for example, would a tight conserver budget accomodate some fantastic bargain on the whatsits that the family won't need for another year or two? *Opportunity buying* for future needs is a legitimate long-term money saver for any smart shopper. What gets violated - good sense or this year's budget? Obviously, good sense should prevail. The question is how to break the news to the budget? There are really only two ways; make room in this year's budget by chopping something else, or extend the budget over a longer period. If you were going to buy the whatsits next year anyway, a two year budget would include the cost. Looking at these upper limits over the longer period may show that there will be an overall saving by taking advantage of the bargain now. Do, however, keep the potential cash flow problems in mind. Spending income before you've earned it, bargain or no bargain, is a short-cut to trouble.

Finally, a budget is a poor respecter of good intentions. Like harsh medicine, it won't do you any good if you can't keep it down. The budget is the place for predictions, not for resolutions. Save those for New Year's Eve, and stick with accuracy rather than good intentions for this exercise. If you do manage to cut down on expenses during the year, that's teriffic. You'll have a surplus at the end of the year. Invest it or blow it, it's your reward. Then change *next* year's budget to reflect your new, inexpensive lifestyle.

3

Needs

There's a story, supposedly true, that Betsy Bloomingdale, wife of a wealthy credit card executive, proudly does her bit for conservation by ordering her servants to turn off the self-cleaning ovens during the evening period of peak energy demand. It's nice to know that we're all in this together, and the world is certainly a better place for Mrs. B's restraint. But the thoughtful matron also does me a favor by underlining, in more graphic terms than I could ever have imagined, the major premise of this chapter - *that need is very much a relative concept.*

NEEDS ARE RELATIVE

Take my relatives for example. The cost of cleaning an oven with electricity rather than elbow grease would have been daunting to say the least. And servants - though it was rumored that we once knew people who knew people who had them - servants were somewhere in the Cinderella class. A servant with a self-cleaning oven would seem as absurd as a farmer buying food, or a credit card mogul paying cash. If servants didn't clean ovens, what on earth did they do?

We used to be shocked, even embarrassed at times, when the annual "poverty line" was drawn by some all-knowing, and no doubt highly paid bureaucrat who would pronounce via unquestioning press that "it now costs umpty thousand dollars for a family of four to live in this country''.* We never knew whether to feel lucky or poor to realize that we were incapable of existing, much less of enjoying the comforts and happiness we have. Now we're merely amused. *Our needs are simply different from the bureaucrat's. Our needs are different from the poor.* Needs are as different and unique as each individual that defines them.

The problem is that so few of us bother to define our needs. We accept them, ready made, from television, peers and advertisers. Letting others determine our needs might be acceptable in a stable, traditional society. It is quite another thing in a dynamic society like ours whose economy is based on obsolescence and growth. North American economists abhor a stable GNP. Not only must the economy expand continuously, but it must expand rapidly lest we hear wails of *stagnation* and *recession* from industrial leaders. Common sense, the Club of Rome, and the second law of thermodynamics all tell us that such continuous expansion is impossible in the long run, but here and now we seem to be stuck with it as a political necessity. Commerce must either continually create new customers, through population growth for example, or it must persuade each of us to consume more and more each year...whether we need it or not. If we accept that persuasion without resistance, if we don't bother to define our own needs but let society do it for us, then the constant inflation of *needs* and consumption is inevitable.

There's nothing inherently wrong with progress, with improving our material lives. Increasing consumption may get more difficult as we exhaust cheap energy resources or face third world demands for a fairer sharing - but condemning it is not the purpose of this book. I won't presume to quibble with those who find that more is better. May Betsy Bloomingdale's servants continue to enjoy clean ovens the easy way, if that's what they really want. But right there lies the real tragedy of the consumer society; the gulf between what so many of us may really want and what we've been persuaded we ought to have.

Not all North Americans aspire to jet set luxuries, but our aspirations - our material expectations - certainly aren't what they used to be. How many young couples have you known who expected to begin married life where their parents left off? A fully furnished house, a car, and all the trappings that their parents

* In 1990 the poverty line for a family of four in the U.S. was $13,360.

took a lifetime to acquire are seen by the newlyweds as normal, a starting point, something on which to build. Rising housing prices and interest rates are putting a crimp in that little illusion of birth-rights, but sadly, the imposition of such realities does not seem to lead as readily as it should to a closer examination of needs and resources. It seems to be leading instead to a new middle class militancy seething with frustration from what has been denied. How much healthier it would be if that energy were turned to the question of what have we earned, and what, *really,* do we need?

EXPERIENCE TELLS US WHAT WE NEED

Needs are relative to each person's experience and tastes, to time and place. Experience - each man's material history and environment - is the most obvious arbiter of need. If you were to ask a street urchin in Dacca or war refugees about their needs, the answer would almost surely be centered on food. Housing of any kind, or decent health care, might be considered as optional comforts. But *need,* to someone facing imminent starvation, is food and water...physical survival. The notion of the North American poverty line - high enough to include plumbing, TV and telephone as basic needs - would seem like a cruel joke to someone facing starvation. Self-cleaning ovens wouldn't even be credible.

If your experience has been one of hard work and few comforts, then the needs relative to that experience might be more elaborate than mere survival, but still more basic than what most of us take for granted. For nearly a century North Americans have felt alternately amused and threatened by the spectacle of new immigrants arriving from poorer countries and - though working at the most poorly paid jobs - quickly amassing capital to buy houses, sponsor relatives, and send their kids to college. They seem to succeed so much faster than the natives. In our conceit we too often attribute such success to the superiority of this society. It may, however, have more to do with needs. The immigrant is consuming according to needs established in the old country, and now he is earning new world wages. As he gets assimilated into the American experience, he and his children begin to discover new *needs* that never existed in the old country. Consumption catches up with earnings; and by the next generation they're slogging along with the rest of us, trying to meet the mortgage payments, keeping up with the Visa account, and wondering how the newest wave of immigrants manage to get ahead so fast.

Another of our pioneer diarists, Anne Langton, observed how much better prepared were the workers than the gentry for success on new world homesteads. Those with upper class experience felt they *needed* carpets, pianos and servants, and wore themselves out trying to lug around and support those encumbrances. Their hardworking servant class, unaccustomed to such frills, got on with clearing the land and succeeded where their "betters", trying to satisfy more complex needs, went broke.

TASTE AND CIRCUMSTANCE

Needs are also relative to individual tastes and circumstances. Obviously families with children have greater, more complex needs than adult couples. Some people need music in their lives. Others have essential attachments to pets. Illness may demand drugs. And some people are as hooked on a space and privacy as others are on neighbors. Any assessment of needs must account for these differences.

Time is also a determinant of needs. Some needs such as food are immediate. Others, like health care, may be equally vital but can be deferred. Warm winter clothing is a periodic need, shelter a constant need. Not every need must be met as soon as it is felt. It is worth money to the conserver to understand the time demands of his needs.

Needs, finally, are relative to place. Living in the country may create a need for a car, but in the city public transport may suffice. U.S. residents may need private hospital or medical insurance that would be provided through the public plan in Canada. Northerners need to heat their homes in winter, while southerners don't.

Looking at the nature of needs is not just an academic exercise, it's a vital process to the conserver. It could help anyone who has to sit down with a budget and decide what he can and cannot afford next year. It doesn't have to be a conscious process. The cartoon character who staggers parched and ragged from the desert may need clothing, food, a ride to town or a hundred other things. He may not examine the character of his needs, set priorities and budget his resources, but he knows enough to get a drink before worrying about any of those other things. By knowing the nature of our needs it's possible to set priorities, budget for them, and most importantly, decide whether the need can be eliminated more easily than it can be satisfied.

It's an old story, but it still says a great deal about the nature of needs. It's the busy executive from the city who spent two precious weeks each year fishing in one particular Northern lake. Each year he fished with the same local guide, and after twenty years or so of this he was emboldened enough to ask the guide how much he earned. Shocked at the pitiful amount, the businessman offered to find the guide a job in the city paying twice as much. The guide refused. The executive was confounded. "Why don't you want to better yourself?" he asked.

The guide asked the executive how much he earned. "And what's the most expensive, most satisfying thing you can buy with all that?" the guide asked.

"My annual fishing trip", was the answer.

"Well, you see, I don't need that much money," the guide replied, happily casting his line across the water.

There is no standard or absolute when it comes to needs. They're related to a whole array of other determinants. That's why it's so ridiculous to talk about a poverty line. Can you imagine creating a corresponding *wealthy line.*

"...and, finally, the wealthy line has gone up again this year. It now costs $97,241 a year to support the average rich family in North America. The Chamber of Commerce has called for a federal investigation into the cost of being rich, and the Rockefellers have demanded an immediate increase in oil depletion allowances..."

Why is that little scenario any more absurd than a poverty line? $97,241 might mean poverty to parents of teenagers in need of braces, or the man who promises to keep Mrs. Onassis in clothes. On the other hand, working people win that much in lotteries and are driven to drink and nervous breakdowns by such overwhelming wealth.

INCESTUOUS NEEDS

If needs are determined by all sorts of relevant individual circumstances, then the most relevant determinant of all is *other needs.* Needs themselves are interrelated to a remarkable extent. If there is any law of family spending, it would have to be that meeting any need is bound to create at least three more needs. This concept will be obvious to any parent who has ever bought a battery operated toy. Other examples abound.

Most North American households, for instance, now feel they need nuclear powered clothes dryers, hooked into giant utilities and metered for their consumption. But the cost of having a dryer is a great deal more than the cost of the appliance itself and the electricity to keep it running. The dryer creates other needs. It needs special wiring, extra space, another hole in the wall for venting, special (and expensive) additives to cope with "static cling", fabric softeners and sprays to make the clothes as *fresh as all outdoors*. Our poor ancestors managed to get their clothes as fresh as all outdoors by using solar powered dryers for nothing, and static cling was something you got on the radio. We solved one problem - rainy days - and created half a dozen more that need to be solved with hard earned cash.

Not long ago we decided to join the twentieth century by discarding the old hand pump in favor of pipes and an electric pump to bring water on demand. In the first month of modern living the labor-saver pump spent three days in the repair shop while we hauled water from town (plumbing was to save us from hauling it from the well by the back door). Then lightning storms and errant cars knocked out the wires that power the pump on what seemed like a daily basis - and always at bath time. Leaky pipes, balky taps, and threats of underground freezing have all left us wondering if it's the unmixed blessing we welcomed so uncritically. We're now in the process of resurrecting the old hand pump. It, at least, was reliable enough to deliver water no matter what the weather, and the only mechanical failure was a broken handle - solved with the help of a nearby locust tree in ten minutes flat. There is nothing wrong with indoor plumbing. 360 days a year it's terrific. But we do know now that it takes more to have indoor plumbing than a pump and some pipes. The labor-saver has appetites and demands of its own.

For most of us, there's no going back to the simple life where needs are basic and easily met. It's an idyll and perhaps an ideal, but modern comforts, once known, are not that easy to discard. Even Thoreau, whose "Walden" is synonymous with simple needs, moved back to town after two years at the pond. "Simplify, simplify," was Thoreau's motto. But, in the long run, there wasn't enough at Walden Pond to satisfy his more complex needs.

If it is neither possible nor particularly desirable to stem all of our expensive modern appetites, it is at least worthwhile to work at controlling them. And the key to that process is to recognize the difference between the needs we accept for ourselves, and the needs that are created by the things we accumulate around us. We might need clean, dry clothing for example. It's the electric dryer which needs anti-static agents, $20 an hour repairmen, and a nuclear reactor to keep it going.

If spending money is a matter of making choices, it's axiomatic that we can make better choices if we're more consciously aware of how our needs arise and whose needs they really are.

EXAMINING NEEDS

Whenever we set out to spend money to satisfy some need or another, we go through a fairly rigorous examination of just what we're doing and why. It's not a formal process, and it isn't exactly the same for every purchase. Much of the process is automatic and internalized. We ask the questions without thinking about them. It is, for us, simply the way we behave as consumers. If I describe the process of examining needs in some detail, it's not because the process is complex. It's the possible needs and situations that are complex. The process of examination may take some time at first, especially if you're not already a natural skeptic of commercial blandishments. You may have to consciously reach for reasons to keep your wallet unopened, but once the habit is formed, you'll find that saying NO to the salesmen isn't really that difficult or time consuming. The process of examining needs is based on six simple questions:

1. What's the problem?
2. Who needs it?
3. What would change the need?
4. How long will it last?
5. What are the alternatives?
6. What are the costs?

1   What's the Problem?

The usual consumer response to a problem or need is not to look at the problem, but to look at the solution, the normal expensive commercial solution. Consumers say, "we need a new car," when they ought to be saying, "we need a means of getting to work, getting out of town on weekends, to the in-laws at Christmas". The answer may well turn out to be a new car, but if you're going to start with the solution instead of the problem you'll never find out if there might be other, less expensive answers. One young couple I know asked themselves that very question, and by examining the true nature of the need, realized that they didn't need a car at all. Now they take the bus to work, take taxis for evenings out, and rent a car for weekends out of town. They're dollars ahead and no longer have to worry about parking spaces, repair bills and having "one for the road" at parties. That's not everybody's solution, but it suits them. More importantly, it's a solution that never would have occurred to them if they had accepted the obvious solution and bought a car like everyone else.

The process begins with asking; "What is the problem? What objective must be accomplished? What function has to be performed?" What you need to buy (the solution) is the end of the examination, not the beginning. *We begin by asking what needs to be done.*

My long-suffering mate, having brought one baby through the diaper years with no more than an outdoor pump and a clothes line, finally raised the question of an automatic dryer. I was surprised, mostly because she, herself, had always resisted the notion of a dryer. The high temperatures were hard on the clothes, moreover, she preferred the smell and feel of clothes dried in the fresh air and sunshine.

"The problem," she said, "is the winter. The wash takes two or three days to dry outside when the weather is cold and damp. The kids are running out of clean clothes for school. I still prefer the clothes line, but - in winter - we need a dryer."

We stopped right there and backed up one step. "Do we need a dryer or do we need dry clothes?" I asked.

"Dry clothes," she agreed, "but they have to dry faster."

"Would they have to dry faster if we had more clothes? Is there anything wrong with leaving the wash on the line for two or three days in bad weather...as long as nobody runs out of clothes?"

As the one who balances the checkbook, she hit me the standard family line, "Can we afford all those extra clothes?" And so we took an inventory. It turned out that with less than $100 worth of extra clothing, nobody would run out of anything if the washing took a few more days to freeze itself dry in a snowstorm. By looking at the problem instead of accepting the usual solution, we saved hundreds of dollars and made everybody happy. *We examined the need in terms of the objective, not the solution.*

I should warn you, though, that this approach drives salesmen frantic. I have a lot of respect for salesmen, and really hate to ruin anyone's day, but it often comes to that when a conserver shopper meets a high-pressure salesman. There was, for instance, the day we bought the mattress. We found the one we wanted, tried it out, and were down to discussing the price.

"The price is $$ dollars for the mattress and the box spring."

"We like a hard bed."

"We'll take the piece of plywood."

"Of course," said the salesman, "it's much better for the back. We have a box spring that's so firm, you'd think you had a piece of plywood under the mattress. Just the thing for health conscious people like yourselves."

"We'll take the piece of plywood."

"Ha. Ha. Ha."

57

"We're serious."

"You need a box spring."

"No we don't. We need to support the mattress firmly."

"That's what a boxspring does," he argued, still smiling but with a telltale flush of red creeping up his neck.

"So does a piece of plywood."

"What's the difference?"

"Fifty-six dollars."

We finished our shopping at the lumber yard. It wasn't the solution the salesman wanted, but it fulfilled the functional need.

Not long ago I heard a gardening expert fielding question on a radio phone-in show. The caller had a stump in her yard that she wanted to get rid of. "What can I *buy*?", she asked the expert, "that will dissolve the stump?" Following her cue, he responded by suggesting several ready-made commercial solutions (with appropriate warnings about keeping kids and pets away from the treated stump). If the lady had asked "what will make a stump disappear?", instead of "what can I buy...?", he might have thought to tell her that stumps, made of wood, will rot all by themselves; and that they will rot away even faster if surrounded by moisture, air, and helpful bacteria that come free from the earth and from other rotting vegetation. Knowing this, our early pioneers, surrounded by the stumps left from clearing land, heaped leaves and other organic "garbage" over the stumps and planted squash in the rotting mounds. Here in the midst of dead elm country we have the same problem as the lady who asked "what can I buy...?" We, however, have followed the lead of unlettered homesteaders instead of professional gardening experts, and gotten rid of our stumps by growing pumpkins on them - worth a dollar apiece at Halloween - rather than buying ready-made solutions. It has a lot to do with how you ask the question. "What will perform the function?" leads to more interesting, and cheaper, answers than "what do I need to buy?"

2 Who Needs It?

The process of examining needs gets downright introspective at times. When you begin to ask *why* you need to buy a particular thing, or better still, ask why you *want* to buy a particular thing, the answers can reveal more about yourself than about the state of the economy or the cost of living.

It's just possible that some of us, some of the time, are influenced in what we think we need by those around us whom we respect, admire, or wish to emulate. There's nothing profound in that observation. That's why advertisers use movie stars and athletes to shill their goods. The fashion industry lives by that urge to emulate. They count on us emulating not only the beautiful people, but also emulating each other. Now advertisers have twigged to the idea that it's not even necessary to tell us that Mr. and Mrs. Rich and Famous use Acme soap, drive an Acme car or drink Acme beer. It's sufficient to tell us that Mr. and Mrs. Average Jones down the street are doing it..."For five years now, Average and the boys have been getting together to shine their Acme cars and quaff a few Acme ales."

There's nothing inherently wrong with emulation. Self-improvement is a fairly healthy urge. And maybe the Joneses really are the most tasteful people on the block and the neighborhood would be a better place if everyone dressed, looked, and acted just like them. Maybe. But then maybe the Joneses ostentatious lifestyle has brought them to the verge of bankruptcy and they're waving goodbye to their repossessed Acme car and wishing they were solvent like everyone else on the block. Maybe. The point is that in spite of industrial America's urge to have us all keeping up with the biggest spenders on the block, some of us are not yet convinced that the Joneses have all the answers.

Children are perhaps the most gullible conformists. Perhaps it's because they're so busy learning everything else by emulation, that they conform to our superficial tastes and habits as well. Our six year old, for instance, loves dessert. You can get him to do just about anything but clean his room by promising to give or withhold dessert. It's the ultimate weapon. What he hasn't figured out yet is that, in fact, he doesn't really like dessert at all. When it is awarded, he never finishes it. It's greeted with frantic applause and giggling, then it sits there virtually untasted while he goes off to more interesting things. In fact, it's his big sister who loves dessert, and what he really wants is to be just like her. She sets the fashion.

Fashion is a neutral term, though. There are good fashions and bad fashions, just as there are traits in others we could very well emulate. What then does fashion mean to the conserver? It means two things really: *obsolescence and the creation of artificial needs.*

Obsolescence, planned and programed, is a fact of our commercial lives. I needn't belabor you with tales of light bulbs that are designed to burn out, cars that are built to disintegrate, and children's snowsuits that are fiendishly made to last just slightly less than one winter. Not only are they predestined never to become hand-me-downs, but the intent also is obviously to ensure that each child needs *two* to get through the winter. This sort of structural obsolescence is well known to every frustrated consumer and well documented in most consumer guides. What is not so well understood, however, is the link between obsolescence and fashion.

Fashion is obsolescence through changing tastes and preferences, persuading us to buy replacements, not because the old ones are worn out, but because they're no longer in vogue. Skirts get shorter and longer, ties get wider and narrower, and woe betide anyone caught in last year's model. Did you ever notice, though, that those things which change by the dictate of fashion, never seem to wear out? It seems easy enough to build durability into those goods which changing fashions will render obsolete. It's only where fashion doesn't apply that structural obsolescence is required to ensure that we have to buy some more.

If light bulbs could be made to change their shape and size each season, and we had to replace them to be socially acceptable, then they might be made to last for years. And who would spend an extra forty bucks to get a fashionable snowsuit for junior? You just need something to keep him dry, right? Snowsuit fashions couldn't be sold to parents, so they have to be made with structural obsolescence built in.

Cars used to be made to last. Sturdy frames, wrinkle-free bumpers, and panels that took a decade to rust. But then they had fins and chrome and stylish features that had to be changed each year for fashion's sake. When buyers began to ignore the fashionable style changes, the makers had to ensure that if fashion wouldn't bring them back to the showrooms, then rust would have to do the trick. Structural obsolescence seems to have replaced car fashions.

Look again, however, at the goods that fashion does change. They are the ones that don't need to have structural obsolescence built in. They last forever. When is the last time you wore out a necktie? And a Nehru suit, like a diamond, is forever.

The real conserver is impervious to the dictates of fashion, but is a victim, nevertheless, of planned obsolescence. He may not change his ties to match the current width, but his light bulbs will burn out like everyone else's. Knowing, however, that fashionable goods are discarded because of style rather than wear, he can often find best value by deliberately seeking out-of-fashion bargains.

The conserver, examining his needs or reaching for his wallet, asks himself: "Whose need is it?...Mine or the Joneses?" By ignoring artificial needs created by fashion and emulations, the conserver concentrates his money on the things that are really important to him...not on the straw men set up by the electronic snake oil peddlers. If my son understood this simple concept, he would never again be suckered into anything with the promise of dessert.

Twenty-five years ago grandmother was cleaning out her rag bag, scissoring up wool for a rug she was making. She pulled out a

I just love your new coat!

heavy camel hair coat gleaned from a rich and distant cousin's discards. There was absolutely nothing wrong with the coat except that camel hair and narrow lapels were just a year passé. Over protests, I salvaged the intended rug and wore it simply because it was delightfully warm. I'll be wearing it twenty-five years from now. It's indestructable. And, in at least two years out of the last twenty-five, my coat has been back in fashion! At least I presume it was back in fashion; those were the years when acquaintances would admire and marvel that I could afford such a wonderful coat. In the other twenty-three years I got sympathy and was treated to coffee a lot. All that mattered to me, though, is that for twenty-five years the coat has kept me warm and comfortable. It has fulfilled my need perfectly. It hasn't always met others' criteria of what a coat should be, but distinguishing clearly between their needs and mine has saved the cost of twenty-five years of topcoats.

3   What Would Change the Need?

Conservers are self-directed people. As such, they never accept that things must remain as they are. They can arrange and rearrange their lives in ways that make sense to them. Needs, then, are never wholly given; they are set in response to other variables. In other words, *a conserver examining his needs looks not only at the need itself, but also questions whether the need would be the same under other circumstances.*

The need for warm winter clothing, for example, is not an absolute, but might disappear if the conserver decided to move far enough south. A conserver who needs a lawnmower also calculates that if he dug up the grass and grew vegetables instead, the need for the lawnmower would change. A heating bill can be lowered not only by shopping for the cheapest source of fuel, but also by insulating and caulking, issuing sweaters and living at cooler temperatures, closing off little used parts of the house, and so on.

4   How Long Will It Last?

Needs change with time. When we examine needs we not only ask *what* is needed, but also *when* and for *how long*. Will time make the need more acute, or will delay allow the need to abate?

Asking *when* a need must be satisfied is an essential part of planning purchases, as we have seen in the budget chapter. The purpose is not only to plan expenditures for when money is available, but to plan them for times when the price is right. End of season clearances, annual sales, and just plain lucky finds, all make waiting worthwhile (more on seasonal buys in Chapter Nine). Considering the time frame of any need is another way of asking yourself, "how long can we put this off?"

Some needs disappear whether you satisfy them or not. Knowing for *how long* you may require something does occasionally provide an excuse to let procrastination do it for you. Most young families, for instance, feel the need for extra space - room to relax without sitting on sticky toys. At that stage I know it seems improbable, but the day does come when the house is empty and parents are trying to talk the youngsters into staying home for a change. The house eventually gets more spacious whether you add the extra room or not. I'm not suggesting that such needs are less important than the ones that don't go away, but knowing that the difficulties are only temporary can affect what you decide to do about it. It's a little bit like a snowstorm in March. Shovelling out the drive gets lower priority when you know it's going to melt soon anyway.

Checking the time frame is especially important for those needs that arise from your non-human dependents: the car, the house, the TV set, and so on. Unlike we immortals, those things have finite lives and we have to judge their needs against some measure of their remaining usefulness. Consider, for example, the driver of an eight year old car on the day his friendly neighborhood mechanic tells him that his clunker needs a new battery. Now anybody driving an eight year old car is part conserver to start with. As such, he might have expected his clunker to live another two years. Everybody in such a pickle winces at the thought of parting with sixty bucks for a brand new battery. But the conserver does more than wince or give up on the clunker in disgust. The conserver figures that the sixty dollar battery may have a life expectancy of eight years (that's how long the old one lasted) and the clunker will likely need a battery for only two more years. He knows he doesn't need a new battery, he needs a quarter of a new battery. Even the cheapest new battery is made to last longer than the clunker. So the conserver get a used battery from a wreck, from the junkyard, or from a less careful consumer who has just worn out another clunker with a perfectly good battery in it.

We're unlikely to ever be so calculating with human needs, but when our "things" need "things", it's useful to number their days before deciding on the best way to meet the need.

5 What Are the Alternatives?

By this point, anybody who has subjected a need to such rigourous examination can't help but have an obvious solution or two in mind. The market place makes it so easy to think of things that will meet our needs, that it takes some effort now to *blank out* the obvious solutions and spend a little time trying to think of less obvious ways to meet the objective or fulfill the function.

It's a mini version of brainstorming, if you like. The faster the ideas come, the better. If they get a little absurd, don't worry, you can weed out the nonsense later. The important thing is to keep the initial problem in mind, and not waste time trying to think of things that are substitutes for the standard commerical solution.

We use a woodstove in a place where, for safety's sake, the wall must be shielded from the heat. It's a common problem and most wood stove dealers also sell heat shields. Most are simply a sheet of non-combustible material (metal, ceramic, or asbestos) mounted on insulated fasteners an inch or so from the wall. Decent ones cost from eighty dollars and up. Even the ugly ones were beyond our resources, and so we had a closer look at the need. As long as we were thinking of heat shields, all that came to mind were variations of what we had seen in the shops, and so we went back to the functions that had to be fulfilled. What we needed - functionally - was a sheet of non-combustible material and some insulated mountings. The mountings were easy. A little brainstorming came up with the ten cent ceramic insulators used for electric fencing. And since we were then down to looking merely for a sheet of non-combustible material (preferably attractive), the answer came soon enough. Within a week I'd found a pile of antique ceiling tin at an auction. We only needed a couple of pieces, but had to buy the whole pile for two dollars. The total cost of the heat shield was $2.40. The leftover tin will eventually make more heat shields for presents or profit.

Finding alternative solutions brings out the inventor in people. It's one of the things that makes surviving on the cheap an intellectual challenge rather than a physical challenge. It means that we're constantly involved in examining processes, functions, the way things around us work. It's no accident that the best survivor in my acquaintance is in fact a scientist, a freelance scientist no less. He and his wife live and work in a van, traveling about the continent from contract to contract: consulting, building, fixing, lecturing, and yes, inventing. At last report they had gleaned and stored a year's supply of food in the van. It meant they stopped for a summer to grow a pig and a garden on borrowed land, and spent some time during the rest of the year gathering wild foods. They literally lived off the fat of the land for that year. In other years, when he lived alone (sort of) in a smaller van, our inventor friend would stop occasionally on his way through town and ask if we were using the shower. Then he'd bring in his soap and towel and lather up...his alternative to plumbing.

The amateur inventor is bound, of course, to make mistakes. Since the object is to avoid the pains of commerce, the mistakes are usually cheap ones; but it can, at times, be more serious. There was, for instance, the summer I decided that the most efficient way to shower was to take a cake of soap out into the rain. It was cheaper than plumbing and a whole lot easier than hauling water in to heat on a stove and then trying to squeeze my bony frame into the old-fashioned round tin tub. Waiting for rain was a great alternative, and all went swimmingly until the day my soapy aria was interrupted by a crescendo of thunder overhead. I froze, one foot raised like a stalking heron and peeked, one-eyed through a lather of hair, at the distance between me and the back door. And then - with a crash - there appeared a thick white line, arcing from the nearest puddle to the end of my upraised toe. I broke the world's record for the one-legged fifty yard dash for naked men with soap in their eyes. The reek of smoking toe and ozone turned the air as blue as my oaths, swearing I was through with crazy ideas.

The next crazy idea was to put a fifty gallon barrel of water on the roof where the sun could warm it. A garden hose from the barrel gave us hot running water in an outdoor shower. Being solar powered it didn't work so well on cloudy days, of course. But then, it was a long, long time before I could bring myself to remove my boots on cloudy days, anyway.

Not all of our crazy ideas and money saving *inventions* are that outlandish, and certainly not all of them work. Enough of them have worked, however, that a pause to consider alternative solutions is an automatic part of any purchasing decision.

6 What are the Costs?

By now you should have some alternatives in mind, as well as an obvious commercial solution or two. The next step is to compare the cost of each of the several ways of meeting the need. Establishing the cost goes beyond the initial price, however. For most material purchases, there is also the useful life to consider (how long is this thing going to last?). In effect, then, you are looking at the *annual* cost of a drier compared to a clothes line, the annual cost of a home encyclopedia (remember they get out of date) compared to X trips to the library a year, the annual cost of one good pair of shoes compared to several cheaper ones that wear out faster. The initial price, divided by the expected life, gives an annual cost that makes it easier to compare apples to oranges...easier to compare the obvious commercial solution to the crazy alternative you just dreamed up.

On big items, you might want to make the comparison even more realistic by including the possible resale value. Comparing the cost of a car, for instance, with the cost of taking buses and cabs, would mean starting with the initial cost of the car, deciding you plan to keep it for...let's say five years...subtracting the resale value of the five year old car from the initial price, then dividing that *net* cost by five to arrive at an annual cost of owning the car.

If you plan to actually drive the car you'll also have to add operating costs: gas, oil, insurance, repairs, parking, tolls, etc. These operating costs are so often overlooked that it's little wonder consumers have so many unpleasant surprises at the end of the month. And it isn't just cars either. Nearly everything we own consumes *something*. It's a pity price tags aren't required to list operating costs along with ingredients. A frost-free refrigerator, for instance, consumes up to 50% more electricity than an ordinary model. Even the furniture consumes cleaning materials. It's part of the cost of owning something. And, no, this is not being picayune.

Consider something as innocent as music. Most North American homes have record or CD players. New music costs $10-20 a shot. Tape equipment, at a comparable initial price, makes it possible to record high quality stereo music direct from broadcast to tape. Instead of throwing last year's hits away, it's possible to keep changing the music in your collection for nothing. It's possible, but because so few consumers consider these operating costs when choosing music machines, the record industry is in no danger of collapsing.

There's one more cost which is harder to put a number on. That's your own time...the time it takes to cope with all the new problems the solution brings. If a car is the answer to your transportation problems, consider the time you spend waiting in the garage while they fix the balky whatsit, the time you spend washing it, the time you spend stuck in traffic jams, and the cold winter mornings when you can't get the damned thing started. All the maintenance, extra problems, aggravation and frustration that are part of owning *anything* should be considered as part of the cost.

With all of these costs in mind, one can at last make some reasoned judgement as to which alternative solution may best meet the need. In fact, one of the most useful results of such a thorough examination of needs is that finding out the *real* cost of all the solutions often shocks us into asking what would be the cost of *not* meeting the need. Would life, with the need unfulfilled be any more difficult or unpleasant than it would be with the extra problems ' rought on by the solution.

My favorite fishing partner decided one summer that paddling the canoe was altogether too much like work. So he got a motor, and all the tools, gas cans, mountings, and other paraphernalia to make it go. The motor had to be cleaned, tuned, tested, hauled around and stored. And, instead of pausing only to dig a can of worms, fishing trips had to planned and started earlier. Packing the motor and all its needs was only slightly less pleasant than humping all the mechanical gear through the bushes and over the bank to the lake. Then it had to be mounted, hooked up and started...and usually restarted half-way across the lake. *We were working harder at the solution than we had ever worked at the problem.* When I suggested that we switch to river fishing and let the current move us along, he readily agreed...and I haven't seen the motor since.

Thoreau, who exorted us all to "simplify", was at his best when scorning the human urge to own things. "I see young men, my townsmen," he wrote, "whose misfortune it is to have inherited farms, houses, barns, cattle, and farming tools; for these are more easily acquired than got rid of...They have got to live a man's life, pushing all these things before them, and get on as well as they can. How many a poor immortal soul have I met well-nigh crushed and smothered under its load, creeping down the road of life, pushing before it a barn seventy-five feet by forty, its Augean stables never cleansed, and one hundred acres of land, tillage, mowing, pasture, and wood-lot."

The examination of needs, then, ends not with the question of "do I really *need* it?", but with a more introspective note: "given all the aggravation, do I really *want* it?"

There's a bit of Betsy Bloomingdale in all of us, though; and we regularly decide that, yes, there are things we need and want and, yes, we are going to pay the costs. The best things in life may be free, but we do need some of the other things, too. What then?

PROCRASTINATE

What then? Nothing. We do nothing. Not for awhile anyway. Mind you, there's some discord on this point and my excuses about the shops being closed or pressing business elsewhere aren't always received with good grace and understanding. My wife says I'm just a plain old procrastinator. When pressed for action, I will often go so far as to put it on the list -" Things We Need". The next time the matter is raised I can be goaded into transfering it to another list - "Things We Need Right Away!" Rarely do we go right out and buy whatever it is we've decided we need.

Procrastination has several effects - all of them profitable. The most common is that eventually we decide we don't really need it after all. Or we forget about it (losing lists periodically helps), which is simply a less conscious way of deciding we didn't really need it. Some needs, however, are even more enduring than my capacity to put them off. They survive for months on the lists. Sooner or later we see just what we were looking for on sale, or at an auction, or in somebody else's castoffs. The longer we can put it off, the more likely we are to get it for less than we had planned on.

One room in the house has a flagstone floor. In it was a gaping hole that led to a cellar cum pit, wherein resided the pump, a few pipes, and a frog or two. Unfortunately, the hole lay right in the path to the coat rack. Since the floor was of stone, the standard wooden door on hinges would be difficult to fit. The junk yards had nothing that would do. Custom made iron work was much too expensive. We put it on the list of things we need and forgot about it. So did several assorted guests, who disappeared - with some discomfort - down into the frog pit. When a couple of children took the plunge, we moved the trap door onto the list of "Things We Need Right Away", and promptly put it off again. Months later, at a party, someone was describing the horrors of renovating old houses and happened to mention a large iron grate he'd had to rip out of his living room floor. Pressed for details, he remembered hauling it to a dump some five years previous. He even remembered just about where he'd dumped it, which was just about where we found it. It's a perfect fit, a perfect solution, and didn't cost a penny - thanks to procrastination.

REVIEWING NEEDS

No matter how careful we are with the initial decisions on whether and where to spend our money, there are certain expenses that continue on a regular basis. The problem is that circumstances change, and the wisest choices may become money wasters as time goes on. It pays to take up the checkbook occasionally - budget time is a handy occasion - and review the regular expenses that are usually kept up without the close attention they might have received initially.

Insurance is a good example. Cars depreciate quite rapidly, and yet many drivers continue paying "collision" premiums, only to discover that even a minor fender-bender can't be fixed on an older car for less than the "write off" value. Time alone will leave a car overinsured, and leave you paying the bills. On the other hand (though I hesitate to ever counsel spending more) remember that household insurance may have to be raised periodically to cover the inflated replacement value of your property.

I once had a student, a single lady in a professional job, who had done well enough that she was on the verge of taking an early retirement in order to travel. She handed in a budget as part of a class assignment, and - to my amazement - she was still spending hundreds of dollars to ensure herself against income loss should she become too ill or injured to work. The decision might have been sound when she had family responsibilites and needed the income to survive, but she had failed to review her needs as her other circumstances changed.

The point of this somewhat tortuous examination of needs is neither as difficult nor as academic as it might appear. Not spending money may begin as a difficult exercise, but after awhile it gets to be a habit. It becomes as ingrained and natural as smoking cigarettes, reaching for the charge card, or any other habit. At first you have to think about it. It may even hurt a little, but in time it becomes easier not to spend than to spend. Thinking of needs as problems to be solved rather than solutions to be bought, leads naturally to alternatives, and to time and cost considerations. It often leads as naturally away from the marketplace to a greater use of your own resources. Alternatives usually include the prospect of doing it yourself, doing it for less, or doing without. With a little practice, your own skills and resources - whatever they may be -

70

will become as familiar as the brand name resources of the marketplace.

The critical point is passed when consumers begin to realize that most possessions cause more problems than they solve, that *convenience* is often a nuisance. It was no accident that the last great wave of anti-material sentiment, the flower children of the sixties, were the progeny of the affluent upper middle class. They had learned from experience that material possessions didn't solve their problems. Neither did flowers and grass solve their problems, but that's another story.

Most consumers - those of us with kids of our own to raise, and with grass that only gets high when the mower is broken - most of us have to learn the hard way that what we choose to buy, consume, and own are precisely that - *choices!* We can learn to say NO as easily as we've learned to say yes. Our needs can be what we say they are. If we need the time to make pottery, grow gardens, or write the great novel, that need can be just as valid as the electric knife or the pet rocks we might otherwise be tempted to buy with our time. *It's a matter of choice.*

There was a time when we accepted that what we owned defined us. Our stature rose with the grandeur of our possessions. When we discovered that those things didn't always bring us joy, we began to ask ourselves just what did we need...and learned that life can be simpler than we thought.

4

Getting Ready

Just about everybody has days at work when it doesn't seem to be worth the effort. Days when you begin to wonder if that's really what you want to do for the rest of your life. My weak moments were always in spring...those first warm days when the sun made a suit too sweaty and prickly for comfort, when I began to plan the garden on the backs of unread memos.

Those were days for dreaming. And when dreaming was no longer enough, they became days of planning and preparation. Those were the days that made surviving without a salary possible. Thorough preparation is essential to a self-sufficient life. The years of idle afternoons and coffee breaks that we devoted to *getting ready* have paid more dividends than any amount of good luck or meagre talent we could muster.

Economic independence, happily, is one of those great leaps that can be made with tiny steps. It takes longer that way than winning the lottery or being born into the proper family, but working at it slowly, over the years, is the only way most of us can make it. Getting ready - mentally, physically, and financially - is the practical way to begin a new lifestyle. It happens gradually, step by tiny step, until finally - someday - the pieces are all put together and you know you can make it on your own.

The alternative, of course, is to move when the impulse strikes. Tell the boss exactly what he's doing wrong, and hope to goodness you can find another way to meet the mortgage payment before the end of the month. There's a lot of visceral satisfaction in following urges spontaneously, but being prepared is easier on the nerves.

DEBTS

The biggest obstacle, naturally, is money. And the easiest way around that hurdle is not making more, but spending less. The last chapter dealt with reducing *needs* to minimum levels. That's the most important step, and one that anybody can begin to practice now - but it's certainly not the only step.

Those of us raised with the standard array of middle-class, North American appetites usually end up with a raft of financial entanglements that must be rearranged to make self-sufficiency possible. The chief villian here is debt.

Good Debts

It's time to be fair. I don't like it, but I do have to admit that debt sometimes does have advantages. If you're clever, or lucky, or both, it's one way to beat inflation. The principle is really quite simple: *borrow to buy resaleable things whose value is inflating faster than the rate of interest on the debt.* That turns inflation to the borrower's advantage. For example, anybody who borrowed money to buy gold when it was $200 an ounce might have paid 15% interest on the debt. But gold, in the next year, was inflating 100% or more. After a year, the buyer of a single ounce owed $230 for principle and interest on the debt, but by then the gold was worth well over $400. It cost $30 in interest to earn over $200 in inflation.

Of course, in the long run, interest rates will never be lower than overall inflation rates. The gnomes of Zurich, or whoever sets the interest rates will see to that. But, from time to time, certain commodities do inflate faster than interest rates. The housing market has periodically boomed faster than the bankers could raise the mortgage rates. Most people who have bought homes in the right place at the right time have seen their property values rise fast enough to match the interest on the mortgage.

When interest rates are fluctuating, borrowers should do some comparison shopping before deciding what to pay off and when. Take a simple mortgage for instance. Many of them are now for five year terms. Other interest rates can change significantly in that time.

When the Joneses renewed their mortgage four years ago the rate was 15%. By now they've whittled the balance down to $30,000. In the meantime, Jones has managed to save $30,000 and is tempted to pay off the mortgage. He checks the alternatives:

1. He can pay off the mortgage now, saving $4500 a year in interest payments. The mortgage, however, carries a penalty clause for early payment. If the penalty is equal to three months interest, his net savings for this year will be reduced to $3375.

2. He can put his $30,000 into a one year term investment with a 10% return. This would earn $3000.

3. He can buy a five year term investment at 12%, earning $3600 a year.

On the surface, it appears that he should keep the mortgage debt and invest his money at 12% instead. Both time and the taxman may change the conclusion, however.

First, taxes. Investment earnings are taxed. Savings are not. If Jones is up in the 33% tax bracket, his net return on the 12% investment is really only $2400. Paying off the mortgage is relatively more attractive.

The tax picture is further complicated in the United States where mortgage interest is deductible. In Jones's bracket the deduction on a $4500 interest payment would be worth $1500. The loss of that deduction, combined with the penalty for early payment, means that he actually saves only $1875 by paying off the mortgage. For U.S. Jones, the term investment is a better deal . . . this year. Next year, when the mortgage is up for renewal, the penalty does not apply and Jones expects mortgage rates to be down in the 13% range. So next year U.S. Jones can save $3900 in mortgage interest and lose a deduction worth $1300, for a net saving of $2600. Next year he would be ahead by paying off the mortgage — so he may wish to put his savings into a shorter term investment now, and pay off the mortgage when it comes due.

The point is that when the cost of a debt is lower than the return on alternative investments, debt is not only defensible, but is also business sense. But do remember that the comparison must include the effect on taxes, deductions, and penalties.

Leverage

You don't have to be a stock market whiz to make money with investments. Everybody who spends is constantly making investments. The problem is that so few expenditures return much profit. Nevertheless, we find a good investment from time to time: a bargain used car that can be sold for more than you paid, a house whose value is rising, a spare room that can be rented out, a profitable hobby. All of those things can be good investments, and a good investment can be made even better with a little *leverage.*

A lever is a simple thing that lets us use a little muscle to move a lot of weight, and financial leverage is much the same...using a little money to return a lot of profit. The financial lever is debt - using someone else's money to invest.

Some years ago the Smiths set out to buy their first house. They had $10,000 saved for a down payment. They weren't particularly fussy about looks, or cupboards, or color schemes, but they were determined to buy into an area where property values were sure to rise. The house was to be an investment as well as a place to live, and as such, it was to be judged on investment criteria. Consequently, most of their house shopping involved foot-slogging research to find the area that might next become "trendy"...where property values could be expected to rise the fastest. When they finally found the neighborhood, they were confident than any house on the street would increase in value by ten percent a year or more - and that proved to be on the conservative side. It only remained to pick out a house.

At the time, a $25,000 house would have been more than adequate for the Smiths. If values rose by ten percent, a $25,000 house would increase in value by $2500. With $10,000 down, they would borrow the remaining $15,000 from a credit co-op at 8%. Interest on the mortgage would come to $1200. The increase in value would be $2500 - a profit of $1300 on their $10,000 investment.

But the Smiths knew they had an advantage as long as real estate was inflating faster than the mortgage rate. A $50,000 house would require a $40,000 mortgage...which would increase the interest costs to $3200 a year. But a $50,000 house, inflating at 10%, would be worth $5000 more after a year. The profit on a more expensive house would be $1800, compared to $1300 on the cheaper house. The debt would be bigger, but the returns would be bigger still. The *leverage* would allow them to earn 18% on their down payment, rather than the 13% they would earn on the house that was merely adequate.

For the Smith's, buying the more expensive property was justified by the interest rates alone; but I should complete the story by adding that the Smiths were not the type to rattle around in a house that was twice as big as they needed. They rented out the excess space and paid all the mortgage, tax, and maintenance costs with the rent money. They had "free" housing for themselves, a healthy return on the $10,000 invested, and a very hefty capital gain when they sold out three years later.

The classic example of leverage is in the stock market. Speculators, buying on margin (on the cuff if you like), can use a small amount of their own money to obtain credit to order much greater values of stock. If the stock increases in value, the speculator profits on his credit as well as on his own capital invested.

The trick, of course, is to only pick stocks - or any other investment - that return profits larger than the cost of the debt. Leverage allows the investor to profit on someone else's capital, but it works the other way too! If the investment turns sour, the speculator must cover the entire loss - including the credit portion. That's what put all those ambitious young men out on the window ledges of Wall Street in 1929. As long as the market was rising they could make large paper profits by operating on margins, but when the market started to drop, and they had to pay off the credit extended by their stockbrokers, the result was financial ruin.

Risk

Using debt is a perfectly acceptable way to make money, but there are always risks involved. For the investor who can accept the risks, understand the investment thoroughly, and still have confidence that the investment will make money, debt and leverage can build up his capital far faster than simply investing his own money could do.

For a family living without the security of a salary, the element of risk takes on a whole new character. A speculator hit with a loss on an investment presumably has the means to recover his losses with a salary or income from other investments. Without a salary, the capacity to recover from financial loss is greatly limited. When those losses are multiplied by debt and leverage, the unsalaried person of little means is doubly vulnerable.

Bad Debts

Some debts are risky but worthwhile. Others have all the risk with no possibility whatever of earning a profit...no redeeming features at all. These are consumer debts. Money borrowed - not to make money - but to consume. When borrowing money to invest, the very worst that can happen is that you will have to repay the loan from your own resources rather than from profits on the investment. Consumer debt, where you don't expect to recover costs, much less make any kind of profit, is a deal that's guaranteed to be at least as bad as the worst investment.

"Hi! I'm Mr Debt. I'll be staying with you for a little while."

"Buy now, pay later" is as insidious as any other form of bondage. The consumer trades his future working life for immediate gratification. The poor working stiff who signs away future earnings to borrow for today's consumption is guaranteeing his dependence on a salary for the rest of his working life.

The average American spends almost one-fifth of his take home pay trying to keep up the payments on consumer debt. The cost is enormous. Even the charge cards - which can be paid off within thirty days with no interest charges - are not wisely used. Only one-half of Canadian bank card holders pay up within thirty days. The other half pay 18% or more on their balances. Department store cards cost the consumer up to 28% interest. The total comes to a billion dollars a year.

The distinction between good debts and bad debts has little to do with how much you borrow or from whom. The distinction centers on what you intend to do with the thing you've bought. If you're going to use it up, like a new suit, a stereo, or a holiday, then it's clearly a case of consumption. If it can later be sold, at a profit if possible, then the expense is not consumed...*it's invested*.

Investment debt is always risky, but it can bring rewards. Consumer debt is 100% risk. It's absolutely certain from the beginning that you'll have to pay the whole thing back, and then some, from future earnings.

In Canada, there's one more reason to distinguish clearly between consumer and investment debt. The cost of investment debt (money spent to make more money) is deducted from income for tax purposes. For someone in the 33% tax bracket, an investment loan at 12% interest actually costs only 9$^{1}/_{4}$%. The rest comes back as tax refund. A consumer loan at 12% costs 12%. So if you want to buy a car and some bonds when money gets tight, borrow to buy the bonds rather than the car.

If you ever hope to walk away from a salary, make the distinction between investment and consumer debt. Judge the first on its merits and your skills as an investor. Avoid the latter like the plague.

Breaking the Charge Card Habit

It's no accident that one of the costliest forms of consumer credit (only the sharks with baseball bats charge higher interest) is also one of the slickest and easiest. If it wasn't so darned easy to whip out the card, the costs would deter any would-be borrower.

The costs are more than the interest on the account. Paying the bill within thirty days helps, but there is a hidden cost as well; you don't count plastic money in quite the same way as the real stuff. When you have to pull out the actual cash and count it into the seller's hands, there's a tug of pain at the parting. At that point it *matters* that the same thing is on sale cheaper around the corner. It *matters* that you're having to give something up, something real, to buy this whatchamacallit. The plastic money isn't real. It doesn't seem to matter if the whatchamacallits are dearer here. *The process is too painless.* The casual ease of it puts us to sleep and makes us less discriminating, less careful consumers. The convenience is costly. Paying should be as inconvenient as possible.

The theory of inconvenience even seems to work with cash. That's why I always try to carry small bills when shopping. When I have a twenty to throw on the counter, I'm hardly aware of whether the widgets are six dollars each or two for $12.99. When I have to count out a handful of bills, the price seems to matter more. The theory of inconvenience likewise tells me to take only big bills to the fair or the ball game where one is surrounded by easy temptations to shell out a quarter here and a dollar there for snacks and tidbits. These petty tricks for self-manipulation may only work for fanatic non-spenders like me, but giving up the convenience card can save a lot of consumers a lot of money.

Don't believe me? Try this little test. Put away the plastic money and go back to cash - cold turkey - for a month. Make a note of all the expenses that you normally would have paid by card. At the end of the month, compare the cash total with the normal charge card bill. If the cash method has saved you money, you can cut up the card and flush it down the toilet. That's the easiest way I know to stay out of debt.

Cutting the Cost of Debt

If you really must borrow money, remember it's a business deal, not a favor. Don't fall into the arms of the first friendly finance man who kindly offers to help you out. You pay a price to borrow money and, like any other expense, it pays to shop around.

A mortgage is usually the largest debt for home owners, and the interest can be one of the most expensive items in the family budget. Interest varies from source to source:

✔ Credit Unions and co-operatives often have cheaper mortgages than profit institutions like banks.

✔ Bank mortgages are usually cheaper than finance companies and other *near banks* that specialize in riskier loans.

✔ When buying a house, assuming an older, existing mortgage may give you a break in interest.

✔ Private mortgages, held by the seller or another individual, may be less costly than an institutional loan.

✔ Mortgage rates vary widely over time. If rates are high and expected to go down, you might save a bundle by waiting to buy when rates are right.

Some borrowers take low interest loans from their life insurance policies. We'll look at insurance more closely in Chapter 10. Suffice it to say here that the rates are low because you are borrowing your own money.

For small amounts of money, cheap (sometimes free) loans can be obtained by deferring payment on other bills. Most of the people who receive your monthly checks charge penalties for late payment. These penalties are the same as interest paid on a loan. Credit card companies have even taken late payment the final step by slapping on an 18% interest penalty and implicitly encouraging the practice with higher limits. In many cases, however, the penalties charged by other creditors are cheaper than the interest on regular commercial loans. Check the penalty clauses on your accounts and compare them to commercial rates. Do, however, keep track of changes. When banks were getting 15% for loans, the U.S. Government charged only 11% for late payment and Canada charged 12%. Consumers "borrowed" by deferring tax payments and governments learned a lesson. Now tax interest rates change in step with bank rates, and penalties are tacked on top. Late tax payment is no longer a bargain.

If it seems slightly underhanded to borrow money by deferring bills, consider that institutions are constantly borrowing from you, the consumer, by soliciting and accepting advance payments. "Lay-away" plans, where you pay now and pick up later, is a form of interest free loan from the consumer to the department store. Many utility companies now send "interim bills" before the meter is read…their way of borrowing from you for nothing. Taxpayers give the government interest free loans by overpaying income taxes and getting a refund at the end of the year.

The Psychological Cost of Debt

Debts, even the cheaper ones, can be a burden to the person who has to pay them. It's not so much the money as the obligation - the commitment of a part of the future and the lack of freedom that entails. Any debt is an impingement on future freedom.

This is doubly true for those who are preparing themselves to live without salaries. Debts require a future income to pay them off. Giving up future income (of the predictable, salaried kind) means giving up debt. Even if the bankers would trust anyone crazy enough to quit working, debt is too hard on the nerves if you haven't a predictable means of repayment. For people like us, there is always the horrifying thought that we might have to go back to a regular job to pay the damned thing off. That alone is enough to keep us away from borrowed money.

The surest measure of the psychological cost of debt can't be known until the debts are paid. The joy of being out of debt - of not owing a penny anywhere - tells us what we really paid to borrow money. That kind of freedom, that many harried consumers have forgotton, is one pleasure that can't be bought on any of the plastic cards.

Getting Out

The first and most important task, then, in preparing for life without a salary, is getting out of debt. Burning the credit cards and swearing off consumer debt forever is a great first step.

The second step is a long hard look at investment debt. Some of it, a mortgage on rental property for instance, may be self-supporting. In other words, the income from the property will cover the mortgage payments whether you have a salary or not. Other investments may be equally profitable, but without the capacity to carry a debt on their own. A mortgage on an owner-occupied home for example. The house may be appreciating rapidly - a great investment. But you can't profit from that increase until the house is sold, and the mortgage is due for payment every month.

When there's a regular salary coming in, any kind of investment debt that promises to make a profit is open for consideration. When the salary stops, the investor should be more discriminating. Investment debts, at that stage, should be self-supporting. They should be able to pay themselves off.

For the peace of mind it brings, that's not a bad approach for people still on salary too. Do without rather than get into consumer debts, pay off non-income investment debts like a mortgage as rapidly as possible, and set up income-producing investment debts to pay themselves off with or without your salary. Any family which can put itself into such a position is well on the way to economic self-sufficiency.

The prospect of paying off debts, as incomes or interest rates change, is reason enough to insist that mortgages (or any contracted debts) include a clause allowing early payment without penalty. If you have a mortgage with a penalty for early payment, wait until the new mortgage rates are *higher* than the rate on your own mortgage. Then ask the lender if the penalty clause can be renegotiated or deleted. Eager to re-loan his money at the new, higher rate, the lender may be quite willing to encourage early payment by dropping penalties.

SAVINGS

No matter how carefully you've laid your retirement plans, something is bound to go wrong. It's the very same logic that ensures a slice of bread will always fall butter side down, and a three year old will always get his boots on the wrong feet - the laws of probability notwithstanding.

Given that, there's great security in having some money set aside "just in case" the purple Tahitian nudes don't sell, or the kids need an orthodontist as well as the dewy meadows and home grown veg. Having a mistake fund set aside separates the realistic planner from the romantic dreamer. It might not convince your in-laws that you're sane, but it will help your insomnia on the night before you resign.

The motive for setting something aside may be security, but that's not to say that savings can't also have some more active function. Like earning their keep for instance.

As a security blanket, your nest egg only needs to be accessible, and to earn at least enough income to keep pace with inflation. Those criteria are met in varying degrees by these common forms of savings:

Bank Savings are perhaps the most common repository. They are safe, easily accessible should the need arise, but rarely pay enough to cover losses to inflation. A good place for emergency funds, but hardly the most profitable investment around.

Term Investment Certificates, offered by banks and other institutions, pay higher interest than demand deposits, but commit the investor to leaving his money in for one to five year periods. You can usually have access to the money before the term is up, but there are penalties. A better investment, but not an adequate emergency fund.

82

Stocks and Bonds have the potential of earning much more than bank investments. Funds are accessible, since stocks can be readily sold, but stock prices can fall as well as rise. Without a very reliable advisor, the "market" is not the place for the casual investor. To make the most of these investments, you must know the market well and follow it carefully.

Mutual Funds vary widely, but are usually invested in some particular sector of the stock market. Experts handle the buy and sell decisions and investors share in their success - or failure. Funds are generally safer than the stock market for the amateur investor, and returns vary widely depending on the fund and its attitude to risks. The safer the approach, the less the income payout. First time investors should check the administrative fees charged by regular funds as opposed to the "no-load" funds.

Real Estate can be a profitable place for savings. Since they are a major component of the cost of living, housing prices usually appreciate at least as fast as the general rate of inflation. Rental property may provide a tidy income as well...especially for the investor who can spend some time looking after it. Property is easy to finance and not too complicated for the amateur who is willing to spend some time researching his market. Land speculation, with no rental income to cover the costs, is a more professional game. Although returns can be quite high in real estate, and (unless you're very rash) it's usually one of the safest investments outside of a bank, the money invested is not easily accessible. Not a place for emergency funds.

Mortgage Investments can be as simple as using surplus funds to pay off your own mortgage faster, or as complex as lending your money to another home buyer. Current rates compared to alternate investments will determine the advantage of paying off your own mortgage. Lending mortgage funds to someone else is a safe investment, but only if you can be nasty enough to foreclose should the need arise. No mortgage investment is easily accessible if you need the money in a hurry.

Rarities such as stamps, art, or even comic books have been money makers for the experts, but it is essential to know what you're buying, and even then the markets for rarities are volatile. Not an amateur sport.

Commodities such as gold, silver, or soybeans are another sphere best left to the pros. In the last gold boom, hordes of eager buyers lined up outside banks to put their life savings into a few thin wafers of metal. A lot of people made a lot of money. The ones in the lines got burned.

Retirement Savings are particularly attractive for the working person who plans on being without a salary in the near future. RRSP's in Canada are 100% tax deductible. That is, up to a limit, any money saved under a registered plan is exempt from income tax. Although regular interest is modest, the tax advantage can be very lucrative (see Chapter 10). In the United States, the Keogh and IRA plans are more restrictive than the Canadian RRSP, but if you can qualify, the tax advantages are the same.

Depending on what you want your savings to do, no one plan may meet all of your needs. Some families find it practical to divide their funds into three separate plans: an emergency fund at the bank, a less accessible but more profitable investment for income purposes (real estate, bonds, term certificates, etc.), and a risk fund with speculative potential. The emergency fund is there whenever it's needed. The income investment may be the largest reserve. And the risk fund is just that - something they can afford to lose.

The management of savings will certainly effect other kinds of financial decisions. A healthy emergency fund, for example, may eliminate the need for certain kinds of insurance. The total reserve fund may affect the need to contract for retirement plans through employment.

Likewise, other circumstances will determine the type of savings plan best suited to each family. Your own skills and interests will guide investment plans to areas you know best. The family's health, number of children, nearness to pensionable age, all these things and more will shape decisions on how much money is enough and where it should be kept.

HOW TO SAVE: THE MATERIAL FAST

A savings plan, like a diet, is one of those simple and reasonable things that's easier to describe than to do. Savers put quarters into big glass jars, have regular amounts deducted from paychecks, save whatever happens to be left between paychecks, moonlight and put all of the extra pay away...there are as many approaches to saving as there are diets - and for much the same reason. Dieting and saving both involve a degree of personal sacrifice - curbing appetites. And just as every dieter has a choice between the cheesecake and a youthful figure, every consumer has a choice between buying everything he thinks he needs and having money in the bank. It's a matter of overcoming appetites.

Each would-be saver knows his own psyche best, and how he can trick himself into curbing the material appetite. My favorite, however, *is the material fast - buying nothing but essentials during a predetermined interlude of spartan discipline.*

Saving in little bits and pieces never worked very well for us. Skimping here and there forever was just too unappealing. In the face of eternal deprivation, however slight, the temptation to cheat was ever present. Worse yet, the money never added up fast enough to make the sacrifice seem worthwhile. Like the thought of never eating another pastry - forever and ever - with the object of losing a pound a month, the short-term result never seemed to justify the permanent sacrifice. Crash savings, like crash diets, were more our style. We could give up anything if we knew we could have it back some day.

Crash savings require a specific objective, a specific time period, and a mutual willingness to sacrifice every expense for that period. The plan is carefully laid out at the beginning. A bare-bones budget is set that includes nothing but the simplest food, housing and essential bills. *Nothing is sacred.* Rent can be lowered by moving (who cares if it's too small, it's only for a year). You can give up the car (we'll walk for a year), clothing (everything that wears out will be mended, and we'll buy clothes next year). Once the budget is set it's inviolable. Even rational exceptions are put off until after the fast. Every other penny of income is saved. It's a radical change in lifestyle. But it works. And it doesn't seem so bad as long as there is an end in sight.

Sue and Mark started married life with brand new jobs at the bottom of the ladder, where visions of the future are supposed to compensate for the meagre pay. They had nothing else, no savings, no car, no TV set, no stereo, not a stick of furniture to their names. They decided to continue the material fast for six spartan months, putting most of the two paychecks in the bank. Six months later they left on a three month round-the-world tour, traveling in comfort and paying cash. A three month feast for a six month famine. A matter of choice.

Because you know it's going to end, the material fast is never as grim as it sounds. It's different. Like traveling in an unknown land, you may even find that it's better in some ways than what you left behind. Not surprisingly, many families who submit themselves to radical savings binges find their lifestyles permanently altered. Some find that walking feels better than driving, that evenings spent in conversation do more for a marriage than a television does, that old shoes are more comfortable than new ones. The material fast can actually start to become an attractive way of life in itself. *The sense that less might actually be better is the beginning of becoming a conserver.*

A TOE IN THE WATER

Getting ready to live without your regular job can be more than idle dreaming and saving your loot for a sunny day. Outside the silver spoon set, most of us who contemplate leaving jobs also have to contemplate other means of earning a living. Of all the people I've met who've realized there must be more to life than what they're doing, most already have something else in mind. Something else they would rather do instead of what they're doing now. The usual problem is making it pay, or finding something else to do for money that doesn't dominate your life the way a regular job can do.

More than half the battle can be won by simplifying needs. But there tends to remain a stubborn residue of bills that just won't go away. Sooner or later you are going to need some cash. Not much, mind you, but always enough to know you must improvise some casual source of income.

Income schemes centered on hobbies, crafts, scaled down versions of your present job, or freelance anything, are a major part of getting ready. This is the time to find out if your schemes will really pay, if you can really do it, if you can really enjoy doing it.

Putting a toe in the water simply means testing those alternate income schemes to make certain they work...*before* you kiss your seniority goodbye. This is the time to:

Test your skills - making sure you have the talent to paint or pot or farm or whatever it is that draws you.

Test the market - making sure your paintings or pots or whatevers will sell.

Test your confidence - knowing you can do it makes all the rest (budgeting, saving, etc.) a whole lot easier to endure. On the other hand, knowing you can't do it, or finding it's not everything you thought it would be, may help you reconsider.

One old pal of mine, a PR man at the time, decided at a par-ticularly stressful period in his career that the simple life in the country appealed to him more. He bought an old farm and a new straw hat, and resolved to grow cucumbers for the pickle factory. The romance went out of cucumbers as soon as he saw you had to bend your back to pick them - somehow, he had envisaged trees. Louis, the walking porkchop, refused to die at butchering time; the septic tank backed up; and the house burned down. He's back in the city now, and refuses to grow so much as a petunia. *Trying a new lifestyle before you buy it is just plain good planning.*

GATHERING WHAT YOU'LL NEED

Ironically, a simpler lifestyle can often involve more complex needs. Growing your own food is about as basic as you can get, but it requires land, tools, fences, materials, and then all the gear needed to freeze or preserve it. Wood heat is making a regional comeback as a cheap alternative to oil, but to keep the old pot-belly going takes tools for cutting, hauling and splitting, a storage shed and a woodlot. It's simpler than drilling your own oil well, but there's still a lot of work and expense between you and the cozy glow.

Getting ready is the time to start acquiring all the tools and resources the new lifestyle will require. That's not to say you should rush out and buy everything you think you'll need. It's enough to start with making lists: what you are going to need, where it can be found, costs, and alternatives.

Planning the acquisition of such resources ahead of time permits the luxury of spending slowly and biding your time until the bargains and special opportunities come to you.

When we planned our own move to the country, one of the first and biggest items on the list was "tractor". I rushed around gathering specs and prices and catalogues. That was ten years ago. In the meantime we've found a dozen different ways to do without a tractor for the small scale jobs we had in mind. The tractor is still on the list somewhere, but gradually finding its way to the bottom.

Moving to the country, or changing your lifestyle in any direction, is a little like an expedition. Knowing what you'll need ahead of time solves problems, but you don't have to take it all with you.

BUDGET (AGAIN)

Cheaper lifestyles are fundamental to surviving without a salary. Spending less is the only way most of us can afford to live outside the forty hour week. It's clear then that the post-job budget could, or should, differ sharply from the budget of a working family.

Budgeting for a new lifestyle takes the same form as the budgets discussed in Chapter 2. The numbers and the categories, however, should change significantly. Regardless of where you may be going, or what you may be doing, certain needs will disappear. Without a job, you may not need a house in town, a new suit every year, or a second car, for example.

This preparatory period is the time to estimate just what the financial situation will be in your new circumstances. In other words, *make a budget.*

During the years that it can take to prepare for financial independence there is one overriding question that is asked more than any other; *how much money does it take to be independent?* How long will it take to get there? The answer, of course, depends entirely upon your needs and your capacity to earn casual income. It depends even more on how secure you like to feel. Everybody's answer is unique, but for what it's worth, our own financial goals (at the getting ready stage) were to hang onto salaries until we:

- were out of debt;
- owned a house in a low tax area;
- were set up to raise most of our own food and fuel;
- had enough in the bank to cover several years of expenses.

By virtually eliminating the cost of food and housing, and by knowing we could do without much of the rest, it didn't take much to make us feel secure. Less self-sufficient lifestyles would doubtless need more cash reserve. Smaller families might require less.

Whatever your own needs might be, an evening spent making up a "what-if-I-didn't-go-to-work" budget will help you to answer the big questions in terms of clear financial goals.

WEANING

Regular paychecks can be addictive. Regardless of what the job is like, leaving payday behind is an awesome thought. To cushion the shock, some folks prefer to wean themselves gradually rather than go "cold turkey". The gradual approach also leaves an escape route back to security for those who aren't quite sure about the merits of a brand new lifestyle. Like my friend, the would-be pickle farmer, some find that idylls aren't all they're cracked up to be. He kept his city job and commuted for awhile...just to keep a foot in both camps until he was sure it would work. It didn't.

Some firms offer employees a Leave Of Absence for educational or other purposes. How about for lifestyle changes? LOA is usually without pay, but it does leave open the option of going back to the old grind if the new grind doesn't work out. The biggest hurdle to giving up a salary is often the grim prospect of giving up long-term security. If you can gather the wherewithall to live for a year (or whatever term the LOA policy offers), your security lies in being able to go back to work when the leave is over. If being your own boss suits you, and if you can still balance to budget after a year, you may not want to go back. LOA is a sort of year's free trial.

Some jobs, in sales for instance, are less structured than others and the would-be retiree can wean himself by gradually cutting back on his time...fewer calls, fewer hours. The paycheck drops accordingly, but the prospect of going back full tilt remains until you actually give up and go back, or drop the apron string altogether.

In other jobs employers can be persuaded to allow a switch from salaried to contract work. You continue to do the same work, but are paid as an independent supplier rather than an employee. There is less security in such an arrangement, but the money is often better and you can control your working life more independently. Employers are often willing to pay more for contractors than for employees because the overhead (pensions, holiday pay, etc.) is lower and because it's easier to drop a contractor than an employee if business gets bad.

PREPARING YOURSELF

Enough of financial preparations. What effect will life without a salary have on *you?* Is your psyche in shape for independence? There are several differences between life on and off the job. Expect them and be prepared.

Self Discipline

The greatest and most obvious change is discipline. Work goals, deadlines, the structuring of time and objectives, are imposed on most employees. When you are on your own, such discipline is up to you. You can structure your time to suit yourself. No surprise in that - that's one of the reasons for leaving jobs. The surprise comes when you realize just how quickly a totally unstructured day can disappear.

Jobs seem to consume such an enormous part of our lives that one tends to think that - without the job - there will be unlimited time to do all those things that are now crammed into weekends and evenings, plus time to do all those other projects that have been put off for "when there's time", plus all that extra leisure time to enjoy the freedom. Oh, if it were only so!

Granted, you can gain forty or so hours a week by leaving a job. But those precious forty hours don't last as long at home as they seem to last on the job. Only if you husband them with a careful discipline will they serve all the ends you have in mind.

Our own failing was leisure. Sitting behind a desk all week, I relished the chance to get outdoors on the weekend to dig the garden, chop wood, hammer nails, anything. For a desk-bound paper pusher, all that constructive physical activity was recreation. When we finally packed up our compost heap and moved to the country we were suddenly free to do all those things we enjoyed most - like digging, chopping and hammering - plus all those things that had to be done - like finishing the house and digging, chopping and hammering. Six months later we were physically exhausted and thoroughly fed up with digging, chopping and hammering. We had been playing "weekend" for six whole months, forgetting that our former recreation was now our work and that we needed time off from that too. Waiting for the leisure to happen, or putting it off until the chores were done, just didn't work for us. We had to impose a discipline and set aside regular, inviolable, family recreation time.

Five years later our time discipline extends even to divisions within the working day: a certain portion for creative or mental work, and another part for the physical chores. There is still never enough time to finish all the goals we set ourselves. Indeed, we seem to be working harder at retirement than we ever did at jobs. But with the discipline to maintain a happy balance between mind work, muscle work and leisure, nothing gets too neglected and we can enjoy a little progress on every front.

Self discipline is not at all in contradiction to the freedom of retirement. The discipline is merely one defence against the rush of time. And, unlike an employer's discipline, self discipline can be arranged to suit ourselves. The family day, for instance. In the summer months we keep a Tuesday sabbath, simply because the parks, beaches and museums are least crowded then. In the summer, when there is lots of physical work to be done, a cup of tea and a quiet read are *de rigeur* after lunch. In winter, when chores are more cerebral, the after-lunch break turns to skiing in the woods. When the children got to the stage of spicing dinner with spills, spats and inane riddles, we invented a new tradition of adult dinner one night a week. They get packed off to bed early to read or play or do anything that can't be heard downstairs, and the grownups get candlelight and wine. We structure time to suit ourselves, but without the structure it soon degenerates into a morass of endless and undone chores.

Other families, infected with milder strains of Calvinist guilt, may need discipline to keep them working; but few of us are able to balance all the demands on time without some form of rules to keep us on track.

Administration

In the age of the paternal employer, much of the nitty-gritty paper work of life is taken care of "at the office". Part of the result is the jigsaw of numbers, deductions, and indecipherable codes that make up the modern paycheck. Cutting the umbilicus means, among other things, becoming your own administrator.

Making budgets, keeping records, scheduling tasks, making sure the medical insurance is up to date, and sorting out the tax and pension tangles aren't complicated jobs when you get right down to it. It's just that they are so easily put aside or forgotten when you are accustomed to leaving such headaches with "the office".

We're quite accustomed to shuffling our own papers now, but we still use "the office" for other things...like complaints. All complaints are immediately referred to the office. All dumb questions like "do you think it will rain next Tuesday?" or "can I have a motorcycle when I'm twelve?" are politely answered with a suggestion that they ask at the office. It's somewhere beyond the trees there. Very difficult to find...but keep looking.

The Rhythm of Life

Most jobs have a rhythm of their own: the pace of production, the end of the month, the fiscal year, or whatever; the work is geared to the ebb and flow according to some pattern of time. At the very least, most jobs force us into a cadence of weekend leisure, Monday blues, Friday's high, and regular checks. Our minds and bodies become so attuned to these rhythms that they disappear into our internal woodwork.

It comes as a shock, then when we leave the workplace, to discover that other lives have other rhythms. If you are not prepared, the adjustment can be hard.

Coming to the country, we had to adjust to the rhythm of the seasons. I expected to work hard, but my internal clock wanted to work and rest on a weekly pattern. For the farmer, planting, haying and harvest seasons set the schedule of work, and his "weekend" is the winter.

Changing lifestyles may mean changing life's rhythm as well. If you are not as young as you used to be, it may take your bones a while to catch up.

The Family Compact

Idylls are largely private things. Daydreams can be built into vivid and detailed shape in the recesses of one's own mind. The rose covered cottage, the painting loft, the rigging on the schooner - we can privately blueprint dreams to the last nail and hue. That's a splendid way to plan the future if you are on your own.

When the future involves families of more than one, however, it helps to air those dreams with your partners from time to time. Better to find out ahead of time that the kids are allergic to roses, or the wife can't stand drafty lofts, or the husband has his heart set on a yawl.

Getting ready is the time for shaping and amending idyllic dreams into practical and affordable forms. If the planning isn't done with the full participation of all the crew, then the dream may very well founder on a mutiny...and deserve to.

WHAT IF IT DOESN'T HAPPEN?

The biggest part of getting ready is organizing your financial life to spend less, get out of debt, and set aside some investments in reserve. For most of us, that's a slow, hard job. It is, however, a "can't lose" approach that takes the risk out of preparing for a crazy project like living without a regular job.

The worst that can happen is that the project fizzles to naught. You stick it out at work and leave the Tahitian nudes or the trout farm or the polar photography until you're 65. All that getting ready to survive without a salary was in vain, right? Wrong! All that getting ready should leave you out of debt, with cash in the bank, and a cheaper style of living. Not a bad sort of a flop.

5

Casual Income

It's one of nature's nastier laws that makes earning a living so much easier when you don't really need it. When money needs are reduced to simple maintenance - no debts or Joneses to keep up with - survivors learn that it's a whole lot simpler to earn small amounts of money than to find and keep a big-money job. Earning a small scale living becomes...well, a casual affair.

It has something to do with changing the rules. A regular career is usually conducted with a tight little set of unwritten but immutable laws:

Never take a job paying less than the last one!
Never take a job with less status than the last one!
Never take a temporary job if you can get a permanent one!
Never take a job outside your own trade or profession!

The effect is to limit job prospects to that narrow range of openings on the next rung of your own occupational ladder. Like going out for a walk and insisting on only walking uphill in a straight line. No wonder the going gets tough!

Prospects change, however, when you throw out the rules. When earning a living is reduced from ego gratification to the simple matter of regularly obtaining small amounts of money, the possible sources of money expand like magic.

WHATEVER HAPPENED TO AMBITION?

Is it merely weakness that causes many of us to walk away from careers that get too demanding? "When the going gets tough, the tough get going", and all that. Ambition is a fine and noble thing, and God forbid that anyone should abandon distant goals just because they're hard to reach. What is too often overlooked, however, is the simple idea that ambition and employment need not be synonymous. Ambition can exist outside the workplace.

Some of mankind's most noted over-achievers have succeeded precisely because they abandoned careers to pursue other goals...and regarded money as a minor but necessary nuisance. If ambition and success were confined to regular jobs, Gauguin might never have painted and the Wright brothers would have stuck to fixing bicycles in Dayton.

Someone, somehow, has tricked Western man into believing that security and self-worth come only from what we are paid to do. We become our jobs and we're worth only what we're paid. What rubbish! Esteem ought to come from everything we do and not just what we're paid to do.

DECIDING WHAT TO DO FOR MONEY

When ego has been removed from the minor but necessary nuisance of money, deciding what to do for income can have a whole new set of rules...or no rules at all. Being a structured type, I function better with lists and rules and don't mind sharing them here; but you make up your own as you like...it really doesn't matter in the least since the object of the new rules is to make paid work small and unobtrusive rather than large and self-enhancing.

1. The very best source of casual income is getting paid for things that you do because you like to do them. Getting paid for enjoying yourself. I write stories because I like to write. If someone decides to buy them that's terrific, but it has nothing to do with what and whether I decide to write. A sale is "found money", not the object of the exercise.
2. When that's not enough to pay the bills, casual income is generated as a by-product of work we would normally do for

ourselves. Growing food for instance. We haven't the land, the skills, or the capital to be real farmers, but we do enjoy raising animals and vegetables for our own kitchen. One pig a year is plenty of pork for us, but it's no more trouble to look after five than to raise one or two. We'd be doing the work anyway, so we plan on a little saleable excess of most of the things we produce for ourselves.

3. The most unobtrusive way to make money is with paper investments; and don't dismiss that option as the preserve of wealthy, coupon-clipping matrons. It may take some hard work to raise the capital in the first place, but once invested it's the money's turn to work for you. We began by considering investments as an alternative to insurance, keeping our own emergency fund rather than buying corporate protection - so now we collect interest instead of paying insurance premiums. Personally, I find the investment field a total bore. So our rule is to pick safe investments that don't require our time or attention.

4. When these dribs and drabs of income still won't stretch to meet our limited needs, and we reach the point of having to devote time to producing income, we look for projects that might prove interesting or projects that are easily started and stopped.

In general, if it's going to take time away from the things we would really rather be doing, casual income has to come from jobs that are interesting, or short-term, or both. Finally, it helps if the job can be related to some specific goal: "Three weeks work will pay for the trip to Florida." It makes drudgery more bearable, and makes it easier to curb extravagant impulses.

Those are our rules. They suit us and still allow enough cash flowing in to keep us afloat. More importantly, earning a living is rarely allowed to interfere with living itself. Too often friends have said, "That's fine for you, but we haven't the skills to sell on a casual basis like that." Such false modesty is usually a whacking load of cod's wallop. *It is confidence, not skill, that is lacking.* Nearly everyone who has spent some time in the work force has both material and personal resources that can be turned to profit.

ASSESSING YOUR ASSETS

No money to invest? Spent it all? On what? Unless you're an unlucky gambler or a hopeless gourmand it's difficult to get rid of all those paychecks over the years without having something to show for it. Equity in the house? Some land, a car, cameras, tools? You can't eat it all! Look around and do a quick assessment of your material resources. How much cash have you already invested in *things?* And they are investments. The problem is, you probably haven't been collecting the interest.

Space can be rented. The spare room, the garage, storage space in the basement. The basement's full? Of what? Stuff you don't use anymore? Sell it, and then rent the space to store somebody else's junk.

You have $500 worth of woodworking tools which you've used to make a $50 bed? Use them to make another bed, or something else that might sell. If you didn't enjoy woodworking you probably wouldn't have bought the tools.

You have some country property for that retirement dream? What's it doing now? Good fields can be rented to farmers. Forested land needs regular thinning. That's firewood, and perhaps pulp or lumber to sell.

One friend owns some acres of scrub too far from town to serve as anything but an occasional retreat. He retreated once too often and has now become a proud and happy first-time father. The retreat hasn't changed; it's still a leaky cabin amongst the trees. Fatherhood, however, has changed the owner's perspective. Now he sees the young trees as an investment. Thinned and nurtured by neighbors who are happy to get the firewood, the timber will be mature enough to harvest in time to pay for baby's college education...a neat little case of financial justice!

If you don't wish to sell or rent the things you own, at least consider using them yourself for money. It may double your value on the market. Your skill as a driver, for instance, may be worth only $5 to $10 an hour. Using your own car, however, makes your services much more valuable. Part of the payment is for your time and the rest is a return on your investment in the car.

Putting your possessions to work pays a double dividend. Not only do you get some return on that investment, but also a share of the costs may be deductible at income tax time. The basement workshop, the attic studio, the family car that does evening shifts delivering pizza, may all pay off in tax advantages. A friend who does freelance TV interviews even deducts her hairdos.

WHAT ARE YOUR PERSONAL RESOURCES?

I was going to call this section "skills", but that always makes folks think of their jobs. It's really much broader than that. The inventory of resources should be expanded to include not only the things you already do for money, but also the things you do for yourself, the things you can learn to do, and most of all the things you're really interested in doing.

A lady once told me that she wanted to work her way around the world but had only one saleable skill. With a little prodding she admitted that she could also drive, cook, shop efficiently, speak English and take quality photographs...all skills that can be profitably used by travellers. It's just that she had never *worked* at those things before and thus had not considered them as skills. The last I heard, she was half way around the world, busily photographing the South Pacific. Another zero-budget traveller I know went from England to India *working* as a bicyclist...he asked and the bike makers agreed that the ride would make a worthy testimonial for their ad campaign.

Deciding what to do for money should be as much an assessment of your interests as it is of your finances. Just don't make the assumption that because you enjoy it, someone else won't pay to have it done. Remember that just about everything you do for fun, someone, somewhere, gets paid to do.

CASUAL EMPLOYMENT

For some, the surest way to make a living - short of hanging on to a career - is to continue selling time or skills to employers, but on a part-time, temporary, or contractual basis.

For the worker, the trade-offs are obvious. You make less money, but spend less time doing it. You gain some control over where and when you work, but lose the sense of security that goes with a full time job.

Some careerists have the false impression that casual employment is only possible in the less skilled jobs; the sort of thing that moonlighting cab drivers, short order cooks and summer camp staffers do. The temporary hiring agencies do seem to specialize in unskilled placements, or easily transferable skills like typists, but casual workers abound in the professions as well. They're harder to see simply because they often have more fanciful titles, like "supply teacher", or "sub-contractor", or the ubiquitous "consultant".

The range of casual jobs is almost endless. When I was eight or nine the neighborhood was blessed with an elderly couple who grandparented for all the kids around who flocked in their cherry tree and hammock. The old man suddenly died, and poor old Mrs. S, who had no other family, was all on her own. She asked if my brother and I would spend a few nights at her place, just to keep her company. She owned the only TV set for miles around, so the treat was really ours. Nevertheless, she gave us each a quarter in the morning and sent us off to school. Naturally, the teacher picked that day to poll the class on the perennial classic, "What are you going to be when you grow up?" Still fingering my new quarter, I allowed as how I would earn my living sleeping with widows. The reaction that provoked in more puritan Bible-belt days was enough to put me off sleeping with widows forever.

Sleeping with widows may be on the outer limit of casual jobs, but just about anything else goes. One active young man worked his way through college as a deodorant tester. He had to go in to be sniffed every day, but most of his time was his own. I know people who've made their living as part-time preachers, evening teachers, truant officers (who only work when the weather's nice), and snow plow operators (who only work when the weather's bad). I've also known seasonal sales clerks (who only worked at Christmas), construction workers (who only work in the summer), a musician who does his work on Saturday nights livening up parties, and a hotel detective who's paid to make them quiet down again.

Many of the casual jobs around are filled by "moonlighters", full-time workers augmenting incomes with extra jobs in their spare time. Others, with smaller debts or simpler needs, manage to make a living on casual jobs alone.

Ray was a personnel officer in the civil service. He had a young family and a small salary...not a happy combination in a city where already sky-high housing costs were continuing to shoot up faster than his already inadequate salary. Ray decided the only way to make it was to start by working even harder. He went to the firms who were conducting weekend training seminars, and hired on as a part-time trainer - the same sort of work he was doing full-time for the government. With the weekend job added to his regular salary, they soon had enough for the down payment on a run-down, ramshackle house in a more desireable part of the city. It was bigger than they needed for themselves, so the third floor was rented out to help with the mortgage payments and the cost of renovations. Evenings were devoted to plastering, patching and painting. Ray was virtually working at three jobs. When the renovations were done, the house was worth almost twice what they paid for it. So they sold it and bought another cheapie. He did another year of the three job schedule: a full-time civil servant, part-time trainer, and evening renovator. By the time they sold the second house, they could afford a third house all to themselves -without a mortgage! Life was getting cheaper. The last I heard Ray and his family had settled in a permanent house of their own, he had left the civil service and was living happily on the income from the week-end training sessions, he was calling himself a "consultant", and - oh, yes - he had just reached his thirtieth birthday.

FINDING CASUAL JOBS

Casual employment is a common practice partly because it has so many advantages for the employer. As the pace of business changes, it's easier and cheaper for the employer to add and subtract casual workers than it would be to hire and fire permanent staff. Regular employees must be paid whether business is booming or slack. An employer filling a permanent career position must be very careful with his hiring. Mistakes can be corrected and poor workers weeded out, but often at the cost of severance pay, union battles, and a lot of hard feelings on both sides. Getting a permanent job is, therefore, a long and drawn-out process. Because casual workers can be dropped more easily, they are usually hired with less fuss and bother too. The process is the same...it just doesn't take as long.

The shortest job hunt on record surely has to be the day I arrived on the island state of Tasmania. The ferry left me in the little town of Devonport: travel weary, T-shirt and shorts, and three days wages away from the price of a ticket back to the mainland.

Devonport didn't appear to offer very much; one long street of low-slung shops and pubs, wooden facades, and a sleepy afternoon heat. Hardly the makings of economic miracles. At the far end of the street was a brick building, the only one in town - and it was two stories at that. If anybody along that drowsy street held the prospect of three days wages it had to be the monied looking place at the end. So I trudged through the dust and, still mystified (there wasn't even a sign outside), pushed through the big glass doors into a cool and spacious office lobby. The carpet was wool and deep. I could wiggle my toes in the thing. Across the center of the room was a long counter of dark, polished wood. Behind it were a dozen or so desks, the front ranks filled with young ladies typing earnestly and looking prim. Behind them were ranks of earnest young men in white shirts and ties. I wiped my hands on my T-shirt, hid my toes in the carpet and cleared my throat. The nearest typewriter stopped. There was quite a flutter of tics and squints across her face before she settled on a cool, superior look that suggested I might be mistaken. "Can I help you?"

Obviously not, but after walking all the way up the street I figured what the hell. "Yes, I'm looking for a job," says I.

Instantly, the necktied chap at the very back of the room jumped to his feet and blurted, "You're hired!" I put my little finger in my ear to ream it out. He was halfway to the counter already. "Can you start right away? I'll drive you to the job site..." I was on my way to the mountains before I discovered I'd be laboring to build a hydroelectric dam. Christmas was approaching and the regular gangs of casual laborers were drifting back to mainland families.

It's not always that easy. Getting a casual job usually follows the same rules as those that govern permanent jobs. The major difference is that letters and formal applications more often give way to the telephone and personal contacts. You still have to do the rounds, knocking on doors and making appointments until you find the places that have more work than workers. You still have to sell yourself and your abilities (though employers are usually more willing to take a chance with casuals). And you may have to work even harder as a casual than you would have as a permanent - remember that casuals are easier to fire as well as easier to hire than the career staff.

In certain occupations (secretarial, clerical and domestic for instance) casual workers are commonly placed through agencies or labor pools. You'll find the agencies in the "help wanted" ads, or in the yellow pages of the phone book under "employment agencies". The agencies make the job hunt even easier, but they will also collect a healthy fee from the employer and thus pay you that much less. If you find job hunting distasteful, by all means try an agency, but do find out the size of the agency's fee and ask yourself if job hunting is really *that* distasteful.

It really is more profitable to decide what you want to do, what time you have available, then look for an employer whose needs might coincide with yours. Don't wait for the dream job to surface in the "help wanted" columns. The market for casual jobs moves faster than that. This is the place for knocking on doors and making your pitch. One enterprising fellow in need of some extra cash was getting nowhere in his search for a part-time job. The problem was that he was only available for work on Thursdays. There were jobs around, but none seemed to fit his schedule. His final solution was artfully simple. On his next free Thursday he did the rounds of the bars, striking up acquaintances, and asking them what they did for a living. When he struck an interesting answer, he asked his new-found friend what he was doing in the bar. "It's my day off," was the hoped-for answer. He paid for the drinks and made straight for the company mentioned, offering his services as a relief man to fill in when the regular staff was off. It turned out Thursdays suited the employer just fine.

When economies slump and jobs get scarce there is a natural desire to hang on to whatever threads of permanence one may have. Ironically, it's at just such times that casual workers become an even more attractive option to employers. Loathe to hire permanent staff in troubled times, employers are more likely to look upon manpower needs as a possible short-term situation. If business does go sour, the employer knows he can cut causal workers more easily than full-time staff. Career personnel, however, are only marginally more secure. When business gets worse, the careerists go too.

The only real security any worker has is in his hands and between his ears. The casual worker's position may be a little more precarious than regular staff, but in the long run there's very little difference. Indeed, if the casual worker is familiar with the temporary job market and accustomed to the mobility, he may be back on someone else's payroll before the careerist has time to recover from the shock of a layoff.

The public service always seems to attract a particularly large swarm of camp followers: consultants, contractors, temporary and casual workers. Periodically (almost ritually) governments take new brooms in hand and vow to clear the deadwood out. Such reforms most often lead to even more scope for the camp followers. No bureaucrat would ever admit that the *work* of his department could be trimmed...that would make it seem unimportant. So when staff controls come down from above, the "work" is shifted from the insiders, who can be controlled, to the outsiders, who can't be controlled so easily. There are no fewer memos - just fewer typists to type them. So the typing agencies are called in to fill the gap. The press releases are pumped out by free-lancers instead of information officers. As much or more money is spent to accomplish the same tasks, and everybody is happy...especially the casual workers. If part-time bureaucracy appeals to you, avoid the regular civil service route and offer yourself to the nearest, over-worked department head - one with a budget of his own.

BUYING AND SELLING

If Western culture ever organizes economic alternatives into castes, working for others would still be somewhere near the bottom. The elite, the aristocrats of unemployment, the prima donnas of casual income, would always be the ad hoc salesmen, the entrepeneurs of anything that comes to hand. Such people were once affectionately known as "horse traders". They were more than survivors - they were "artistes". Horses may have left the roads long before the Edsel, but the knack of buying and selling as the opportunity arises survives.

The rattly old pick-up was dribbling ice water into the dust beside the forsaken country road. "How far ya goin'?" I shouted over the clangor of errant pistons.

"Next pub...maybe farther,"he roared back.

There hadn't been another car all morning and it was hot, dry walking. So I found a narrow perch amongst the litter and junk in the cab, carefully adjusting the springs that snaked through rents in the seat.

Conversation was impossible over the din, so I slumped at the window and took what I could of the breeze coming by. The forward progress was barely enough to keep up a breeze, but it seemed to be all the lopsided, jolting, shimmying hulk could manage.

Mercifully, he killed the motor as he turned off the road and coasted over the thirty yards of gravel to the front of the country pub, peeling in the white of the sun. Even after we stopped, it took awhile for the heaving squeeks and wheezes to finish their codas and fade away. The final sound was the steady rivulet of water trickling over the battered tailgate.

My companion walked exactly like his truck - a noisy, rolling waddle wherin forward progress was less than half the total motion. Filling the doorway, he snapped his suspenders. "Two beers!"

The publican looked twice at the fat old codger in the doorway before he saw me trying to squeeze in from behind. He seemed to be only half grateful for the company.

The old man put the glass to his mouth and sucked half a pint of foamy lager off the top. He belched. "Gawd it's 'ot!"

The publican mopped the puddles off the bar with a towel, then wiped his face and draped the towel around his neck.

"Wot's for lunch, mate?" the old man asked.

"Pies," said the publican, turning towards the kitchen.

"No bloody fish?" roared my driver, full of indignant surprise.

"No fish around here." The publican paused, his hand on the swinging kitchen door. He sounded tired. "Ya wanna pie or doncha?"

"How come there's no bloody fish?" The fat man winked at me as he finished his question with a swig of beer.

"It's too bloody hot and we're too bloody far from bloody Sydney, ya silly bastard." The publican was getting a mite cross.

The old man relaxed and smiled at him in a genial, conciliatory way. "Come on out 'ere mate, I got summit for ya." The publican had to think about it for a minute, and he still looked dubious as he followed us out to the rusty blue hulk, disintegrating in front of the pub. The sun was merciless.

The three of us peered over the side of the truck at the homemade plywood box. It sat soaking in those few puddles that hadn't found the tailgate or a rust hole yet. The fat man reached inside the box and drew out a long, dripping knife. The publican knotted his jaw.

"How much can you use?" he asked the publican, raising the lid higher with his other hand so that we could at last see the enormous carcass of a single grouper awash in the remnants of ice. The publican finally smiled. In fact, the smile got downright grinny as the old man hacked off an armload of cold, wet fish. It might have had something to do with the cool and delicious wash of air that rose from the box as we leaned in to admire the fish.

"How much can you use?"

The publican gave us a couple more beers and the old man got a fiver for the fish. "Where'd the fish come from?" I asked him as we squeezed back into the rattletrap truck.

"Some dumb tourist at the coast give 'im to me three days ago. Said he just like spearin' 'em, not eatin' 'em."

Ten miles further on we stopped for gas, and the manager let the old man take a half a dozen discarded tires from the heap at the back of the station. By evening, most of the fish and all of the ice was gone. The back of the truck, however, was loaded to the gunnels with tires. The tire center in the next town took them all to be retreaded. The old man counted his roll as he squeezed back in behind the wheel again. He peeled off a couple of bills and handed them to me.

"What's that for?" I asked.

"Helpin'." He ground the motor into its usual cacophony and we rattled off to find the best steak dinner in town. We were both more or less headed for Melbourne. Me more and him less, however. After three days and barely 150 miles of net forward motion I had to leave the old man to catch a faster ride, but I never found a more instructive one. It was slow progress, but we ate and slept in first class places, had a beer in every pub along the way, and parted company with more cash than when we'd met. For all I know he's still on his way to Melbourne, selling everything along the way.

On our last night together we split the day's profits and headed for an evening at the local. "Take one beer and sip it all night," he muttered as we ambled into the bar. Not my choice, but I knew enough by then to trust him. He stopped in the doorway, snapped his suspenders, and offered a round of beer for all. The dozen or so workmen propped against the bar responded in kind and within a few hours it was the most jovial and...well...relaxed bunch of good old boys in town. All except me. I slumped in the corner feeling a little left out until the old man, with more slurring of words than I knew was really in him, neatly turned the mostly incomprehensible talk to the subject of arm wrestling.

Amid the bantering and stumbling, the old man roared, "Ahh, you puny lot of poufters couldn't even beat the likes of him!" and he pointed his glass at me, then drained it with a sly wink in my direction.

"That skinny bloke in the corner?...Put up or shut up you silly old bastard!" and other words to that effect filtered out of the uproar. A table was cleared, bets were laid, and (suitably handicapped) most of the aspirants were hardly capable of taking a grip...much less deciding in which direction they should pull. We left shortly after - by separate doors of course - and split the take in the truck. The master salesman strikes again.

I never managed to catch the old man's flair for drama, his sure touch at timing the "pitch", but I did learn that you can sell just about anything to anybody if you screw up the nerve to try...and try again if it doesn't work the first time. It can even be fun.

UNDERSTANDING THE MARKET

Few of us are really cut out to be itinerant, ad hoc salesmen. It's hard on the liver as well as the nerves. There remains, however, a great deal of scope for casual, penny-ante buying and selling for profit. The key is to keep it on the smallest scale (so it doesn't take too much time from more important things), and to thoroughly understand what you are selling and the market for it.

That approach coincides exactly with the best way to shop for home consumption; understanding the goods and the market. Consequently, buying and selling for profit doesn't require a lot of extra effort; it's simply an extension of careful shopping. We rarely make major spending decisions until we're satisfied that it's the very best deal obtainable anywhere. When we're that sure, it doesn't take any more effort to invest in a little excess. If it's a bargain for us, it will be a bargain for others too.

Building materials for instance. One year we needed an inside door. We shopped around and learned that solid, pine inside doors were in the neighborhood of $100 new, and half to two-thirds that price in the places that sell used doors. Weeks later, at a country auction, a whole pile of discarded doors was on the block, and at the bottom of the pile were three that looked as if they might be suitable. The bidding was slow and the price was right so I took the whole pile for six dollars. I knew it was a bargain for the door we wanted, so it must be a bargain on the excess too.

We broke even the next day by selling one of the extras to a neighbor who was building a garage. He got a $6 door and was thrilled. Another was traded for eight pine shutters, two are serving as shelves, four have been joined for a chicken pen, and the rest are still in the barn - every once in a while some one comes by and asks if we have any old doors around...

Urban conservers are even better suited to profit from casual buying and selling: quite simply, there are a lot more customers. The process is exactly the same; shopping carefully for family consumption and buying excess when the bargains are best. When Bradley and his wife got married, they couldn't afford to furnish their home from department stores. So they spent their Saturdays prowling around the garage sales, picking up bits and pieces here and there. When the house was full, they were still finding pieces they liked at bargain prices. Brad kept buying. They made room in the house by selling extra pieces to friends (at a reasonable markup). When friends couldn't keep up with his bargains, Brad and his wife held garage sales of their own. Now they have a house full of valuable antiques and a profitable part-time hobby. Others have done the same sort of thing with bicycles, stereos, TVs, and cars. I suppose somebody, somewhere, is still trading horses in the classic fashion.

As a callow youth I spent a horrible two weeks peddling pots and pans from door to door. The spiel was phoney, the price was too high, the pots were shoddy, and the sound of slamming doors still haunts me. I'll never have what it takes to make a career of selling. But when somebody pulls in the lane and asks if we have any extra eggs, or some corn to sell, or any old doors lying around...well, it's easier somehow. When the neighbor says he needs a TV and you've got an extra one in the basement, or when the garden produces a load of perfect pumpkins for Hallowe'en, making a sale can be a downright pleasant experience. It's the difference between filling someone else's need and trying to create one.

COTTAGE INDUSTRY

There was a time, in the British Isles, when crofters and "small holders" processed goods for the market right in the family home. Weavers kept a loom in the house, crofters spun, smiths and cobblers and all manner of small scale artisans worked in their homes...cottages. This activity, in contrast to the centralized wage labor of factories, was referred to as "cottage industry".

It still goes on today. Stay at home entrepeneurs sew, type, paint, write, make baskets, string snowshoes, and - yes - still spin and weave. At least one lady I know of works at home as a typesetter. My favorite, however, was the young, bearded hitchhiker I picked up on my way to the city one day. In spite of his scruffy looks, he wafted into the car smelling like grandmother's kitchen The bulging rucksack was loaded to overflowing with carob rolls and peanut butter cookies. He was, he said, a baker, making his living from his kitchen stove and wholesaleing the goodies to city bakeries. The delivery system was a little unorthodox, but a small price to pay for the pleasures of working at home.

His approach was unusual, but the traveling baker had all the elements of a typical cottage industry; home based, no paid employees, and labor intensive. Working at home with the immediate family involved, is a familiar model. "Labor intensive" is a term that might require an explanation.

Simply put, goods are produced with three classes of input: the raw material, labor and capital. The capital is whatever is invested in the tools, machinery, buildings, and so forth, that are used to produce the goods for sale. To a certain extent, capital and labor may be substituted, one for the other. Workers can be replaced by machines, and vice-versa. The cookie man, for instance, took all morning to fill his pack with goodies. He put three hours labor into that load, but the capital investment was negligible; a few pots and pans, a rucksack, and a fraction of the kitchen stove (most of it being used for family meals rather than saleable production). Virtually all of the revenue goes to him for his labor. His approach was "labor intensive". On the other hand, he could have invested in automatic mixers and a big industrial oven to mix and bake all his cookies in a single batch. He might have cut his labor down to half an hour or so, but the capital input would have been a great deal higher. That approach would have been "capital intensive".

There's no law that says a cottage industry can't be capital intensive, but in most cases it just isn't practical. The cookie man couldn't afford to leave that big expensive machinery sitting idle for most of the week. He would have to keep it working to pay for itself. That means more cookies than he could carry in his rucksack. So he would have to buy a truck and hire a driver (or pay another baker to stay home and keep the cookie machines going). He would need somebody else to sell all that extra production and somebody else to keep track of the wages and receipts and the payments on the cookie machines and the truck and...and before he knows it he's got a cookie factory instead of a cottage industry. The operation has certainly outgrown his little farmhouse kitchen, so he has to move the business to a larger building and the payments on that mean even more cookies have to be sold. The cookie man may get rich - or go broke. He may retire to Florida, or spend seven days a week at the cookie factory making ulcers. The capital intensive approach may have any or all of those results...but it won't result in a cottage industry.

Cottage industry that hires outside employees, or builds up its capital plant to the point where it moves out of the home and acquires a life of its own, simply becomes another small business. Though the differences are mostly ones of degree, the changes in character between cottage industry and a "real" business are of fundamental importance to readers interested in the quality of life.

A small business has a life and momentum of its own. It must support not only its owner but also its employees, the building, inventory, the capital debt, accounts receivable, and so on. The larger a business becomes the harder it is to stop and start, to close it down for the summer, or to exercise fully independent control.

A central part in the life of most small business is debt. The risks involved in borrowed capital are high. High enough that new businesses go bankrupt with alarming regularity. Potential rewards for success may be high, but so is the risk of failure. It's that high level of risk which keeps so many would-be entrepeneurs from taking the plunge. No one with a good idea should be discouraged from launching a full scale business venture; but it is a pity that so many who are discouraged by the risk, believe staying with a salaried job is the only alternative. If the venture can be started at home, with yourself as the only employee, using labor rather than capital, the risk can be virtually nil. That's the attraction of cottage industry. *Less risk - and greater independence.*

THE HARD PART: DECIDING WHAT TO DO

There are two approaches to picking a cottage industry. The most obvious is to start with something you already know well: your job, past training, a hobby or craft. The other approach is to find a gap in the market that the big guys haven't filled very well; a speciality item or new procedure that may be too small or too new to have attracted organized commerce yet. These are easier to find than most people imagine.

How often have you gone shopping for something and not been able to find what you were looking for?

"Sorry sir, they don't make those anymore."

"Sorry sir, this is all we have."

"Sorry sir, you can only get those in..."(someplace 80 miles away).

110

You have just identified a gap in the market. Faced with such obstacles, enterprising conservers go home to see if they can build it, fix it, or adapt something else to the purpose. The usual outcome is finding out *why* the big guys aren't interested in selling the whatsit you had set out to buy. You discover it really is too expensive, or too difficult, or doesn't work the way you thought it might. Every once in awhile, though, basement dabblers discover that they *can* do it better or cheaper than anything else on the market. That's a gap in the market ready-made for home industry.

Setting out to buy something and ending up providing it, is just what got us into making heat shields. It sparked a frustrated connoisseur into setting up his own wine importing business. And it turned one student vet into a kitchen table surgeon. The poor chap couldn't afford to get his own cats spayed at professional rates, so he did it himself. The story spread and soon he was providing a much needed neighborhood service. He eventually got his license, an office, and a lucrative practice at professional rates. The old neighborhood, I expect, is overrun with cats again.

Ironically, opportunities for home industry seem to be growing rather than shrinking. One would think that - with the passage of time - all of the gaps in all the markets would be filled, that all the profitable ideas would be taken. Seems logical...except for the fact that markets are dominated by the big guys, who continue to get bigger and bigger and more and more standardized. They're too big to be bothered with any items for which demand would be small, or specialized, or regional, or...just the sort of thing a cottage industry is suited for. The big guys want to supply the world. If you want to make whatchamacallits for your neighbors, or elbow patches for one-armed poker players, or anything else where the demand is just about big enough to keep your basement in full production, chances are you may get some competition from your neighbors or from other one-armed poker players, but not from General Motors. The big guys only want big gaps in the market. The cottage industrialist is happy with little gaps.

Setting Up

The details of starting any particular venture as a cottage industry will vary too widely to generalize here. There are three points, however, that ought to be stressed:

1. *Test the market for price and saleability.* No matter how sure you are of your product, it pays to actually build a few prototypes

first and see how they sell. It's easier to change the design or the color, or whatever, *before* you get all geared up with a load of materials for full production.

2. *Minimize capital costs.* Any small scale business goes through innumerable changes in the first few years as you learn more about the market and find short-cuts or improvements in the process. Such changes are easier to make if you haven't committed yourself at the beginning to a shop full of expensive tools and materials. In the beginning it pays to keep these capital costs as close to zero as possible. Borrow equipment, rent it, substitute more labor intensive methods, but start on the smallest shoestring you can. It's easier to make the inevitable changes and there's less at risk.

3. *Find out what licenses, permits, and zoning changes you would need to operate legally.* Zoning regulations vary from city to city. The object is to control development and to keep you from becoming a nuisance to your neighbors. State and provincial bodies require licenses in many specialized areas: cat spaying, brain surgery, and the handling of food, for instance. The object is to protect your customers. Most jurisdictions require a vendor's permit or business license to identify your commerical character. The object is to know where to send the tax bill. For details, check at city hall.

Selling Your Wares

For many otherwise clever and forceful people the actual selling of what they do is the hardest part of independence. It's not surprising. We are, after all, taught from childhood about the virtues of being modest, humble, and self-effacing. Then to survive we find it necessary to tout our skills or wares as the very best there is. Even if we believe it, it's hard sometimes to say it to others. It feels so...pushy.

Don't despair, modest reader, there's a way to be business-like without losing that virtue. It's called a sample. Samples of your work, shown to prospective buyers, can sell themselves. Whether you are planning to make planters or photos or latkes, have some samples ready and let the buyer judge the quality himself. If your income scheme is based on a service rather than a product (house sitting or tax consultation for instance) the sample can take the form of a written description of the services offered, prices, and -best of all - testimonials from previous customers. If the quality of your work can speak for itself, all that remains is to find the buyers and set the price.

There is some advantage, not entirely psychological, in starting with smaller prospective customers. Chances are the big guys are already supplied by the other big guys. Those little gaps in the market that you are looking for are at the other end of the scale. So don't go waltzing into Sears with your first two widgets hoping that they'll put them on the shelf for you. They may like them and ask for a thousand a week, when you're only geared up for two. Build if you will, but do start small.

Wherever you go for those first few sales, set the objective in advance. "This week I'm going to call on these five (or seven or forty) prospects." The objective is set on the basis of how many tries you will make...not on the number of sales. The only purpose is to ward off discouragement from the first few refusals, to keep you plugging away in the face of apparent defeat. Think of those first attempts as practice sessions, trial runs to get your knees to stop shaking and to find out what questions prospective customers want answered.

How Much?

The first question customers ask is usually "How much?" The answer, of course, depends on whether you're selling retail, wholesale, or consignment (where the retailer accepts your product for display and pays you a fixed percentage of the retail price after the goods are sold). The price depends on what the competition charges, what the product costs you to produce, and how many you wish to sell. In short, there is no one right price. You're your own boss and it's entirely up to you. You may wish to ask yourself a few pertinent questions, though.

What's fair? You know your costs of production and what your own time ought to be worth. Covering those costs is the basis of a reasonable price. Someone else, however, may have found ways to do the same thing more cheaply. If your prices are higher than the competition's, your venture may be shortlived. You may have to charge less than a "fair" price until you have found ways to pare the costs.

What will the market bear? That's an even more critical question than fairness. If your price is too high you could end up with a basement full of widgets and no customers. If prices are too low, your widgets will be sold faster than you can make them, and you will spend a lot of time saying "sorry" to disappointed customers. Economists call that the law of demand (the cheaper they are the more you can sell).

If you're lucky, your *fair* price will attract just enough customers to keep you as busy as you want to be. Your supply will meet the customers' demand at a point where everybody is happy with the price and there are no unsold widgets or unfilled orders. If you are not so lucky, you may have to fiddle with the price.

Undercharging, or even giving away free samples, is one way to get things rolling - to get prospects to try your wares and, hopefully, to keep buying after the price goes up.

Overcharging (setting a price that's higher than what you have decided is fair return for your time and costs) is a simple way to control sales volume when it threatens to become a landslide. The idea is to scare off just enough customers to bring demand into line with the level where you want to produce.

Finally, there are times when it becomes necessary to be absolutely outrageous with your price. Times when you would really rather not sell. Last October, the kids and I cleaned out the garden and decided to take the leftover squash and pumpkins into market. We found a spot amidst the other vendors and sorted the future Jack-o-lanterns into a lumpy pile, a good pile, and one absolutely perfect scare-monger that the kids wanted to carve for themselves. When "please don't sell this one, Daddy," didn't work, they tried sitting on it so no would see it.

"How much are they?"

The first question from the first customer was, of course, "How much are they?"

The kids looked at me and I looked at them. "What do you think?" I asked the seven year old, who had already checked on the competition.

"Seventy-five cents for the lumpy ones and a dollar for the good ones," she answered.

What about the one you're sitting on?" asked the lady.

"Ten dollars," says the miniature tycoon, deadpan. Outrageous, but she got to keep the pumpkin.

Think Small

Those who approach income as serious business (driven by avarice, ambition, or debt) often succeed through sheer hard work. "Think big! Aim high!" and all those other inspirational catechisms of the capitalist religion, hang in their heads if not on their office walls.

The survivor, though, keeps a different set of rules. When income is given only casual consideration, a minor nuisance, a means rather than an end, the inevitable outcome is that less hard work may go into any one venture. More of the survivor's income schemes may fail or simply wither from neglect. Let's face it, if the hard-driving, big-money, ulcer-riddled ranks of the real moguls fail at such an impressive rate, what chance does the casual survivor have after spending most of his energy on the non-profit side of life. He decreases his chance of failure by treating debt like the plague, but the casual approach is - without doubt - a handicap to big financial success.

The survivor accepts from the start that his casual income schemes are handicapped, that not everything will succeed. The strategy, then, is simply to keep a number of schemes in motion at any one time. This is what distinguishes you from the "real" businessman. He works hard at one thing, and either fails or gets rich. The survivor works casually at a number of things. Some succeed and some don't. Since all his ventures start small and are free of debt, the flops don't lead to bankruptcy and ruin...they just don't make any money. And the successes don't lead to fame and riches. They're little successes...just enough to meet your needs if your needs are simple enough.

"Think Small" is not an apology for dropping out, or a credo for all of life's little wallflowers. It's no more than a reminder that making a living doesn't have to take over from living itself. *It is a way of scaling down financial risks and financial expectations simultaneously.* Think small and diversify. Any income scheme that gets boring, doesn't pay, or interferes with more important things, can be discarded...with no more effort than ignoring it.

FREELANCE LIVING

So far we've talked about casual approaches to relatively standard ways of making a living: employment, buying and selling, cottage industry...small, controlled attachments to the regular economy. Those attachments can become even more tenuous when the worker (independently) seeks markets for what he does rather than doing what the market asks.

In the confusing days of medieval warfare, the freelancer was literally that: an unattached soldier, a mercenary, later called (less romantically) the hired gun. Those types are still around, but the modern freelancer can also be a writer, artist, photographer, broadcaster, teacher, or just about anything. He sells his skills or creations to anyone he can. I know a freelance bookkeeper, a freelance scientist, a freelance stage designer, and a freelance builder of parade floats. It's like a cottage industry where the owner is also the product. It's like casual employment, except that there are usually several customers instead of a single employer and the freelancer is always the boss.

Apart from the obvious attributes of maximum freedom and independence, being a freelance anything is to enjoy the justice of a system where success is almost solely a function of talent and effort. The freelancer lives outside the usual rules of paper credentials, seniority advancement, and office politics. His work is judged on its merits.

Paradoxically, this makes it easier to enter any field and yet harder to get established. Entry is easier because the work provides its own credentials. To be employed as a salaried photographer, for example, may require professional experience, accredited training, or the crossing of a number of other barriers set up to separate the wheat from the chaff. But the barriers are based on the *person*. A talented beginner may find it tough to cross those barriers, in spite of the quality of his work. But a freelancer is free to call himself a photographer and let his work be accepted or rejected on the basis of whether it's any good or not. There are still barriers, but they are more concerned with the work than with the person.

Getting established as a freelancer requires that your work be seen by a number of potential buyers. Being seen is the hard part. Most people with money to spend on freelancers are busy people. Persistence, patience, the shotgun approach, or all those tactics may be necessary to get your foot in the door. After a few successes, getting in the door is easier. One job leads to another.

Those first few jobs, however, take some special effort. It might help to keep in mind the lessons applied to a cottage industry:

Doing sample work (or even free work) if it will help to have your product seen by more potential buyers;
Diversifying, keeping several projects in the works at once, in the hope that one of them will catch on somewhere;
Refusing to be discouraged by initial rebuffs.

One would-be writer started his freelance career by vowing to always keep at least three articles in the mail at any one time. The first few rejections might have ended his efforts, except that he could always hope the other two prospects might be positive. Every rejection slip had to be followed by another submission. No matter how bad the news in the mail, there was always hope that better news could follow. It did.

CASUAL INCOME: NEW BEGINNING OR A WAY OF LIFE?

There are many independent types who spend their evenings setting up a basement industry or trying to peddle that first short story. Some are compelled by dreams of success in a more independent line - something riskier, more far-reaching, and more rewarding than what they do for a work-a-day wage. They are seeking new beginnings. Others are less concerned with reaching the stars than with simply generating a few bucks to support some other dream.

Whatever the motives, casual incomes are invariably easier to generate than most nine-to-fivers imagine. There are more ways to make a living than ever appear in job descriptions at the employment agency. There are certainly more ways than I ever dreamed of when that rusty blue truck pulled up, rattling and wheezing and dripping water into the dust.

6

The Second-Hand Market

The catalogue beside me shows a simple wooden table. A card table. Four legs and a top. Not even a drawer to hide the aces in. And it's used. Southebys estimate its value at $125,000! They, of course, don't refer to it as "used". Status conscious matrons don't buy used furniture - they buy antiques.

Face-saving euphemisms like "antique" furniture, "heritage" china, and "previously owned' cars are all aimed at covering up the stigma of buying second hand. The euphemisms, naturally, affect the price...hence the fabled sign in front of the country shoppe: "We Buy Old Junk and Sell Antiques".

Thank goodness, though, there are such stigmas. That's what makes it possible for the conserver crowd to maintain a happy standard of material living at a fraction of the cost of shopping in the shoppes. We stick to shops, and buy used stuff and junk. What a difference a name makes!

Unfortunately, more vendors seem to be catching on to the name game. More and more junk is being sold as "junque", and advertisements for antique cars with automatic trans and power steering make one wonder if the term hasn't already been stretched beyond usefulness. When I start seeing ads for "old" antiques, I'll know it's time to discard the word entirely.

If you can stay ahead of the name changers, however, and don't mind being seen in the low-rent district where junk is spelled with a "k", the second-hand market is still a bonanza for cheap living.

Buying second-hand is not the same as retail shopping. The rules are different. If you like the convenience of the big plazas and department stores, you've probably also fallen into the habit of accepting prices on the basis of the store's reputation. One chain is known for cheapie imports and bargain basement prices; others are known to carry medium quality at medium prices; and every town has at least one store whose prices have more to do with snob appeal than quality. When you want something cheap to wear in the garden, you don't shop around for price, you go to the store with the cheapie reputation and trust that the lowest price there will be the lowest in town. It's not that easy in the second-hand market.

The successful second-hand shopper has to judge price and quality independently - for each item - with less regard for the reputation of the seller. I have seen the most upright and honest of country auctioneers selling used household goods for more than the same item would cost new, down the street at the hardware store. I have also found occasional bargains at the snobbiest antique shoppes. In the second-hand market there's just no way of recognizing a bargain unless you know ahead of time what you want, and what it's worth.

WHAT YOU WANT AND WHAT IT'S WORTH

Second-hand shopping begins at home. Unlike retail shopping, the value of the thing you're after is not the same as what the store is charging. You have to decide fair value for yourself. The best place to start is with consumer guides, catalogues, and that enormous free library of price information: the junk mail circular.

The consumer guides (by subscription, or *free* at the public library) provide a wealth of comparative data on products: how they last, which ones work and which ones need loopholes in the warranties, which are safe, and what the average retail price will be. Exhaustive tests and brand-by-brand comparisons provide an encyclopedic review of all the things the ads won't tell you. For most common products, consumer guides will, at the very least, help to weed out some brands or products that will *not* suit your needs.

Of particular interest to the second-hand buyer is information on durability and potential problems. If the brand X widget is prone to wear out in the left rear whatsit, that's the first thing to check when you find a used one. Faults in used products are easier to spot if you know what to look for ahead of time.

The least useful information in consumer guides are the prices. The national averages listed may be irrelevant in your own locale, and price information is rapidly outdated. Current prices, local sales, and store-by-store price comparisons can be easily seen in the chain store catalogues and advertising circulars that come in the mail in a daily stream.

Collecting such information need not be a major research job, preceding every shopping trip with charts and studies and a trip to the library. With me it's more like an habitual tic. I turn to the classified ads the way other newspaper readers turn first to the sports or comics. Knowing what we need to buy ahead of time, and then delaying the purchase as long as possible (remember procrastination) leaves lots of time to register mental notes of prices. If I can't remember the current retail price of any item, it's easy enough to check the catalogues.

What's collecting in the head, though, are new prices; and remember we're going shopping for used. The new price is an absolute upper limit. There's nothing more embarrassing than buying a used anything, then finding it on sale, new, at a lower price than you paid for a second-hand version. And I'm not being picky, because it happens all the time. Not long ago I was in a second-hand shop (which has since become a shoppe) and was surprised to see a modern wine bottle in the midst of a display of antique bottles. The modern bottle was familiar - an attractive earthenware imitation - but the price was a shocker at $9.00.

"You know," I said to the owner, "you can buy that bottle new at the liquor store for $3.85, and you get a litre of wine with the bottle."

"I know," he admitted, "but a lot of customers don't."

WHAT'S A USED ONE WORTH?

If the new price provides a crude sort of upper limit on the worth of second-hand goods, it might save total embarrassment, but won't guarantee you any bargains. For a better idea of second-hand values, shoppers should consider the new price, reduced according to the *age and condition* of the used one. This approach will be familiar enough to used car buyers. The value of a year old car in average condition is a given percentage of its new price.

The declining value from an initial new price is called depreciation, and most things that wear out can be given a value by depreciating them. It's not a precise calculation - more like organized guess work - but it can be a more reliable guide to second-hand values than simply taking the seller's word for it. Here's how it works:

My favorite electrical repairman tells me that the small, portable washing machine we want usually lasts only six or seven years. New ones are being advertised for around $480. That makes it worth about $80 a year. ($480 ÷ 6 = $80)

After finding a used machine for sale, the first concern is to ensure that it is in good working order. That means turning it on, pumping water back and forth through all the cycles, looking for leaks, and listening for groans and rattles. The second step is to find out how old the thing is. The dates will be on the original warranty papers or bill of sale - ask for them. If the machine is three years old, we assume it has used up half its life and is now worth a maximum of $240. ($80 per year x 3 years = $240)

That's a *maximum* and not an average because we know that the last three years of the machine's life are worth less than its first three years. In the last half of its life it may require more replacement parts, and service calls. It may even die sooner than its allotted 6 or 7 years. But we can set $240 as the upper limit, offer $80, and settle somewhere around $160. For that price, we would expect to have two years of maintenance-free washing.

APPRECIATE WHAT YOU CAN'T DEPRECIATE

Not everything loses value with the passage of time. More durable items (like furniture, tools, building materials, metal goods, etc.) must be valued more by their condition than by age. Indeed, the older goods were often better made and of better material than the newest models. Setting a fair value for such goods gets gets a little tricky. It helps to spend enough time at auctions and second-hand sales to get a rough idea of the market value of comparable items. Here, there is no good substitute for experience.

Take beds, for example. Old, wooden bedsteads were more solidly and beautifully crafted than most of the stuff being manufactured today. It would be tempting then to say that an old bed is at least as valuable as any comparable new bed. The price of "antique" beds in the shoppes would seem to bear this out; but, closer to the source, the price of used beds does funny things. Somehow, they seem to be a glut on the market. And it is not at all uncommon to see solid old beds of maple and ash selling at auctions and farm sales for $10 or less. No rule of thumb would tell you that, and an inexperienced buyer who finds a nice old bed in an antique shoppe for a little less than the price of a new veneer one, might think he had found himself a bargain. It would be a bargain, too - except that he could get it even cheaper elsewhere.

WHAT'S IT WORTH AS RAW MATERIAL?

When experience, or depreciation from a new price, doesn't tell me whether a second-hand buy is a bargain or not, I often fall back on a basic rule of thumb; *what's the worth of the material in it?* Like semi-handy husbands everywhere, I make a lot of well-meant but worthless promises to build and fix things around the house, "one of these days". Sometimes I even get as far as drawing a plan or making a list of the materials needed for the shelves in the cellar or the kitchen table or whatever. At some point in my auction habit, It occurred to me that buying a table was often cheaper than buying the lumber to build one. If I didn't like the table on sale, I could take it apart and use the wood to build a better one. In fact, there are usable materials in a lot of bargains that might otherwise be ignored.

One of the more expensive items on our "one of these days" list is a greenhouse. Expensive because of the price of glass. So I keep "glass" on my permanent shopping list, and collect bargains here and there until someday we have enough glass to make the greenhouse. A few weeks ago there was an auction sale nearby that advertised a quantity of glass to be sold. Obviously some others around here had the same idea, and bidding on the glass was brisk. The short guy in front, with the bald and well-tanned head, was getting most of the glass...and paying dearly for the privilege. I wasn't surprised then when late in the afternoon he bought a pile of old storm windows, with two sheets of new glass on top of the pile. I was surprised though when he picked up only the smaller new sheets and started to take them away.

"I thought you were buying the storm windows," I said as he passed.

"No," said the bald man, with the sly grin of a successful bargain on his face, "I'm building a greenhouse, and all I want is the glass. Take the windows if you want them."

I loaded them quickly, certain he would realize at any moment that there was a lot more glass in the windows than he had in his hands.

WHEN IT ALMOST WORKS

Like the proverbial cup that's half empty or half full - depending on your point of view - there are people who can see residual value in someone else's junk. A thing may be worthless if it doesn't work; add the price of what it takes to make it whole again and you may have a valuable bargain.

An axe without a handle won't cut wood, and that's why axe heads are often thrown out or sold, second hand, for pennies. The people who buy an axe head for pennies are the people who know that adding a five dollar handle will make it as good as a fifteen dollar axe.

There was the discarded freezer that wouldn't keep anything frozen. We added a five dollar seal around the door and used it for eight more years, after it had been given up as worthless.

A common form of this talent is the guy on every block who can take someone else's junkyard car and add a whatsit, some body work, and end up with something as good as new. With cars, that talent is worth thousands.

It doesn't always take a special skill, however. Sometimes a different perspective is enough. Years ago, before Liz had learned to pound a nail, she saw the neighbor put out two broken chairs for the garbage. It was a matching pair: a rocker with a broken back and a straight chair with a broken seat. Liz went right over, pulled the broken back off the rocker and replaced it with the good back from the other chair. It's still in use today. The neighbor had seen two broken chairs where Liz had seen the makings of one.

If there is a secret to dealing in the second-hand market, It's buying on the basis of a thing's bad features (the half empty side) and using or selling it for its residual value (the half full side).

LOOK AT FUNCTION

Chapter Three urges that needs be considered in terms of function. It's a simple change in perspective that has no other purpose than to open our minds to a broader range of possible substitutes...including the more unusual substitutes that may be considerably cheaper than the common commercial solutions to our needs.

The *function* approach is especially useful in the second-hand market, where prices and supply are so much more erratic than on the retail scene. The simple fact is that we often can't find what we feel we need, and have no choice but to look for substitutes.

I saw the lesson come home with one lady who cleaned out her cupboards and brought her castoffs to the flea market rather than the dump. She had an old shower curtain in her discard pile.

"I don't know whether to put this thing on the counter or not," she mused. "I can't imagine anybody wanting *this* in their bath!" She finally shrugged and put it at the back of the sales table, hoping that for twenty-five cents some sucker would at least save her the trouble of taking it home again.

Later on we munched a few of her bran muffins that hadn't sold and the talk turned to fixing up houses. She was, she told me, in the midst of painting every wall in the house. "And the hardest part is to keep from painting the furniture and floors at the same time. Good drop cloths are so expensive for what they are!...My God," she sputtered through a mouthful of muffin, and scrambled to salvage her sturdy sheet of waterproof material from the sales table before someone else saw that it could function as something other than a dirty old shower curtain.

One more example. Solar heat, the oil moguls tell us, is expensive and impractical. And if you go to the marketplace to buy solar panels - even small systems to heat the water - their disdain appears to be justified. The darned things are expensive for what they are...basically a grid of tubing under glass or plastic. But in the second hand market there are items that fill that function perfectly: large, elaborate grids of tubing, often copper, made for heat conduction. Most are already painted black, as solar panels are. They are so cheap that most people don't even bother trying to sell them. They're drained of freon and dumped in landfills, or worse. The people throwing them out don't even know they're solar panels though. They call them broken refrigerators and never consider the function of all that stuff on the back! Just like the people throwing out old storm windows. They have no value because they don't fit the new aluminum frames. Those people don't realize they're throwing out covers for solar panels and greenhouses.

A GOOD SELLER IS HARD TO FIND

The thing that buyers must understand about sellers is that the source that's easiest to find is likely to be the most expensive. Take furniture for instance. Retail furniture stores are easily accessible, well advertised, and the most expensive source in the market. The buyer pays dearly for the convenience of knowing where to find furniture without looking. Second-hand stores aren't located in the big shopping plazas, and don't blanket the area with full color ads. They're harder to find and a little cheaper. Small time sellers (who insert little classified ads in the paper to get rid of the old dining room table) are usually cheaper still. In fact, that's where the second-hand dealers get a lot of their stock. The cheapest source of all is often the person who owns such things but never bothers to put it on the market. That's the guy who puts his old dining table in the basement and forgets about it until someone comes along and offers to take it off his hands. He places so little value on his discards that he takes no steps at all to make himself accessible. That's one of the reasons there are so many enterprising souls in the want ads of any newspaper, offering themselves and their pick-up trucks to help clean up basements.

If you want the best deal on the second-hand market, the trick is to imagine who might be discarding the thing that you want, but who is too small or too busy or too something to bother making himself available to buyers. Readers who had to buy their own school books will remember that the rich kids bought their textbooks new at the big bookstore nearest campus. Students on a budget went to the second-hand bookstore that always seemed to be down an alley or in a basement. The real penny-pinchers, though, sought out the rich kids who had already taken the course, and made them an offer for last year's texts.

AVOIDING FADS

If accessibility makes second-hand buys more expensive, used items that are so popular and accessible that they become fads can come to cost even more than the new version. There was a time recently when "barn board" was selling in the cities for a dollar a board foot (one square foot of one inch board). At the same time, the new stuff - the unweathered lumber from which barns were built - was available at the mills for thirty cents a board foot! And yet fad conscious builders continued to buy the more expensive barn board and nail it over outside walls where the new stuff would have weathered to match before the builder could earn the difference in price. These are probably the same people who pay more for "prefaded" jeans.

There are fashions even in the second-hand market, but people who buy second-hand to save money should understand the cost of fashion.

LET'S MAKE A DEAL

When buying new, you decide what you want, the seller tells you what it's worth, and you decide whether or not you can afford it. The buyer's role is mostly saying *yes* or *no*.

In the second-hand market, buyers take a more active part. It takes more effort to find what you're looking for, more effort to find the cheapest source, more careful attention to the condition of the thing, and a lot more fun in making a deal. In this market you see, there really is no price. I know, I know, there's often a piece of paper with a dollar sign and some numbers on it. *Forget it.* That's for the carriage trade and the odd tourist who wanders in.

Neophytes to the scene are prone to edge shyly into junk shops and rummage sales. It's unfamiliar territory. Even the dusty, mothball smells are different. Not at all like the Muzak and bright lights of "normal" stores. Finding that the goods don't have a price tag is one more disconcerting difference in this alien culture. "How much is it?" your wife whispers, edging around behind you in the narrow aisle.

"Can't find the price tag."

"Ask the man."

"It's too dark in here to see the price."

"Well, *ask* him."

"It's probably too expensive anyway."

"Here he comes."

"Can I help you folks?"

"No thanks. Just browsing."

If you are a refugee from Muzak plaza, in a place as strange and foreign as a second-hand shop, finding a price tag is like a welcome sight from home. You can pay it and get out. Or you can be righteously horrified at how high it is and walk out feeling comfortable and superior again.

"Did you see that tatty old chair in there for twenty bucks? New ones, just like that, were on sale at the plaza last week for eighteen. Can you imagine."

When your eyes get accustomed to the gloom and your nose stops running at the whiff of mothball, you'll learn to ignore the price tags. And that's when the fun begins. Anyway, if you've been paying attention to this chapter so far, you won't even go in the door of a second-hand shop until you have some good ideas as to what you want and how much it's worth. You know the retail price of the new ones, how long they last, what is likely to break or wear out, and what possible substitutes might do the same job. You don't need a price tag to tell you what it's worth... You know.

Then, when you find what you want, make the man an offer. Of course you won't offer what you know it's worth. You'll offer a great deal less. The dealer will be shocked, disgusted, mocking or even gently chiding you for offering such a ludicrous sum. Don't take it personally, though. That's the same reaction *you* are supposed to have when he states his price or shows you the tag. He, of course, starts his price at a much higher level than he knows the thing is worth. So you are both in the same game. When you realize that the dealer's offended reaction is part of the sale, it assumes a familiar, almost ritualistic form. A ritual in which you, the buyer, are expected to participate. The dealer doesn't expect to make a sale every time, but there is a genuine disappointment when the buyer drops out at the very first salvo without so much as a counter offer.

In spite of the fact that he's a stranger on the seller's turf, the buyer does bring some weapons of his own to the contest. The buyer is expected to use every visible or imaginable defect to deduct from the price. The scenario goes something like this -after the dealer has made two or three cuts from his initial price and doesn't appear willing to go any lower:

Seller: That's it. Take it or leave it.

Buyer: And a fair price too,..if it were in good condition.

Seller: They don't come any better than that.

Buyer: The left rear whatsit is worn. (Rattle it.)

Seller: Easy to fix.

Buyer: Maybe, but the parts are going to cost me another umpty dollars (deduct that from the dealer's last price). And there's some rust here. I'll have to clean off the whole thing and paint it (make another deduction). And it looks pretty old. Probably won't last very long.

By now the seller is steaming and sputtering about what great shape the thing is in, and how he never claimed it was new, and do you know how much the new ones cost, and...

Buyer: But the new ones are guaranteed. Will you guarantee this old thing? (Of course he won't).

It often happens that buyer and seller get stuck with some distance left between each one's "final" offer. Neither is willing to budge. That is the time to bring up "extras".

Buyer: Well, I'll pay your price...but only if you throw in the...(whatever else catches your fancy that might be worth the difference).

Buyer: Well, I'll pay your price...but only if you fix the whatsit.

Buyer: Well, I'll pay your price...but only if you deliver it.

The Seller Protests....

Buyer: Well, knock something off the price, and then I'll fix it (or deliver it) for you.

If the buyer is lucky, he'll convince the dealer to accept a price at or below what the buyer knows it's worth. A bargain is struck. The handshake is made with both parties protesting at once that they are losing money on the deal.

WILL THAT BE CASH OR...

The buyer pulls out his cheque book and pen, smooths out a cheque, and pauses..."Or perhaps you would rather have cash?" The dealer starts to smile.

"Shall we say X dollars cash?" (naming a sum 20% less than the one just agreed to).

The dealer protests of course, and the haggling starts again.

Your line is one of wounded innocence: "Oh, but I thought that saving on bookkeeping and banking, and the risk that cheques might bounce would be worth 20% to a businessman". It would be crass to add that cash receipts aren't always reported to the tax department. Crass to say it; but a hint will let him know that you know that he knows it.

He will nevertheless continue to protest and may only be willing to concede 10% or so. If the dealer won't make any concessions for cash, go back to writing out the cheque, or better still, pull out a credit card. That will cost him an extra 6% to collect from the credit card company. For all those reasons, the seller has more to gain from a cash transaction than you do. Just make sure he pays you for the favor.

Although you will never catch them saying so in public, most businessmen would rather see cash than the ubiquitous cards. The reason is simple. Every credit card transaction costs the seller from three to six percent of the receipt. The credit card company takes that much off the top before it turns your money over to the retailer. Most cash customers, though, pay the same price as the credit card buyers.Cash means up to 6% more profit for the seller. The cost of handling credit cards is passed on to cash and credit buyers alike. It's up to the cash buyer to demand fair treatment. A few establishments advertise discounts for cash. Others will allow cash discounts if buyers demand them. If they don't, shop somewhere else.

SECOND-HAND SOURCES

Not every shopper enjoys the mock-serious sport of haggling for bargains. But even shy buyers can enjoy the color and variety of places that deal in "previously owned". The retail stores at Muzak plaza differ in prices and decor: higher prices, thicker carpets and lower lights. A rummage sale, however, is as different from a pawnshop as a garage sale is from an auction. There are a lot more differences between them than price and decor.

Finding What You Want in the Want Ads

Most newspapers have a section of "want ads", properly known as the classified section. Businesses and high volume dealers use them, but the "for sale" columns are mostly for the little guys - individuals with personal discards to sell.

These can be the best or worst bargains in the second-hand market. It depends entirely on the individual selling the goods. There's no easy way to tell, short of calling the number and asking for details.

The worst buys are often those advertised by inexperienced sellers who simply cannot accept that their nearly-new whatsit is no longer worth a little bit less than what they paid when it was really new. This is particularly true of cars and big appliances that may have been bought on credit, and have depreciated faster than the monthly payments. It's hard for the seller to accept that the resale value may be less than the amount still owed.

On the other hand, inexperienced sellers tend to undervalue goods that may require only minor repairs, or older goods that don't depreciate rapidly like solid furniture, good tools, lamps, and dishes.

Sellers differ, too, in their bargaining flexibility. Some have clearly been guessing at prices and are quite willing to consider your view of the market value. Others get stubborn and insist that the asking price is a final price, whether it's reasonable or not.

When shopping in the ads, be careful to follow all the possible sources. The big daily papers offer the widest choices, but the smaller weeklies, local neighborhood flyers, and shopping circulars often carry more interesting ads. They may not be as current as those in the daily paper, but prices are often better because sellers place so little value on their goods that they are reluctant to pay for a more expensive newspaper ad. It also pays to check neighborhood bulletin boards for the casual hand-written ads stuck up with a pin. These are often found in places like supermarkets, laundromats, and community centers.

In urban areas there is a particular advantage in following the ads in neighborhood flyers and bulletin boards. It saves you the trouble of travelling all over the city for bargains that may not be bargains when you get there. You can, of course, be almost as picky - geographically - in the city papers by noting the first three digits of the phone numbers listed and starting with those exchanges nearest you.

Shopping the ads is a popular sport and the best buys are quickly gone. It helps to be the first one on the scene. That means getting the paper early (don't wait for home delivery) and start calling immediately. If you do find a bargain, don't dither and think about coming back later after you've checked out the other prospects on your list. The real bargains won't be there when you get back. Offer cash, and close quickly.

When you've been reading the ads for awhile, some of them will start to look familiar. Some of these are merely dealers, fishing in another pond. Others, however, are genuine, one-time, clear-out-the-basement, civilians. Chances are their initial prices were too optimistic. The first rush of bargain hunters said "no thanks" and now the stuff is still sitting there. When you find an ad like this that has been running for a week or more, call back, even if you tried them on the first day and found the asking prices too high. Given time, and the inconvenience of all that unsold clutter, they may come to appreciate your view of a more realistic price.

The Second-Hand Shop(pe)

These are the people who buy old junk and sell antiques. The problem, usually, is prices. The range of types is wide:from classy antiques to wreckers' yards. What they have in common is their middle-man status. They buy the goods from the people who have used them, and sell them back to the second rank of users. There's nothing inherently wrong with that position. They do, after all, provide a service in making all those scattered sources more accessible. If you want an old table in a hurry, it's much easier to walk into a shop that may have a dozen tables to choose from than to spend a week trying to track down sellers through the want ads. The second-hand shops are selling convenience.

The thing to remember is that you have access to the same sources as they do. Attending auctions was a great educator in this respect. After awhile I began to recognize a few antique dealers and kept an eye on what they were buying. Walking into one dealer's shop on the day after an auction, I was astonished to see a bench with a price of seventy dollars...a bench that I had seen him buy the night before for two dollars. A hundred other people could have had it for the same price.

There are no give-aways in second-hand shops, but it is possible to find decent bargains from the dealers. The knack is to avoid the carriage trade. Stick to the low-rent district. Shopping off-season to avoid any tourist traffic helps. So does buying mid-week and other slow periods when the dealer has time to dicker awhile.

Remember, too, that even second-hand dealers have waste. An antique dealer, for instance, may buy his stock at auctions or in bulk lots (a whole estate). Only part of the purchase will be old enough or good enough to display in his shop. The rest is sold to other dealers, sent back to be auctioned off again, or sold from the back room to bargain hunters who wander in and ask for a whatsit...even if they didn't see one in the window. A goodly chunk of our own home library is from a rare book dealer who casts off the modern paperbacks that clutter up his purchases. Asking an antique dealer "What's new?" isn't just a bad joke, it's also a legitimate request to see his cheaper goods.

About the best you can hope for from second-hand dealers is to come close to scrap prices: furniture for the price of the lumber in it or metal by the pound.

We set out one year to buy the cheapest old woodstove we could find. All it had to do was make smoke for the smokehouse, and be sturdy enough to be left outdoors. After three days of trekking around sales and stove stores, I finally drove into a second-hand shop. Hope quickened at the sight of hundreds of old cast iron wood stoves heaped carelessly in the weeds behind the building. The dealer was understanding, but the cheapest relic in the pile would still cost me $50, broken or not. Scrap iron, he explained, was worth eight cents a pound. The average stove would bring $25 as scrap. To pull one out and help to load it would cost another twenty-five.

Discouraged, I bought a single door (by the pound) and went home to build a stove from a salvaged oil drum. I was just about finished bolting the door on the barrel when a neighbor, a retired school teacher, stopped to watch. "Why didn't you tell me you were looking for a stove?" she scolded. "I've had an old one sitting on the back porch all fall. It's too darned heavy to get to the dump. If you can move it you can have it."

The lesson stuck like on of those little light bulbs that pop into the lives of cartoon characters: The heft of an old stove made it valuable to the second-hand dealer, but the same heft made it difficult for others. Those hundreds of stoves piled up in the weeds must have come from a lot of individuals who were just happy to get the darned things carted away. I was free to use the same sources the dealer had.

Pawnshops

For the buyer, a pawnshop is not much different from any other second-hand shop. In general, the wares are a little more specialized, with the emphasis on the more valuable, portable items like watches, jewelry, cameras, radios and musical instruments. Pawnshops warrant special mention only because they acquire their stock somewhat differently from other shops.

A pawnshop is basically a lending establishment. They lend cash to customers who are, in turn, required to leave some item of value behind as collateral to secure the loan. If the loan is not repaid, the collateral is sold from the shop.

There's a touch of Hollywood mystery about the pawnshop. Its image flickers in that grey gulf between good guys and bad guys. Maybe it's because of the role it plays in personal hard luck stories, where the loan is not reputable enough to warrant the lower interest rates available at the bank, or the borrower is too romantic to sell his collateral outright at the higher prices regular dealers could offer.

Because of its shady aura, some buyers are reluctant to shop at the pawnbrokers'. There is no need. The edge of desperation may taint the people who borrow there, but as far as the buyer is concerned, it's a second-hand shop like any other.

Swaps and Exchanges

Anyone with children will understand the very short, useful life of anything bought for them: skates, skis, bikes, toys, even clothes and books. The cheap ones disintegrate in their little hands, and the higher quality items are just as quickly outgrown. Parents can't win...except by dealing with other parents.

We started with skates, buying castoffs that were fine for our little ones but pinching the toes of some older skaters. The skates that we then outgrew were sold back to the exchange for a little less than the bigger ones cost. Then we discovered ski exchanges that work on the same basis. A nearby town boasts a lending "library" for toys, organized by parents. Bikes can be an even bigger problem. Here, local parents have organized an annual trading day at the school. The only bikes that aren't eagerly snapped up are the wee ones, where first-time parents have not yet realized the cost of keeping fast-growing kids fitted out with new ones.

The organization of such swaps and exchanges is mostly a local initiative. In some towns, commercial stores operate swaps and trade-ins as part of the business. Sometimes it's a co-operative, ad hoc effort organized by parents or scouts, or done informally on a neighborhood basis. If your area is not already teeming with such activity, it's easy enough to get it started. Just mention the problem to a neighbor whose kids are younger or older than yours and watch the response.

I was first tempted to label this a newer phenomenon, an informal offspring of the cooperative movement. Then I remembered that passing around hand-me-down clothes was a regular part of my own childhood. Cribs and baby furniture were rotated around the family and around the neighborhood until they fell to pieces. And the candy store had a comic rack where used ones were traded back three for two.

Flea Markets

The good burghers of old Europe, suspecting that the plague was carried from town to town by fleas, kept itinerant merchants (and their flea infested goods) from entering the city gates. Undeterred, the pedlars set up shop outside the walls. The customers came out - more mindful of prices than the plague - and the flea market was born.

There are few North American towns today that don't have at least one flea market in the vicinity. In most cases, modern city fathers still keep them on the outskirts of town, but it's fear of lower prices and not the plague that arouses the emnity of the downtown merchants.

Modern flea markets are as wildly individual as the craftsmen and pedlars within. They range in style from permanent, indoor, commerical space (that calls itself a flea market only because it is divided into many smaller booths), to the once-a-year neighborhood bash, where residents bring a card table and their gleanings from cupboard or basement.

However they may be organized, most flea markets offer a very wide variety of both new and used goods. Prices vary almost as widely as the goods. In general, though, it seems that the more informal ad hoc markets usually have lower prices than those that operate in established commercial premises.

When second-hand goods appear to be too pricey, remember

that you can go to the same sources that the dealer has found. And, of course, a flea market is another of those marvellous places where the buyer is *expected* to haggle over the price. Timing, too, is important, particularly at those markets that don't operate on a full-time basis. At a once-a-week, or once-a-month market, dealers are reluctant to leave too much stock unsold at the end of the day. In these places, morning prices may be sticky, but as closing time approaches dealers tend to be more generous with hagglers.

Finally, if prices don't attract you as a discriminating second-hand buyer, consider becoming a seller - even if it's only for a day. In most markets, the manager will rent you a booth, or space to set up a table, on a daily basis. Clean out the cupboard, gather the best of your hobby products, garden surplus, or granny's butter tarts. Mark every item with an asking price (felt pen on masking tape works well), spread it out on a card table, and you're in business. It may not be Neiman-Marcus, but you'll have all the fun of a flea market and come home a little richer. You may even learn something about the art of being a seller.

First-time flea marketeers invariably find some surprises in the experience. One friend, who was selling all his old paperbacks for a dime apiece, thought he had the knack as the boxes rapidly emptied. Then he discovered that his best customer - that nice old lady who was such a voracious reader - had a booth around the corner where she was reselling his books for a quarter. Another lady was so delighted with the flurry of interest in her crochet goods that she sold her friend's hat in the excitement. The nicest surprise of all, however, is when first-time sellers are suddenly struck with the realization that the things they produce, the things they collect, the things they have all around them that might otherwise be put out with the trash...that all those things have a value, that somebody wants them, that money can come from someplace other than a paycheck.

Garage Sales

Garage sales (or yard sales for people without garages) are a great excuse for a neighborhood party. They may also offer good value to the second hand shopper...as long as you don't have to travel far.

The problem is the limited variety. It's rarely worth the drive across town on the slim chance that someone may be selling just the sort of widget you're looking for. Of course it's sometimes fun to go just to see what's there, but that's entertainment, not serious shopping. We go if they are close or we happen to be passing by.

Prices are erratic. Since sellers may have limited experience at second-hand values, some goods will be overpriced and others will be cheaper than you could find elsewhere. As with private sales through classified ads, sellers may wrongly assume that resale values are some uniform percentage of what they paid when the goods were fancy and new. Thus modern furniture tends to be overpriced, and older (more solid) pieces are under valued. Appliances are worth less than most first-time sellers imagine, but small items of household surplus can be genuine bargains such as books, pictures (for the frames), sports equipment, toys and dishes.

For most families, garage sales are one-time affairs. They may be as interested in cleaning out the garage as they are in the revenues. This has a definite effect on pricing. Although it pays to go early for the best selection, the prices are often lowest at the end of the day when the weary vendors are facing the prospect of stuffing all the leftovers back in the garage. If you see something you like in the morning, but are unable to strike a bargain on the price, try coming back in the evening. If the thing is still there, the price may be getting better.

Rummage Sales

These are the church basement and charity bazaar sales, where the goods are usually donated and sold by volunteers. There are two critical differences between this format and a run-of-the-mill second-hand sale that you might find at a garage sale or regular shop. In the first place, prices are generally quite low in comparison with other second-hand sources, and secondly, dickering over prices is *not* usually accepted practice. Without the motive of personal profit, sellers have less interest in maximizing sales profit. So they start low and stay there, for simplicity's sake.

It also seems that donors are more careful of the quality of goods collected for rummage sales. Perhaps it's like listening for the tinkle of coins in the collection plate — one doesn't like to be seen giving less than the best. Whatever the reason, rummage sales rarely offer valuable merchandise, but there's less utter junk than you'll find at other second-hand sources.

Quite apart from the bargains, rummage sales are worth visiting just to meet the people there. They're invariably staffed by everybody's favorite Aunt. It's the one place where I have no qualms about buying used clothing and fresh mince tarts.

Because prices start low and rarely go lower, the best time to visit a rummage sale is in the opening minutes.

Charitable Institutions

Goodwill, Neighborhood Services, Salvation Army, and Superfluity Shops (a favorite, simply because of the name) are all like rummage sales writ large and given permanent status. Like rummage sales, goods are donated, and paid help or volunteers handle the selling. Thus prices are usually low and not negotiable...unless you are down and out.

The institutions offer good value on smaller items like books, clothing, sports equipment, and small appliances (sometimes!...always try out appliances).

Because of the larger size and permanent character of these outlets, they do lack some of the qualities of the informal basement rummage sale. Donations are more impersonal, and thus less subject to social comparisons of who has given what. The result is less uniform quality of merchandise than the rummage sale offers...more junk. Furthermore, the large volume institutions attract more attention from antique and second-hand dealers than the rummage sales do. The competition for things like old furniture gets fierce, and the casual shopper would have to be very lucky to find an antique bargain there.

Trade-Ins

This is a relatively unknown side of the second-hand market that is part gimmick and part real. Everybody knows that most used cars on the market were traded in to dealers for newer models. The "trade-in", though, is also used as a sales gimmick by many other merchants. Carpets, appliances, home equipment and other durable items are often sold with trade-in discounts: "bring in your old whatsit and get $50 off the price of a new one!" Every such ad means that the dealer is going to end up with a back room full of used whatsits. He won't advertise them for sale (it might cut into his new whatsit business), but he will sell them to a used whatsit dealer or to an enterprising bargain hunter who appears at the back door with cash in hand. They are sometimes even given away when the back room gets too crowded. I once carpeted an entire six room apartment that way...for nothing!

Government Surplus

One of the all-time most popular myths of second-hand deals concerns the army surplus jeep: "still in the crate and only $200"...or $50, depending on how far removed the teller is from the actual purchase of an actual jeep.

Government surplus of all types is most frequently sold at special auctions. The disposal of U.S. government equipment is handled through the General Services Administration and Department of Defense. Write for application forms from:

> General Services Administration
> Federal Supply Service
> Personal Property Division
> Washington, D.C. 20406

or

> DOD Surplus Sales
> P.O. Box 1370
> Battle Creek, Michigan 49016

The application specifies your region and the type of goods you are interested in. You will then be notified when goods of that type are auctioned in your region.

In Canada, Crown Assets Distribution Group is the agent. Prospective buyers may contact Crown Assets Distribution Centres at:

> 933 Gladstone Avenue
> Ottawa, Ontario K1A 0T4

or 6205 Kestrel Road
> Mississauga, Ontario L5T 2A1

Unfortunately for the individual, the sheer volume of merchandise falling from the back end of the tax machine demands that such sales be organized primarily for large quantity deals. The system is geared to jobbers, wholesalers, or dealers who can buy a thousand desks or pencil sharpeners on a single bid. One gets the impression that dickering over the condition of a single jeep would constipate the entire system.

By and large, the systems in both countries are set up to deal with the middlemen. The merchandise does eventually appear in stores that advertise "army surplus" or "government equipment" or some such thing, but these outlets are run by private enterprise, not by the government. Wares are priced according to what the market will bear, and there are no special deals just because they once belonged to the taxpayers.

If you do find such a store, it may pay to keep a few general guides in mind:

- Governments buy the best. Even the surplus is usually high quality.
- Military clothing is heavy, durable and well-made.
- Not all surplus is used. You may find brand new discards at less than new prices.
- The worst buys will be on the most popular items: desks, furniture, filing cabinets, etc. But if you want a terrific bargain on parade gaiters...!

AND LAST BUT NOT LEAST

And the very best second-source, for sheer entertainment as well as for bargains, is the auction. That's a chapter all by itself...

7

Auction Buying

We set out to buy a pig last week, and ended up perched on a tier of high plank seats, looking down through a haze of tobacco and sweat at the sawdust pit below. There were a few buyers from the packing houses. They arrived in the dusty Cadillacs, wearing city shoes and smoking tailor-mades. By custom and clout, they jostled noisily into the luxury seats - the padded vinyl ones, salvaged from a school bus and set up front row center. They began to pass the gin along the row.

The ones wearing mucky boots and baseball caps with Mack and Deere and Massey on the fronts filled up the smoky bleachers, nodding and whispering to one another.

Like every other auction, this one had its own cast of characters and unwritten constitution. Dean, the meat buyer from the big city, chainsmokes and stays quietly engrossed in the Pepsi can...sipping it, rolling it around in his palms, and topp'ng it up from the flask. Everyone knows that he bids with his eyebrows, though, and the farmers who want to see if the price of beef is headed up or down keep both eyes rivetted on Dean's mobile brow.

Acton, the local vet who is usually buying goats for the Greek restaurants, is concentrating on pigs today. He slumps forward, left hand holding his chin, right hand shielding his eyes. He watches Dean for the first few bids to make sure that Dean is not buying pigs this week. When he's certain that Dean has orders not to buy any more pigs, Acton flicks up the little finger on his right hand over his eye. The bid is topped by someone else behind him. Must be a farmer. Acton's finger flicks twice - a jump bid. The farmer drops out. Acton just bought himself a pen full of pigs for $9 each. Half the price they were going for the previous week when Dean had orders from the packing house to bring back some pork.

Auctions are entertainment as well as business, and variety is a part of their charm. The goods and the actors are different at every sale. So, too, are the quirks and corny jokes of the auctioneer. The unwritten rules, and even the bidding systems, change.

There are "dutch" auctions, where the auctioneer starts with a high asking price and gradually reduces it. The first bidder wins. In progressive bidding, prices start low and bidders compete by increasing the price. The last bidder wins. In a mail auction the highest bidder wins, but participants submit only one bid. There is no second chance to outflank the opposition.

If you already have a nodding acquaintance with auctions, chances are you'll be most familiar with the system of progressive bidding. The auctioneer asks for a starting bid and would-be buyers keep topping it...until no one is left to raise the price again. The auctioneer says "Going...going...gone!" (or some such thing), and the goods are sold to the last and highest bidder. That's the usual approach to auctions.

Auctions are used to sell everything from antique things to zirconium rings. Ordinary bargain hunters, however, will most often be involved in a few common types:

ESTATE SALES

It usually happens that our possessions outlive us. Unable to take it with us, to retirement haven in Florida...or to even warmer places, we leave it behind for the next generation. The next generation would rather have the cash, thank you very much, and so the auctioneer comes in to convert all those family heirlooms and broom closet leavings to nice long green for the next of kin.

The estate sale is more than an appendix to the wake. They also happen when people move, divorce, or just clean out the basement. What makes them different is that they commonly include everything from the family car to the kitchen sink, and the half-finished jar of shaving lotion.

Such variety is not only the spice of life, it's also a great advantage for the second-hand shopper. Specialized sales, like those that concentrate on cars or building materials for example, tend to attract large crowds of buyers interested in those particular things. The competition pushes up the prices. The estate sale, however, may offer only one used car, or a single roll of roofing felt...not enough of any one thing to attract the dealers and big money buyers from miles around. You may be the only one at the sale interested in a car or a roll of roofing felt. When that happens you can virtually name your own price.

Estate sales often do attract the interest of antique buyers, and competiton can be fierce for anything old and collectible. But, if you need a kitchen sink or half a jar of shaving lotion, it's hard to beat the prices at an estate sale.

Farm Auctions

A farm auction is no more than an estate sale that happens to be on a farm. They usually offer an assortment of farm tools and machinery, sometimes livestock and land as well. The crowd is different from those at a run-of-the-mill estate sale, too. Farms are often harder to find than numbered houses on well marked streets, so farm sales tend to attract a higher proportion of locals, and fewer day-trippers out from the city. The antique dealers still manage to get there if the sale is a large one. In general, though, as sales become smaller and more remote, the competition and prices diminish as well.

Get yourself a good, detailed map - one that shows all the dirt roads and lanes. Look up some small town weekly papers at the library (farm auctions aren't always advertised in the big city dailies), and make a day of it. Take a hat and a folding chair for comfort, and a picnic basket if hot dogs and home-made pies aren't your fare.

Livestock Sales

There was a time when the meat packing companies sent buyers around from farm to farm to pick up livestock. Prices were as low as the buyers could get away with, and with only a few buyers in any one district farmers were usually faced with take-it-or-leave-it propositions. In self-defence, many rural communities have sales barns now where local farmers bring their stock, and buyers (in theory) bid against one another.

Sales barns operate on a regular basis (once a week is common), and are usually not advertised, or even very well identified. You are supposed to *know* where and when the sales barns are in session. Ask a local farmer.

Some farmers add to their herds by picking up bargains at a sales barn, but it's a risky business for neophytes. Animals can be inspected before a sale, and with a practiced eye, you might be able to spot most of the sickies, runts, and genetic defectives. Those who don't know scours from scabies, however, might be better off buying from places where there's time to ask questions.

Meat is a different story. Even apartment dwellers are free to buy the family bacon from the same source the meat packers use. You don't even need a farm. Haul your walking bacon straight to the nearest slaughterhouse, and then take it home all cut and wrapped for the freezer. Do make arrangements with a slaughterhouse *before* splurging on a four-footed steak, however. They may be closed that day, or booked up for appointments only. That predicament is hard to explain to landladies.

Specialty Auctions

Some large scale auction markets specialize in a single commodity group: cars, construction equipment, coins, and works of art are just a few examples. Government surplus is often disposed of at specialty auctions. Advertisements for such sales can be found in the classified section of most big city newspapers.

These sales attract dealers and professionals. They know the market value of everything on the list. Consequently, it's next to impossible to find the real give-away bargains that happen when there's no competition. On the other hand, these pros and dealers are buying to resell (at a profit) in another market. A clunker at a car auction won't be a steal, but chances are you can buy it more cheaply there than you could at the used car lot. (Look over your shoulder...that's probably the used car dealer standing beside you stocking up for next week's customers). Check with a local auction house to see if there are restrictions on public attendance. Some car auctions, for example, are restricted only to dealers.

New Goods

Not all public auctions are part of the second-hand market. Retail businesses rid themselves of slow-moving or out-of-season stock by turning it over to an auctioneer. Bankrupt businesses can be liquidated by selling off whole inventories through auctions. Some centers have established auction halls to handle such sales. In other places, the auctioneer goes to work in the parking lots or warehouses of the firm being liquidated.

These sales are usually well-advertised for the convenience of the general public. Consequently, they are also well attended...always a disadvantage for the bargain hunter.

Functionally, it's an auction like any other. In reality, it's quite different. It's the crowd that makes it different. They are people who are looking for new things cheap. Their bench mark is the usual retail price, and anything less than that will be considered a bargain by someone in the crowd. In the usual auction crowd of dealers and second-hand scroungers, anything more than half the retail price is exorbitantly expensive. Dedicated second-hand buffs don't find much to get excited about at new-goods auctions.

One other difference bears watching. Unlike estate sales or farm auctions, liquidation and clearance sales frequently offer multiple quantities of whatever happens to be in stock. At an estate auction, you may find one bidet and two people bidding on it (and the price goes up). When the plumbing factory goes belly up, the inventory sale may offer a hundred bidets - one at a time. The two civilians who are interested will bid up the price of the first two fixtures, get what they came for, and then the rest will be sold to dealers at prices that resemble wholesale. Just remember that bidding patterns change whenever a number of identical items are offered.

Police and Customs Auctions

The law regularly finds itself overstocked with orphan goods. Customs seizures and unclaimed stolen property are common examples. These goods are periodically auctioned off at public sales. Police auctions are good sources for tape and stereo equipment, bicycles, and cameras. Customs auctions are less predictable. All such auctions are advertised in the classifieds. Remember, though, that they will attract large crowds, and you will be competing against wholesale buyers again.

Charity Auctions

These are the ones that get all the publicity. They offer name-dropper gimmicks like the mayor's necktie, or a date with a bunny; fun for voyeurs and uninspired feature writers, but not a fruitful place to look for bargains.

Prices are high for the same reason that rummage sales have higher quality junk: at a rummage sale the wares are publicly donated and donors want to be known for the quality of their discards; at a charity auction it's the buying that takes place in public and the Joneses don't like to be seen as cheap. The only advantage to this type of auction buying is that some purchases can be deducted from taxes as a charitable "donation".

Consignment Sales

This is the essence of the ordinary, run-of-the-mill, rural auction hall. Sellers arrive through the week with boxes of old paperbacks, granny's fur, the old TV, or the heirloom chest. On auction night everything is sold, the auctioneer collects the money, takes a percentage off the top, and returns the rest to the sellers.

The auction halls are normally set up to handle small estates and liquidations, as well as the consignment trade. It makes little difference to the buyer, however. There are three features of these "bits and pieces" auction halls that are particularly attractive to bargain hunters:

1. The wide variety of goods offered makes it more likely that you can always find at least a few of the items on your "things we need to buy" list. Even if the entertainment value begins to pall, the outing remains worthwhile as a regular shopping trip.
2. As is the case with regular estate sales, there is rarely enough of any one line to attract dealers or specialist buyers. The antique buyers are omnipresent, but otherwise the competition is scattered. When only one kitchen sink is being sold, and only one buyer interested, the buyer can name his own price - literally. I have seen perfectly good stainless steel sinks sold for less than a dollar.
3. Most consignment auctions operate on a regular basis - an indoor hall with parking, seats, and a regular weekly schedule. Unlike farm sales, you don't need a map and an entire day to attend.

145

BUT DON'T SCRATCH YOUR EAR

Given the entertainment and bargains there, I'm always amazed at the number of people who have never been to an auction. They all know the myths, though: scratch your ear and unwittingly buy the nine foot, glow-in-the-dark, plaster of paris Elvis statue and coin bank. Get carried away with the competitive spirit and pay twenty bucks for the tacky lamp that Woolworth's couldn't flog for ten. The myths do have some small basis in fact, but perhaps it's the fear of committing such *faux pas* that keep the uninitiated away.

For the stout of will, the best advice is to attend a few auctions determined not to buy a thing. Watch. Listen. *Don't* panic when the gorgeous old cuspidor (that's probably brass under all that green paint) is being almost given away to the clutzy couple who bought the Elvis statue. Let them have it. Keep your hands in your pocket and watch.

If you're like me though, you can't be trusted in such situations. I can last a month without so much as a tickle in the throat, then go to a concert and (in that dainty pause before the music starts) have an absolutely uncontrollable urge to cough. And I still can't go to an auction without developing an overpowering itch somewhere on the top of my head. If that's all that's keeping you away from the auction halls, first spend a little time here to find out how they function, and *then* go to a couple of auctions with your hands in your pockets.

THE AUCTION HALL

The mechanical functions of the auction hall are simple enough. The auctioneer and the owner of the goods agree on the auctioneer's commission. These are usually posted in the hall and will read something like this:

Commissions
15% on furniture
25% on small items
Special rates for whole estates

The goods are given a "lot number", which identifies the owner.

It helps the bookkeeper, but means little to the buyer unless you need some help to identify a specific item examined before the sale.

On sale night, buyers register as they arrive. That just means find the office, sign your name, and take a number. The number is on a card. You'll need it to bid and to pay up at the end of the evening. Your bidding number is the means by which the auctioneer and the bookkeeper keep track of who is buying what. No money changes hands until you are ready to leave. Then you go back to the office, or the registration desk, and turn in your number. The cashier tallies up your purchases, you pay your bill, load up the Elvis statue and leave.

Have a Good Look

Part of the hall, and likely the outside space as well, will be given over to displaying the goods to be sold. It won't look like the nice displays at Muzak plaza. More like spring cleaning day at the dump. Don't despair. It's the price of the art deco windows and indirect lighting that you are about to save. The goods are the very same ones that made their debut in the plaza.

Buyers are free to wander around, before or during a sale, to have a closer look. When an item is on the block (being sold), there won't be time to have a look underneath, open the drawers, or read the label; it's going, going, gone before you can really judge its condition. The pre-sale examination is vital unless you really like surprises. Don't be shy. It's not like peeking in the neighbor's drawers. Take a tape measure to be sure the table will fit the dining nook, and a retail catalog to check what the new ones are worth. Poke, prod, plug it in if it's electric, count all the pieces to be sure they're there, try the chairs out for comfort. The only thing you cannot do is ask the salesman for help. The hired help at the auction hall are mostly furniture movers. All they know about the stuff being sold is how heavy it is. The salesmen are all back at Muzak plaza where the money is. These are the cheap seats.

Don't Ask Us, We Just Work Here

They don't sell programs at an auction, and the only ones wearing numbers are in the audience. How do you identify the players?

The cashier you met when you first arrived. That's where you got the number, and that's where you come back later to settle the bill.

The auctioneer is obvious. He's the one doing all the talking. His role is to conduct the bidding. Since his commission is a fixed percentage of the final sales price, his chief interest is to coax the bidding up to the highest possible price. All the jokes and cajolery are most disarming, but never forget that he is on the seller's side - not the buyer's. When the auctioneer tells you that the clock used to work, don't assume he means that it probably still does.

Within whispering distance of the auctioneer will be the recorder, a silent presence with clipboard and pen. His job is to record each purchase, the winning bid, and the person who bought it. If you can't control your arm and do end up buying something, show the recorder your number.

The other semi-official types fluttering around the action are the auctioneer's helpers. They fetch and carry, and hold up the item being sold. If you can't always tell from the auctioneer's babble just what it is that's being sold, it will be whatever the helper is holding up for display. If it's something like a fridge, he may just be holding the door open and looking tired. It's perfectly kosher to ask the helper to turn it around for a better look (not the fridge though), open the drawers, or read out the brand name. It's better if you've already done that inspection yourself, but don't hesitate to ask if the helper isn't displaying it clearly enough.

What Did He Say?

The patter of the auctioneer is often difficult to follow. Complaining is pointless. It took the poor fellow years to learn to be that incomprehensible and he's not about to revert to articulate speech now. Relax. The ear gradually gets accustomed to the rhythm and starts making sense of the nonsense. It helps if you know what he is *supposed* to be saying.

He first establishes what it is that's being sold. If in doubt, see what the helpers are holding up or pointing to. At this stage the auctioneer should also clearly state the *units* of sale. If, for example, the helper is holding up one of six chairs, the auctioneer might say:

"How much am I bid on *this* chair?"...you're buying only that particular chair.

"Next we have this *set* of chairs."...the price will include all six chairs.

"How much for *choice* of chairs?"...the price is for any one chair. Take as many as you want.

"So much apiece - take them all."...the price is for one chair, but you must take the set.

Likewise, the auctioneer might indicate that he is selling an entire tray of small items, the suitcase *and* its contents, the rabbits but *not* the cages. etc. Do pay attention to exactly what is being sold. Last summer I saw a lady dancing about in great delight at the fabulous bargain she had just obtained on a dining room suite. Then someone told her she had only bought one chair.

If you are not absolutely certain just *what and how many* are being sold, put your hands in your pockets...or lash yourself to the mast and listen more carefully to the siren's song.

The auctioneer is next obliged to suggest a starting bid. He may mumble something like., "Gimme ten ta starter off!", or "Who'll say five for the three-legged chair?" Many auctioneers will suggest a starting price in the range of what they expect the item to ultimately sell for. There is, in short, no need to be the first bidder into the fray. The starting bid will drop. The auctioneer will lower it himself to get things going, or a buyer will offer a starting bid at some lower point.

When he finally does get a starting bid, the auctioneer double clutches and puts his patter into high. If you thought he was incomprehensible before, wait until he really gets going. You'll know the real bidding is underway when it sounds like Alvin Chipmunk singing an old Philip Morris commercial on the trading floor of the stock exchange. But even that can be understood if you know what to listen for.

In spite of the auctioneer's frantic pace, you are not being left behind. The actual bidding moves much more slowly than the auctioneer's tongue. The chant you hear is mostly the sing-song repetition of a number - the asking bid. It means the auctioneer has a bid from the audience, and is asking any other bidder to top the last price with the higher number being repeated in the chant. He may also occasionally repeat the bid already given. Thus if $1.50 has been bid, and the auctioneer is asking anyone in the crowd to raise the bid to $2.00, his chant might be: "I have one and a half, gimme two, gimme two, gimme two,...one and a half gimme two (someone nods), two and a half, have two, gimme two and a half." If at this point, the bidding ends, the person who nodded at two has won the bidding and pays $2.00 for the article. Of course I can't write those bids as fast as he can chant them, and you'll have to let your ear get used to working at 78 rpm. But if - out of all the gibberish - you can hear a number being repeated, chances are it's the asking bid.

When the bidding ends, the auctioneer will often repeat the winning bid more slowly for the recorder's benefit. The last exchange may end with something like, "Sold to number 79 for two dollars." It's a good time to check your first impressions of what you *thought* he was saying in the chant.

The hyperactive sing-song of the auctioneer's performance is not just an oligarch's exclusion of the unchosen, like a doctor's Latin or a bureaucrat's jargon, but is a deliberate sales technique. The whole intent is to speed up the action, create the impression of frenzy, the possibility of being left behind. It's opportunity knocking, and move quickly before you miss the fleeting chance at a real bargain. In fact the underlying message is: don't stop to think about it! Don't stop to consider whether you *really* need a nine foot Elvis coin bank. It's so cheap! Get your hand up! Now! Before it's too late. "Sold!" Arrgghh. Impulse buying incarnate.

It's mesmerizing. Just last night there was a five piece silver tea set that glittered enough to catch everybody's eye, and that's not easy at the auction hall where I often loiter. There are usually a hundred or more people there, gossiping, lying, trading amongst themselves, starting up the chain saws, and yelling at the kids. The kids are under the metal folding chairs, competing with a fat old beagle for unattended hot dogs. It is, in short, an audience not easily rapt. Anyway, the tea set glittered and turned every head in the first ten rows. The opening bidder was a middle aged lady with an instant just-what-I've-always-wanted glaze across her face. She just kept nodding excitedly in cadence to the auctioneer's own frenzy. She ran out of competition at $150. "Sold!" She held up her number for the recorder, then seemed to come out of her trance.

"How much did I pay for that, anyway?"

"$260," said the auctioneer, deadpan. (Hisses and boos from the audience.)

"$150," said the auctioneer, turning the faintest shade of pink. (Clapping and cheering from the audience.) The lady looked relieved.

Few are totally immune from the mesmerizing effect of the

chant. I still have nine steel steps from a playground slide. They were a fantastic buy for a quarter (and get that hand up quickly before somebody else takes them home.) Someday I'll figure out what to do with them.

When You Can't Hold It Back Any Longer

So you want to join the action? Sooner or later the urge to bid overcomes all restraint and the arm snaps up in a Stranglovian salute. Here's what to do:

First of all, catch the auctioneer's eye. He's babbling away with both eyes fixed on the person he's trying to persuade to raise the bid (the guy who's "out"). The auctioneer totally ignores the person who has just tendered the latest, highest bid, (the one who is "in"). As soon as the object of the auctioneer's attention nods, winks, or otherwise agrees to the asking bid, the auctioneer sets a new asking bid and swings back to cajole the former bidder, who is now "out." The auctioneer's head is turning back and forth between the active bidders, always fixing on the one who is "out." If you want to be "in" you may have to speak up or raise your arm.

Once the auctioneer does notice you, he'll immediately ignore you again. You know he had taken your bid when his chant jumps up another notch, repeating a new, higher, asking bid. Now you don't have to worry about being ignored. You're "in". You're holding the highest bid (until another bidder tops it), and the auctioneer won't waste his time by looking your way again. If you still aren't sure that he saw you, you can always try waving again. An honest auctioneer will refuse your second wave and remind you that you're "in". One with less scruples might accept your second wave as another bid, letting you bid against yourself (or trump your own ace in bridge player's jargon).

Better to trust that he's seen you. When a competing buyer tops your bid, the auctioneer will turn back to you with full, unmistakeable interest. He's eye-to-eye, allegro pitch until you indicate (with a shake of the head) that you won't pay that much, or you bid again...

When there is only one bidder left, the auctioneer scans the audience, making one last plea for another bid. Nobody else interested? "Sold!" The last bidder "in" holds up his card and the auctioneer tells the recorder, "Sold to number 79 for two dollars."

The closing ceremony - trying to coax one last bid out of the audience - is a variable routine. If there's a lot of money at stake, the auctioneer may plead and wheedle for several minutes before declaring it sold. But if it's a set of dishes and he's trying to raise the bid from $1.50 to $1.75, the last bid will be accepted quickly, bang, and on to the next item. For 25% of that last quarter, it's just not worth his while to prolong the sale. The moral of that distinction being: on the expensive stuff, you'll have lots of time at the end to think about whether or not you want to get back in (make another bid); but on the cheaper goods, he who hesitates will go home empty handed.

More valuable items may also be sold with a prior warning that there is a *reserve* or *advance* bid. A reserve simply means that the owner of the goods has instructed the auctioneer to refuse to complete the sale unless bidding reaches some predetermined minimum level. The audience is not told what that minimum is, only that there is a reserve. An advance bid is tendered by someone who may be absent, or someone who wishes to remain anonymous. He gives his bid to the auctioneer in advance, and the goods are sold to the highest bidder, present or not.

The audience's role is not entirely passive, accepting or rejecting the auctioneer's asking bids. It's quite common for a buyer to verbally suggest his own starting bid if the auctioneer's start is too high. If the increment is too large, the bidder may signal a reduction. For example, if the price has reached $50 and the auctioneer is asking for $60, you may see a bidder hold up two fingers and get "in" at $52, or make a little horizontal slash with his hand (a common signal for half) as a bid at $55. The *jump* bid is a double increment (in the last example, going straight from $50 to $70), intended to scare off casual competition early.

Who To Watch

An auction, like professional wrestling, is one of those sports where the audience is part of the entertainment. Knowing who's bidding against you is an essential part of the action. At a general goods auction (an estate sale or consignment hall) the crowd will be filled out with a lot of casual bargain hunters and curious neighbors. The key players, however, will be the dealers: antique dealers, second-hand dealers, and special interest buyers.

The dealers are easy enough to spot. They're the ones doing

most of the buying. After the fourth time the auctioneer says, "Sold to number 79 for ...dollars!". look around for number 79. If a distraught spouse isn't glaring at him, chances are he's a dealer. Watching *what* he buys will soon tell you whether 79 is an antique dealer, second-hand dealer, or specialist in some other line (a bicycle repairman buying all the old bikes, a watch maker looking for parts, someone buying only books, or only glassware).

Picking out the main players, post hoc, is easy enough. Keeping track of them, and spotting the participants *before* the bidding is over can be a little tricky. They have a habit of moving frequently, and the dealers are always trying to hide their bids from one another. That's why they're addicted to furtive bidding and elaborate signals that would be the envy of any third base coach.

Dealers hide from one another because they're competitors. No businessman likes to let the opposition know what he's stocking and how much he's paying. Moreover, knowing whom you're bidding against can affect the final price. And that is the major reason that even casual bargain hunters should keep an eye on who is bidding, as well as on what is being sold.

The first thing you can learn is a lesson on prices and quality. The dealers make their living at this sort of thing. If the dealers have been buying wooden chairs all evening at a steady $7 to $10 each, and then refuse to go over $2 for the next chair in the bunch, don't assume that you've caught them napping. There is likely a very good reason for their reluctance. Have a better look. Is the seat split? A rung missing? Is it plywood under the paint instead of solid as the others were?

Quality means different things to different people, though. In the last example, if the chair buyers were all antique dealers, the two dollar chair may have been shunned because the rungs had been replaced with newer wood. If you are mainly interested in finding something to sit on, new rungs won't matter a bit. It may very well be a bargain.

The other reason for watching the bidders is to predict where the bidding is likely to end. Let's take bicycles to illustrate the point - a decent ten speed that may sell, retail, for around $150. Second-hand, and in good condition, that model might sell for $80. Now when you see that bike come up for sale at an auction, the bidding depends entirely on who wants it. The used bike dealer might bid it up to $40 or so. He can resell it for only about $80 in his shop, and must leave a margin for profit and handling costs. A casual shopper, wanting a bike for himself, might bid as high as $80. He knows he would have to pay at least that much at the second-hand bike shop, and anything under $80 is a bargain for him. If you were a dealer, you would probably let the casual buyers fight it out until they each get a bike and drop out of the bidding; and then you would buy the rest of the bikes at $40 or less. If you were a casual buyer, you would jump up and down on your chair, wave your arms, and give every indication you were ready to pay any price. Then, when the dealers drop out at $40, and you scare the other casual buyers off at $45, you might get the thing for $50. Maybe. It all depends on how wily the other bidders are. Which is all the more reason to keep an eye on them.

Finally, there is the bladder factor. Auctions can go on for hours and the players wander in and out, go for a drink or a de-drink. If you are bidding against Jones for the whatsits, watch for the moment he slips away. The whatsits might be selling for considerably less while he's off stretching his legs.

Knowing When To Buy
You can't always rely on nature calling your competitors away. Fortunately, there are other elements of time that may also work in your favor.

There are usually fewer bidders around at the beginning or at the end of a sale. My best bargains have always been in the last half hour of an auction, when the crowd is all rushing off to pack the junk into the truck and get the bill paid before the line-ups start. That's when the pine table in our kitchen was bought...for three dollars!

Pay special attention, too, when there are a number of similar items being offered. When a group of lamps, for instance, is being sold on a "first choice" basis, the winner of the initial round of bidding is entitled to take his pick of the lamps - any one or all of them at the same unit price. If you think you want a lamp, it pays to make a quick assessment of who is bidding and what are they likely to choose. If there is one old lamp in a pack of newer ones and the bidders are antique dealers, the dealers are likely to choose the old one and leave the rest to be auctioned again. Second choice, or even third choice, will be considerably cheaper. On the other hand, if the bidders are all second-hand dealers and there are no possible antiques amongst the lamps, then there's a chance that the winning bidder will take them all. If the bidders are casual buyers, like yourself, they may want only one or two of the lamps. Let them fight it out for first choice, and wait for the cheaper ones on a subsequent round.

Some actual numbers may help to illustrate the point. This week at a local auction, five doors were offered on a "choice" bid. They were all solid, five-panel, pine doors. One differed from the rest by virtue of a bevel on the panels. It was older than the rest. There were four bidders - an antique dealer and three casual buyers. First choice went to the dealer. He took only the oldest door and paid $3.50. Two doors went on the second choice for $1.00 each. The third bidder paid fifty cents for the last two doors. They were indistinguishable from the one dollar doors. Similar doors at a building supply store start at $100! Oh yes, the doors were sold in the closing minutes of the auction. Most of the evening's crowd had left to pay their bills and get out of the parking lot. The fourth bidder? That was me. I'll wait until winter when they get a little cheaper.

Setting Limits

A trip to an auction should begin like any other second-hand expedition - with a well considered shopping list. And a conserver's shopping list, remember, is not merely a list of what you need, but also a clear indication of what you are prepared to spend for it.(See Chapter Six).

Spending limits are essential at an auction. The auctioneer's skill is in hurrying things along, getting buyers caught up in the rapid fire, competitive spirit of the thing. When there is little time allowed for thinking - for trying to remember how much that was at the "nearly new" shop - it's too easy to let the hand fly up and stay in the bidding for just one more round. It's better, and cheaper, to set some limits on each item before you start. When there isn't time to make well reasoned decisions, better to let your pre-set limits put you out of the bidding when prices go too high.

I like to keep two limits in mind: an upper limit and a bargain limit. The upper limit is, roughly, the cheapest price from any alternate source. If lumber is 30¢ a board foot at the mill, and 10¢ a board foot at a demolition site, ten cents would be the upper limit on comparable lumber sold at an auction. When the price hits ten, I drop out - no matter how badly I need the lumber. When it can be had more cheaply someplace else, I quit bidding.

The upper limit is for the things we really need. Like many, though, we keep a second "list" of things that we will eventually need, or things that we might profitably use if the price were right. Those things we buy only if they are real bargains. Doors for instance. When we needed doors, we would pay up to a dollar each for them. That was an upper limit. Now we have a cache of doors on hand, however, and are buying them only for other uses. Now the limit is 50¢. That's the bargain limit.

Look Again

Auctioneers don't like to argue with customers. It spoils the happy frenzy that keeps the prices high. They try, therefore, to describe the goods with some care. Few would tout an appliance as being in working order if they knew it was not. They might say it "used to work" or it "could be working", but few would knowingly lie about the condition of articles being sold. Many auctioneers begin a sale with careful disclaimers to the effect that all goods are sold *as is*...no guarantees.

Nevertheless, anything bought at auction should be examined immediately. If electrical goods have been described as being in working order, plug them in and be sure. Check glassware for cracks and chips. Look inside to make sure all parts are present. One sad lady bought a beautiful, and expensive, grandfather clock. When she got it home, she looked inside and found she had bought an empty case.

If you feel there has been a misrepresentation, the time to argue the point is then and there, not after you get it home. Explain your case to one of the helpers, or take it right back up to the auctioneer. Depending on the auctioneer's style, and on the state of his disclaimers, you may not win every appeal on the condition of something bought; but if you have any chance of winning at all, it can only be by making the complaint immediately, when everyone still remembers just how the goods were described.

Auctioneers are mostly reasonable types and are as capable as any of making an honest mistake. A reasonable complaint about an honest mistake is easily made and easily settled.

An audience, too, can help to keep an auctioneer on his toes...sometimes. I do recall one young auctioneer selling gallon cans of paint to an audience of 100 or so neighbors. He held up a gallon of "ebony enamel".

Three or four bids had already been made when one of the bidders asked, "What color is ebony anyway, Jim?"

"Brown!" shot back the auctioneer, scarcely missing a beat in his patented chant.

"No it ain't," shouted someone else from the audience, "It's sort of an off-white."

Commerce ground to a halt while the crowd divided into three equal factions: pro-whites, pro-browns, and undecided. The few who were pretty sure it was black kept quiet to let democracy run its course. The auctioneer took a vote. "Light brown" was the winner by a narrow margin. The happy buyer, content with the people's verdict, didn't bother to open the can until he got home.

When There's Really More Than You Want

It frequently happens that goods are sold in large, mixed lots. A box of tools when you need a hammer, a ski outfit when you only want the poles, a dozen pigs when two would be plenty. And, for the same reason toast lands butter side down, these awkward lots always seem to be the cheapest. Fate.

At a regular consignment auction, the solution is simple enough. Just buy the big lot, sort out the portion that you wanted, and leave the rest to be auctioned again later. You will have to pay the auctioneer's commission on the resold excess. If there are only a few small things involved, you may prefer to take the leftovers home until you've collected enough to justify a consignment. In either case, if the price is right, don't worry about the quantities being wrong. You can be a seller as well as a buyer.

Alternatively, you can let the big lots go, then deal privately with the winning bidder. Make him an offer for the part you wanted. Private trading, done discreetly (remember there's no profit in that for the auctioneer and it is his hall), is an accepted part of the auction scene.

CHOOSING THE SALE

If you've never been to an auction before, your first surprise may be the realization that there are so many to choose from. You will find them advertised in local newspapers or on community notice boards. The ads often give a partial listing of goods to be sold. Even so, you may want a few criteria by which to winnow out the better prospects.

Ironically, it's often the sale with the least interesting list of wares that offers the greatest bargains. The reason is simple: an auction is a competitive event. Fewer competitors result in lower prices.

In general then, bargain seekers look for sales that *don't* attract large audiences, and buy things there that are of little interest to other buyers. An auction-wise car buyer would avoid the "monster auto extravaganza sale" where prices and crowds would be wholesale and up. He would look for a small, out-of-the-way estate sale where one car might be hidden in the list of doilies, hearing aids, and china.

The value of being the odd man out cannot be too heavily stressed. Even the classy antique auctions may offer bargains in newer goods. The price is lowest when you are the only one in the audience who wants it.

When the idea of "health" food was still a novelty in North America, I saw one old auctioneer come across an electric yoghurt maker in a box of consigned goods. He had to put on his glasses to read the label. "It's a yo-gart maker," he announced to the roomful of farmers assembled to bid on the tools that comprised the main agenda.

"What the hell's a yo-gart maker?!" somebody yelled from ten rows back.

"Makes yo-garts!" the old man shot back. "Now what am I bid?"

One lady there did know what a yo-gart was, but wisely kept out of the ensueing debate and quietly bought it for a quarter.

Location is another useful criteria. It doesn't have to be far away - just hard to find. Get a good map and hope that no one is following you.

Timing, too, is of great importance. Again, the idea is to find the auctions that are too inconveniently scheduled to attract many buyers. Auction crowds - and prices - rise and fall with the seasons. Summer is the busy season. Tourists and day trippers from the cities swell crowds at country auctions and push the prices higher. Weekend sales are worse than mid-week ones, and holiday weekends are worst of all.

Weather plays a big part. Nice sunny days must lull customers into a defenseless state. There always seem to be better buys when it's steamy hot, or - better still - too cold for other bidders to bother with taking their hands out of their pockets.

The ideal sale, in my book, takes place off an unmarked country lane, 60 miles from the nearest city, at five o'clock on a Wednesday morning in January. With any luck, the weather will be terrible and the auctioneer will forget to advertise it. Perfect!

8

Alternatives to Buying

In the economic life of Western man, the rules of normal behavior ask only that we sell our labor in the marketplace and buy what we need in return. Quid pro quo. If we are lucky, we come out even. We work. We earn. We buy. We consume. The rich and the poor are born to their fates - the rest of us try to break even.

The mass of men who plod through life in quiet conformity to those rules are the redcoats - rank on rank in rigid order. They have pretty clothes and plenty to eat. The economic guerrillas ignore the rules and survive. And the rules, remember, are not rules of right and wrong. No one is suggesting that the economic guerrillas should steal, or live on government handouts (like an aircraft company or an automaker). The guerrillas merely refuse to accept the regimental uniform, deciding for themselves what their needs ought to be, and meeting those needs in efficient ways, conservative ways, *conserver ways*...alright, I'll admit it - CHEAP ways. Any way except whipping out the credit card and buying it shiny new at the parking lot plaza.

When wars were fought by ranks of redcoats, lined up neatly on the field, the rules were made to suit the officers who could direct the thing in a safe and gentlemanly way from the shade at the top of the hill: "King's bishop to knight four...Oh, well played chaps!" Economics is no different. Rules of *normal* behavior, from plastic money to fashions in dress, certainly aren't set up to profit the poor schmuck who has to pay the bills. You want to know who decides that skirts are shorter this year? That the candy case is open at nose level for a three year old? That pulling something useful out of the neighbor's garbage is socially unacceptable? That fixing a car can cost more than replacing it?..You want to know who makes these rules? Look up on the hill...there!...in the shade. *To hell with the rules!* There are enough redcoats in the world already.

RENT OR OWN?

The decision to rent or buy has become a cultural decision rather than an economic one. Renting a home is socially acceptable in Paris or Manhattan. In Los Angeles or Cleveland or Scarborough it's strictly déclassé. Renters are people who can't afford to buy.

There's nothing wrong with ownership. It's just that it doesn't always make economic sense. Take this housing situation as an example:

The Smiths have a home that suits them fine. Just what they always wanted. The only problem is that it doesn't belong to them. They pay $1200 a month in rent and the regular obligation irks. The landlord is willing to sell for $100,000. The Smiths work hard and save their pennies to someday realize the American dream. And the dream comes true. They finally have the $100,000 saved. The stash has been wisely invested at 10%, and thus earning a helpful $10,000 a year on its own.

When the big day comes, they sign the papers, hand over the cash, and become owners. No more rent to pay. $1200 a month ahead! There are some new expenses of course. Property taxes come to $2000 a year. Repairs and maintenance add another $2000. Insurance is another $1000. All together their new expenses add up to $5000 a year. Then, of course, their savings are gone - the $10,000 a year in interest is lost. Ownership, for the Smiths, will cost them $15,000 a year. . .$600 a year *more* than they paid in rent!

Even if they hadn't saved a penny, the result might be the same. If they borrowed the whole *$100,000* and paid *10%* interest on the mortgage, the cost of ownership would still be *$15,000* a year:

$10,000 capital costs (mortgage interest or lost investment)*
2,000 taxes
2,000 maintenance and repair
1,000 insurance
$15,000 Total annual cost of ownership
$14,400 Total annual cost of rental

It's not that simple in real life of course. Inflation complicates the calculation. In the year after Smith bought his house, let's assume that inflation pushes housing costs up by 10%. Smith's house is now worth $110,000 at newly inflated prices. The house has *earned* $10,000 in appreciation. Had they decided to keep their money and continue renting, the rent would have increased by $1,440 a year. Does inflation serve the owner and punish the renter?

Not always. The $10,000 in inflationary earnings is mostly illusion. In order to collect such earnings, Smith would have to sell the house. Any comparable house in the area would also have inflated by 10% and Smith's advantage would disappear as soon as he tried to buy another house.

Renters have some additional protection against inflation in areas where rent controls are enforced. The protection may only be temporary, since sooner or later rents have to be adjusted to the owner's costs, but such protection must nevertheless be considered in the decision to rent or buy.

*U.S. homeowners have an additional reason to be borrowers rather than investors: mortgage interest can be deducted from taxes in the U.S. A real comparison would require that this tax advantage be subtracted from the "capital costs".

People buy houses for all sorts of perfectly valid reasons that have nothing to do with financial advantages. For independence, security, the freedom to build or expand, or just to have an investment that can be seen and cared for. Oil stocks may pay better returns, but their values go up and down for reasons that are totally beyond the investor's control. Mowing the lawn or painting the kitchen doesn't help a bit if you put your money in an oil well.

The decision to rent or buy should not ignore the human factors. Such preferences are at least as important as the financial criteria. But *do* get the financial part of the decision straight by including capital costs in any comparison, regardless of whether the capital is yours or the bank's.

FINDING THE COST OF OWNERSHIP

When considering the purchase of anything, the questions most often overlooked are: How often do we need it? For how long?

Everybody asks for the initial price. Few consider the cost per use, or the cost per year. It's these costs that must be compared to the rental cost before a truly sound decision can be taken.

Take garden tillers for instance. The cheapest new ones are about $500. Vibration take a heavy toll on such machinery, but if they're very well cared for they may last for years. I'll be generous and say that with luck and some repairs we might keep one going for twenty-five years. The initial investment would be used up at the rate of $20 per year.

Initial cost ÷ expected life = Annual Cost, or
$500 ÷ 25 years = $20 per year

Now if I weren't buying a tiller, I might leave that $500 in the bank and earn, let's say 6%, or $30 a year. So buying the tiller will also cost $30 a year in forgone interest. Maintenance costs might add another $5 to $10. Operating costs (gas and oil) depend on how much it's used. The couple of hours it would take to do a big garden would use about a dollar's worth of fuel. Owning a tiller would therefore cost us a minimum of $55 a year, plus a dollar everytime we used it:

$20 initial cost per year
 30 forgone interest
  5 maintenance

$55 Total annual cost, plus $1.00 each use

Right now we use a tiller once a year - to turn the garden in the spring. That single use would cost a minimum of $56 if we used our own tiller. They rent locally for $14 for half a day's use - gas and oil included. Granted, some gardeners till more frequently. However, the purchase would be financially justifiable only if they used it at least seven times a year and were of confident of keeping it running for twenty-five years.

Renting and owning aren't the only two choices of course. A high-cost, low-use item like a tiller is just the sort of thing that can be profitably shared amongst neighbors. Spread the capital costs, and use the machine more intensively. That, however, is a guerrilla solution that your redcoat neighbors may find hard to accept.

My urban friends made much the same sort of calculation in deciding not to own a car. They started by estimating their total transportation needs, and the cost of meeting those needs in various ways:

Transportation Needs
Commuting to work. They both worked in the city center, three miles from home. When driving, they shared a ride and paid $5.00 a day for parking. Mileage: 1410

Evenings out. They went out about 50 evenings a year. Most of their outings were into the city, a six mile round trip. Free evening parking. Mileage: 300

Shopping and appointments. They make 150 trips a year back into the city, or to a nearer shopping center. Five miles is an average round trip. On half the trips they pay an average $3 parking fee. Mileage: 750

Weekend excursions. Twenty-five times a year they go skiing or out to cottage country. Ten of those trips are overnight (for a total of 35 days). The average trip is 200 miles. Mileage: 5000

Cost of Owning a Car
A new car might cost them $10,000 or borrowed from the bank at the current 13% that would come to $3219 a year for four years. Insurance adds $500 a year, maintenance $300. The total parking fees are $1400. Total mileage is about 7500 miles a year, which would take about $500 in gasoline. Total cost of ownership: $5869 per year.

Cost of Alternatives
Taking the bus to work and for shopping trips would require 1240 fares at 85¢ each, or $1054 in total. Taxis for 50 evening outings would add $600. Renting a car on weekends costs another $1575.* Total cost: $3229 per year.

Savings
Using public transport and rentals would save $2640 a year. After four years the cheaper alternatives would add up to a total saving $10,560. At that time the car would have been paid for and could be sold or traded for its depreciated value (let's say $5000 maximum). Altogether then, owning the car would cost $5560 more than cabs over a four year period.

My friends assumed that the convenience of having a car at hand was offset by the inconvenience of traffic jams, beakdowns, and parking problems. Being true conservers, they also decided to rent out their empty parking spot at home for twenty dollars a month. Over four years, this will earn them another $960. Total savings anticipated: $6520!

*Based on a typical charge for renting a medium-sized car that's several years old:$12 a day, plus $5 insurance, plus 11¢ a mile, plus gas. Renting a new car would be more expensive.

Now those circumstances won't apply to everyone, and many families with different needs may find more financial advantages in owning a car, but the example does show how a careful look at costs (in any purchasing decision) may undermine the accepted wisdom that renters are people who can't afford to buy. That's a redcoat rule. Sometimes you are better off not to buy.

BARTER'S BETTER

The last time Colby had tried amateur home wiring he was sharing a tiny two-room flat with a fellow student and seven cats. Since the landlady was not aware he lived there, he was hardly in a good position to ask her to turn off the electricity while he moved a few outlets around. When the landlady finally did arrive at midnight, to replace the fuses that were mysteriously blowing, she found poor Colby crouched in a corner, trying to splice two smoking wires in a dim little pool of candle light. The rest of the room was dark as pitch. Even the halo of candle light was dimmed with a haze of electrical ozone smoke. The room was filled with a hulking mountain of furniture, pushed away from the walls and entwined in a hopeless tangle of disembowelled wires. In the darkest corner - opposite Colby - one of the cats was giving birth and obviously having trouble, screaming and shrieking in an unearthly way that was more like banshee than cat. Colby swearing at the wires, and the landlady yelling at Colby (whoever he might be), and the banshees screaming from somewhere in the smoky depths, and a tipsy visitor (awakened by all that screaming) trying to crawl out from under the furniture knocked the pile over in an avalanche that snuffed the candle and finally sent the landlady sobbing into the night. Colby vowed he was through with home improvements.

Years later, when Colby had a house of his own, he broke his vow and built on a large addition. He balked, however, when it came to the wiring. Some nascent, primeval twitch overcame him at the fuse box. He decided it would be sensible to have the wiring done by a professional this time. So he called in a carpenter.

Carpenters, he explained, were so much cheaper than real electricians. Besides, this particular carpenter was also skilled at home wiring. Better still, working without a license himself, the carpenter was more amenable to Colby's unsanctioned shortcuts...like the absence of permits, inspections, and the innocent belief that the building code was some sort of street directory.

Even carpenters have to be paid for wiring, though, and Colby's carpenter was duly paid: four loads of firewood, a used lawnmower, and the loan of Colby's cement mixer. Both got fair value. The carpenter had $120 worth of firewood, a lawnmower that would have cost him $50, and a mixer that normally rents for $17 a day (and he kept it for three months). For three days labor he earned tax free* benefits worth far more than he could have earned at his regular job. And Colby got the wiring done.

Had Colby been a redcoat, the idle mixer would have stayed in the garage until he needed it again, the wood might have stayed in the forest, and the lawnmower would have gone to the dump. He would have had to earn $1000 to get the wiring done by an electrical contractor.

*According to the rules, all such benefits should be reported and taxed. See the next section.

$1000	Colby's earnings
- 400	income tax and payroll deductions
$ 600	Colby's take-home pay and contractor's fee
- 300	contractor's expenses, taxes and profit
$ 300	electrician's gross earnings
- 100	taxes and deductions
$ 200	net benefits left for the electrician

If our fictional electrician, like Colby's carpenter, had then set out to obtain firewood ($120) and a used lawnmower ($50) in the normal way, he would have owed $12 more in sales tax and had just enough left over to rent a mixer for a single day. Though Colby and the electrician might each earn exactly the same wage, Colby must work ten days in order to buy three days of the electrician's time. Barter, at one-for -one, is a better deal. The "normal" way is like feeding the horse to feed the sparrow...a lot of the value disappears between the beginning and the end of the deal.

Barter has one fundamental advantage over the redcoat economy - it eliminates the middlemen. When you eliminate the paper pushers, politicians, financiers, administrators, agents, salesmen, organizers, consultants, foremen, brokers, inspectors, investors and profit takers from the picture, and get right down to the nitty gritty of a producer and a consumer who can look one another in the eye and make a deal, one-for-one,...*then* economics makes sense again.

What Will the Tax Man Say?

Guerrilla economics, though slowly becoming socially acceptable again, still wavers on the outer edge of bureaucratic approval. Specifically - the tax department. Strictly speaking, the tax man sees no difference between earning a paycheck and earning goods or services in exchange for your work. It's all subject to tax.

Although I would not have been so rude as to ask, I expect that Colby's carpenter dutifully listed the firewood, mower, and use of the mixer as "other income" on his annual tax return. And Colby, I'm sure, reported the value of the wiring on his own tax form. Keeping tabs on the guerrilla economy is a lot more difficult than taxing computerized paychecks; but the law, after all, is the law. Right? Right.

The bureaucrats are happier when barter is done in an organized way. Many large scale barter clubs and commercial "exchanges" have sprung up in recent years. Members, or participants, earn *credits* on a predetermined scale for the services they provide to other members. They may then spend those credits by buying goods and services from other members. The clubs have the advantage of giving access to a wide variety of willing traders (not everyone happens to know a carpenter who can wire houses and needs a lawnmower).

Barter clubs have several disadvantages, however. Most add an administrative fee to each exchange. Eight percent is a typical charge, and that must usually be paid in cash. Secondly, an organized exchange can put a disproportionate load on some members. A dentist, for instance, in a club with fifty writers and violinists, would earn far more credits than he could reasonably spend within the group. For that reason, some clubs allow participants to demand a share of the exchange in cash as well as barter. Finally, the greatest disadvantage of the clubs is precisely the feature that so delights the tax men: *all those vouchers and credits are so easy to count and value and report and tax.* "Line up there, you redcoats!"

Because the barter clubs can only eliminate *some* of the middlemen (and the smaller ones at that), the real guerrillas make their barter connections one-to-one with friends and neighbors. Frankly, it is harder that way to find the goods and skills you may need, but it does seem to be worth the extra effort. The bureaucrats have not yet figured out how to tax the mutual benefits of friendship. After all, who is to say what a friendly favor is worth?

Making Connections

The easiest way to find a barter partner is the direct approach. Ask! The next time the dentist looks in your mouth and phones his yacht broker, ask him if he would be interested in something other than another load of mere cash. Some needlepoint for the chair perhaps? A painting for the ceiling? Polish the yacht? Offer whatever you can provide. And don't be shy on the presumption that a dentist would not be interested in something as...well, base as bartering. Chances are his income bracket is higher than yours (unless you happen to be a plumber) and he thus has even more interest than you in something as base as barter. You of course will remind him that the value of your yacht polishing must be reported to the tax department. Of course.

Barter starts with need. Decide what you need, find out who can supply it, and ask them what they would take in lieu of cash. The only general advice that applies is to avoid the middlemen and the hired help. It's futile to ask the sales clerk in the department store about barter. If it's furniture you want, ask the man who makes it or the man who owns it. Deal with smaller firms where the owners talk to the customers, and with tradesmen who can moonlight on their own time.

Barter works in the city as well as in the country. I know of one apartment dweller with a 16 foot canoe. He stores it in a colleague's garage. He gets free storage. His friend gets a free canoe, 51 weeks a year. Urbanites trade rent-free living for "house sitting" service, potted plants for records, car repairs for home cooking. Nearly every service or ware that can be bought, can also be bartered. There are exceptions; public utilities and the tax man still insist on cash, but by and large the things you can get with barter are almost limitless. Just this morning I got the local blacksmith to make up a little part for the pump. Cost me a dozen beets. Try getting blacksmithing done on your American Express card. I even know of one case where a man traded his shotgun for his neighbor's wife (cross my heart it's true). It came to light as a consumer complaint. The wronged party claimed fraud...it seems the shotgun worked but the woman didn't.

The best sort of barter is that between friends and neighbors (with the possible exception of the case above). However, when you need something that your own acquaintances can't provide, don't hesitate to ask a stranger to barter. Chances are he already knows the advantages - just as the redcoats knew the guys behind the trees were better off than they were. The difficulty in dealing with strangers is not in convincing them to barter, but in finding out what they want and agreeing on values.

How Many Apples is an Orange Worth?
In the redcoat economy of middlemen and taxes, all goods and services are given a dollar value, and the handy green units will tell you at once how many apples an orange is worth, or how many hours of labor it takes to equal a TV set. A dollar is a dollar is a dollar. When everything has a dollar value, exchange is greatly simplified.

The guerrilla economy is a little more complicated. Equivalents are easy enough, in theory. Just trade on the basis of theoretical dollars; if filling a tooth is worth twenty dollars to the redcoats, and yacht polishing pays five theoretical dollars an hour, then the filling is worth four hours of polishing. The problems arise when the units are not easily divided. You cannot trade a canoe for a tenth of a car. Nor is it easy to persuade someone to take ten canoes for his car...even if the values are equivalent. Then there's little choice but to trade other things, or look for other traders, (or God Forbid, make up the difference in cash).

When negotiating equivalent values, both traders should value their goods in the same price system. A dozen eggs and a loaf of bread might both be worth a dollar at supermarket prices, and a fair trade one-for-one. But if the egg man claims that Maxim's restaurant gets $5 an egg (served on silver, one at a time), and his dozen are therefore worth $60, he cannot trade them for sixty loaves of bread. He can try, but it won't often work. If he's going to value his eggs at Maxim's prices, then the bread should be priced per slice at Maxim's theoretical dollars too.

Choose the price system that seems appropriate, retail, wholesale, bulk or individual. Keep it fair and be consistent. *And,* if the tax man's looking, keep to the lowest system. For example:

Smith is a plumber, Jones an accountant. They agree to trade ten hours of plumbing for ten hours work on the tax return. During his regular job, each man earns $20 an hour doing work for which his employer charges customers $30 an hour. So if Smith hired an accountancy service in the normal way, he would have paid $300; but only $200 of that would have gone to the accountant. Likewise, Jones would have paid $300 if he had called in a plumbing firm; and Smith would have earned $200 for the ten hours work. No money changes hands in the barter, but legally each must report the value of service received in return for his labor. He must report an equivalent dollar amount under "other income". Should they each report a value on the barter of $300, the amount they would have paid? Or $200, as the amount they would have earned? Or would they have been better off agreeing to trade labor arbitrarily valued at some lower wage? The trade off is exactly the same in any case. The question is whether to pay income tax on $300, $200,... or $25.

COOPERATION AND COOPERATIVES

It can be as simple as borrowing a cup of sugar from the

neighbor, or as complex as the billion dollar system of retail co-ops. Whatever the style of cooperation, it nearly always means savings for consumers.

Consumers save by cutting out the overhead and the middlemen. So simple co-operation, like sharing a lawnmower with a neighbour, saves more than buying your own private lawnmower at the co-op hardware store. Bigger isn't always better.

There are kennel services, taxicabs, tool rental firms, and tow trucks all willing to sell the services that neighbors give and receive for nothing. The only price on the cash-free way is that you are expected to give as well as receive. It seems such an obvious and natural way of life that I'm always surprised that kennels, rentals and other types of businesses do so well.

It's no contradiction that a tight-fisted skinflint like me would counsel sharing freely with neighbors and friends. That kind of generosity is nearly always repaid in full. When our two tykes wanted to play store this summer, they made a sign, picked bunches of wildflowers, and set up to sell them beside the road. Old spoilsport pointed out that they weren't really giving fair value, since anybody was free to stop and pick his own for nothing. It was more of a game than a business anyway, so they shrugged and got the crayons out - changing the sign to "free flowers". Not only did they stop a lot more customers that way, but they soon came bounding home with pocketsful of "tips" - delighted with the joys of giving. I'm neither small enough nor cute enough to get away with that, but I've rarely been disappointed in the rewards for being neighborly.

Neighborliness can be more organized when the group gets too big to remember what's been done and owed, or when friends and neighbors are too mobile to sustain that kind of interdependence. Many urban neighborhoods operate simple co-operatives for common services. Baby sitting, for instance. The one I know best began when Ann and a few friends were discussing the costs and perils of hiring sitters, particularly in a big city neighborhood like that one, where people moved too often to get to know the local teens on more than the briefest recommendation. It wasn't the money so much as the idea that strangers were taking care of their kids - strangers with teenage appetites and boyfriends. They decided they would feel better sitting for one another. Ann bought a ledger book (the only expense the group ever made) and asked if Martha was free to sit that night. Martha spent four hours at

Ann's that night and earned a four hour credit in the ledger. Ann's page showed a four hour debit. They took turns making appointments and keeping the ledger, and the system worked so well that dozens of families got involved. They could always get a sitter at a moment's notice, and never again found an empty fridge at the end of an evening.

Other families cooperate to buy meat in bulk, share the cost of vacation cottages, own tools in common, establish schools, or make larger scale investments than any of them could afford alone. In every case they could act alone and find what they wanted on the retail market, but they gain financial advantage by acting as a group.

One of the newest forms is the cooperative garage, owned by members who hire mechanics to do honest, non-profit auto repairs, and to assist members (with tools and advice) to do their own repairs.

Many of the larger co-ops were formed as protection against the outright exploitation of individuals in the market place. Western agricultural co-ops, for instance, were formed by farmers fed up with selling wheat at give-away prices to the few big buyers who dominated the market. The big co-ops look like any other business, though, with charters and shares and voting rights and dividends, and all the consultants, accountants, lawyers and other non-producing middlemen that go with size. The big co-ops are in the phone book under "C".

The biggest savings, however, are usually found in the smallest groups, where overhead is zero, middlemen don't exist, and members can make decisions over the backyard fence - without a lawyer to complicate the situation.

GETTING IT FREE

If you're reading this book at the public library, you already have the idea. Go to the head of the class. If you bought the book, I thank you. The publisher thanks you. But pay attention, you have a lot to learn about guerrilla economics.

"There's no free lunch", said some forgetttable philosopher. It's true enough in the larger economy, but the individual is surrounded by a veritable sea of freebies. I know, I know, someone has to pay; but as long as the redcoats are convinced that freebies are for the lower classes, it only seems fair to let them get their jollies by picking up the tab.

I'm not talking about food stamps, pensions, or other official aids for those who might need them. I'm referring to the cornucopia of give-aways that are freely available to all. Here's a tiny sample.

Tools. Need a sewing machine to finish the wardrobe, or fancy saws and planers to build a dining suite? Sign up for an evening course at the local high school. There's usually a nominal fee, but you can get access to a roomful of the finest equipment for a fraction of the cost of buying or renting. And if you don't know what you're doing, there's an instructor to help.

Books. There's the library of course, and most of them also offer records and films to borrowers; but if you want new books to keep, join a book club. The introductory offers (you know - four books for a dollar and that sort of thing) are reasonably good value. When you've finished the obligation, there's no reason why you can't quit and join again for another introductory offer. And once you join a club, you're on everybody's mailing list for books. You'll get free samples, special offers, "take the first volume free and cancel the rest if not completely satisfied". You can collect Volume I of every do-it-yourself set published and still not spend a penny.

Fruit. Most city parks plant ornamental fruit trees. Apart from being pretty, they bear edible fruit that clutters up the grass if someone doesn't pick it. Check with your local parks department to be sure they won't object, and to be sure they don't spray the fruit with ojectionable chemicals. In the last city we lived in, I picked crabapples, rose hips, and cranberries, just on the path from office to home. We make up to thirty gallons of wine each year, and every drop comes from free fruit.

Garden Soil. Need fertilizer, potting soil, or just some good rich fill for the lawn? Make your own by composting manure, kitchen scraps and leaves. If it's mixed in a pile, watered and turned occasionally, it will be ready in a couple of months. Suburban riding stables will give away manure, free leaves cover the sidewalks in many neighborhoods, and - if you ask nicely - the local market or restaurant will save vegetable wastes for you. A smelly nuisance? One fall we made over five tons of compost on a tiny city lot, and the only hint the neighbors had was when they saw me raking leaves a block away from home. And the head swami guru at the vegetarian café began to suspect that I was feeding a pig on their daily pail of kitchen wastes...now there's an idea!

Meat. Free meat in the age of $2.00 hamburger? Preposterous? Not at all. Groundhog is delicious if you remove the musk glands first (they're in the armpits). Farmers are delighted to get rid of all the groundhogs you can take. Christmas dinner at our house last year was a succulant haunch of beaver - fur trappers throw the car cass away. Squab and pigeon breasts are gourmet delights and cost a fortune in fancy restaurants - and yet they're free for the taking in every rural barn. Fish belong to whoever catches them. Many slaughter houses give away soup bones and unsightly pieces that other customers don't want (ask about pigs' heads). Free meat isn't the exclusive preserve of hunters and farmers either. My own introduction was in the busy metropolis of Cleveland, when a friend arrived at the door wearing a black, three-piece suit, and carrying a briefcase, a rolled umbrella, and a dead rabbit. He was walking past the opera hall, it seems, when this rabbit hopped out of the bushes. The brolly was faster than the bunny. Delicious.

Commercial Samples. The givers expect the getters to feel obliged and buy a lot more after getting the freebie. That's a cardinal redcoat rule. We took our free 8 X 10 family portrait as advertised and the salesman seemed genuinely surprised that we didn't also feel obliged to take the $37 package of copies that accompanied it. Soaps, toilet articles, new snack foods, cleansers, and many other products are commonly given away as gimmicks. The only cost is the will to say *no* to the ensuing pitch to buy some more. The kids favorite family outing is our annual free tour of the chocolate factory - free samples in the sales room afterwards!

Government Services. Want to know how to skin a rabbit, cook a pigeon, pan for gold or fix your car? Chances are there's a bureaucrat somewhere responsible for that. Federal and local governments are a mine of information. Your local librarian can steer you to the right department. We set out to find some information on planting windbreaks, and stumbled across a government nursery selling seedling trees for a penny apiece, and a trained forester full of free advice on how to do it. Ask.

SOME OF THE NICEST PEOPLE SHOP AT THE DUMP

Even the Lone Ranger and William Tell were kindred spirits in my affection for adopting orphaned goods. All together now...To the dump, to the dump, to the dump dump dump...

Amazing what the redcoats will throw away! Right now I'm writing on a desk that was a door last year - it went out with someone's renovations. The lamp came from a motel - they discarded it twelve years ago when the shade got bent. The file box is walnut, decorated with hand carved inlays - it was an old sewing machine top, thrown out when the handle got broken. I'm sitting on an antique walnut and leather swivel chair. A doctor threw it out for the garbage collection when his teenagers broke off the armrest. With a little glue and the leather restored it's magnificent. If it were for sale I couldn't afford it.

The house is full of it: a walnut dresser, pure wool carpets, antique chests, rockers, chairs, beds and cupboards, lamps, windows, books, doors and even a piano bench. All of it thrown out for lack of a bit of glue and elbow grease that restores it to life again. We have an easy chair in the living room that is broken beyond redemption. The original plastic cover leaks stuffing from every crack and orifice. Some inner collapse has left it listing ready to spill unwary guests. It really is an offensive thing in an otherwise pleasant room. We keep it because it's the only piece in the house that someone else didn't first discard. We actually bought it new, and leave it there now as a monument to the folly of our old redcoat vanity, when we believed that one had to go to the store and pay for nice things. First-time visitors, who know our reputation for shopping at the dump, usually avoid the chair. I mean, it's so obvious...isn't it?

Treasures don't turn up every week on the curbside heaps of green plastic bags. And many large municipal dumps won't allow scroungers wandering around serious, big-time, burn-n-bury operations. Where then? If you don't have access to small rural dumps, you're left with only three good sources: neighbors, special junk days, and industrial waste.

Conservers play a curious symbiotic role with "normal" friends and neighbors. Not closet conservers who do their scrounging furtively in the dead of night, but full-flown, honest-to-God, up-front, here-I-am, out-of-the-closet addicts to the re-use of refuse. Junk junkies. Word gets around...quickly. Before long, friends and neighbors will be seeking *you* out:

"I'm clearing out the basement; would you like to help?"

"We bought a new fridge; do you have any use for the old one?"

"It's a perfectly good coat; it just doesn't fit anymore."

Truly! It happens! It isn't charity. The scrounger does provide a service more personal and useful than the garbage collector. How many garbage men will help you carry your junk out of the basement and then split a bottle of dandelion wine in the bargain? More than that, the scrounger brings some measure of entertainment to the serious business of being a consumer. The game is: "Throw it out - not even Charley could find a use for 12 old shingles (doghouse roof), or a piece of iron bedstead (barbeque grill), or a broken sheet of corkboard (soundproof the pump), or a carpet with a hole in it (a smaller carpet with no hole), or the upper half of a boot (leather hinges)." That's a lot more fun than seeing their expensive consumer effluent scrunched to a green plastic mush in the jaws of a garbage truck.

Most towns that offer garbage service, limit the kinds of thing you may set out for the weekly pick-up. No appliances, furniture, lumber, brush, etc., etc. Nothing but old chicken bones and disposable diapers (not even Charley wants those). But once or twice a year such towns relent and have a special collection for "spring cleaning" or some such euphemism. The towns that don't relent find the bigger junk dumped along the roadsides anyway, so it's cheaper to relent officially. When the clear-up days are announced, the piles of furniture, lumber, fridges, and bedsteads start to grow beside the curb and on the lawns of suburbia. And as the sun sinks slowly into the West, the parades of trucks and commandeered wagons start cruising slowly past the piles, ever alert for carelessly discarded treasure. It pays to be early - the best stuff goes first.

The very best junk often comes from industrial garbage. For all the propaganda about the efficiency of private enterprise, there's an enormous amount of perfectly good garbage going out the back doors of American industry. Admittedly, some of it is sold (steel barrels for $3 each, and sawmill slabs at $5 a load, for example), and the best refuse is picked over first by the people who work there. Ask your friends who work in factories or in warehouses about the kinds of things that are normally thrown out. But a lot is still left for the asking. In steel-making areas many a drive and path is paved with slag from the furnaces. Just outside a nearby marble crushing plant, nearly every driveway is paved with pure white marble dust. Fruit and vegetable packers throw away tons and tons of perfectly good food...culled for appearance's sake (crooked carrots, blemished apples). One friend heats a large house with the hardwood packing crates that were discarded at the neighboring snomobile sales lot. We have pig pens and gates from trucking pallets, workbenches from an instrument factory, and the stone walls are reinforced with broken crane cables discarded at the auto wrecking yard. (That was something of a coup - using the junkyard's junk!) Find out what your local factory throws away and ask (at the back door) if you can help get rid of it.

DO-IT-YOURSELF

By far the most satisfying freebie of all is to find that you can do it yourself. That advice seems almost gratuitious in the face of a recent announcement that over 50% of building supplies sold are now going to amateurs doing it themselves. That's fact. The suspicion is that a major part of those home projects involve kits and assemblies, glue-on bricks and self-stick tiles. All very admirable efforts I'm sure, but not really in keeping with the intention here...saving money.

When conservers do-it-themselves the end result is meant to be cheaper than the commercial version. It may also be better and more fun than buying, but the point is to spend less - to cut out some more of those middlemen. The ultimate in ridiculous do-it-yourself gadgets is the electric cream maker. You take a pound of butter, stick it in this gizmo, and make your own cream. Truly! I do not tell a lie. They sell such things! A conserver would set out a pan of milk and take the cream off the top with a spoon. The middleman economy would have us separate the cream, churn it into butter, and then buy a machine to turn it back into cream again.

Do-it-yourself, in this book, means doing it with less - less money, less energy (the world's energy or yours), less fuss, and less claptrap from the middlemen about how only a machine, or a skilled, licensed and regulated specialist can do it properly.

My idea of do-it-yourself is illustrated by one young family not far from here. They have just completed the building of a two story house with 1700 square feet of brand new space. It took them two years and $10,000. That's right, $10,000! They didn't want to start off life with the handicap of a mortgage, they explained. They started with neither experience nor skill in building. They didn't even have a plan. They copied the outside dimensions of another house down the road, and made up the inside layout as they went along. Nor was it done with kits, pre-built trusses, snap-on siding and glue-on bricks. Bought materials were just too expensive. The walls are cement and local cedar, and cost just $500 to raise.

Not everyone has the confidence to start a house from scratch; but millions of ordinary people have discovered that they can bypass the middlemen with results that are profitable, and often up to professional standards as well. Here are just a few examples.

Haircuts. The last time I was in a barber chair, the price was fifty cents and included a touch-up with a razor and a squirt of toilet water. The minimum trim is $5 now and you'll pay ten or more to be "styled". If you can press a spouse or willing friend into service, it's a simple job that takes less time than finding a parking spot at the barber's. The barber's skill is in knowing how to cut many styles on many different types of hair. With only one or two heads involved, the knack can be learned in a few practice sessions with scissor and comb. You may look a little funny for a couple of months, but when a trim costs $20 and you can look back and remember when you hated to pay five, you'll forget all about the practice cuts.

Legal Fees. The Utopians, More wrote, had no need of lawyers since their laws were clearly written and based on simple reason. We, unfortunately, have left the writing of law to lawyers, so that it is neither clear nor simple. There are cases, however, that are common and simple enough that the law is applied repetitiously, by rote and formula. An uncontested divorce or a straightforward will, for instance, are processed in the courts like so many Big Macs. The language is still mumbo jumbo, but it varies little beyond the personal data of the participants - name? address? who gets the house? catsup or mustard?... It's about as complicated as applying for a driver's license. Most towns have at least one firm selling "legal forms". It's often a stationery store. You'll find it in the yellow pages. Most now sell kits to individuals wishing to act as their own lawyers in simple cases; all forms and instructions included. Don't try it if you want to leave your fortune to the canary, but neither should you waste the expense of a lawyer to fill in your name and address.

Plumbing. Like many expensive tradesmen, the plumber uses his experience and skills on a tiny fraction of the jobs he does. Most of those thirty dollar an hour bills are for simple things that even a teacher, or writer, could master. Putting a washer in a leaky tap, or a shower over the tub, involve a few techniques that a layman could figure out from a how-to book in ten minutes or less (joining copper pipe, glueing plastic drains together, where to screw it off and on, and where to smear the gunk). If you can't figure out the how-to book, the plumbing supply shop will explain it. Even the nasty jobs, like getting the toilet to take it away instead of erupting on the bathroom floor, involve more mess than know-how. The expensive tools (like drain augers for the toilet) can be rented. Beyond that, there's little point in paying a plumber $30 an hour to mop up the bathroom floor. Save the plumber for the really tough problems, like where to eat in Nice and whether to be bullish on gold.

Sales Agents. Selling the house? Trading in the car? Getting rid of Grandpa's boat? Do you call in the agent or sell it yourself? Of course the agents will tell you that they earn their fees in the higher price they can get for your treasure. Consider: most markets for expensive items vary widely over time, or from city to city, but at any one point there is a standard set of values that is easy to establish and hard to buck, no matter who your agent is. If you're selling a three bedroom bungalow on a 40 foot lot, look at similar properties in similar areas and see how much they are selling for. That's the "market price". You can get less (quickly) or more (with hard work and patience), but chances are that you, or your agent, will have to sell pretty close to the market average. The agent's fee is a percentage of the sales price. It varies, but let's say 5%. If the market value is around $100,000, the agent expects a $5000 fee. If he is in a hurry he can get $4800 by finding a buyer at $96,000. Or he can spend ten times the effort and perhaps get a buyer at $104,000. The difference to you is $8000; the difference to him is $400. Doubtless, many agents are scrupulous enough to hustle all those extra buyers on your behalf, but there may just be one or two who would just as soon take the $4800 for a sure quick sale. You, the owner, have more at stake and a greater incentive to hold out for the best possible price. On an hourly basis, your return for the extra effort is twenty times as great as the agent's.

Car Repairs. Understanding the internal combustion engine is as easy for me as water divining or telling if the goat is pregnant. The color-coded, cut-away drawings were clear enough in the text-books, but a real engine is closed up and covered with all sorts of mechanical red herrings that didn't show in the drawing. Deciding what might be wrong under all that greasy tangle has, I'm sure, more to do with alchemy than science. The cost of buying auto repairs, however, leaves a conserver little choice but to do what he can himself. When our friendly neighborhood garage merged with the drive-in bank, we knew it was time to dig out some how-to books and start looking for the engine. It's still not easy and I still hate it; but knowing how to unstick the choke and change a tire and jump the battery and wire the muffler back in place has saved us many a dollar. Moreover, it's car repairs that convinced me that lack of knowledge and talent still can't stop us from doing it ourselves. If I can make the Ford start, anybody can do anything.

And Anything Else You Can Think Of. So far this year, Liz, who learned nothing more practical than Latin in school, has taught herself how to fix the washing machine, tan a hide, knit left-handed, castrate a pig, upholster a chair, spin, cure ham, make three kinds of cheese, lasagna noodles, and rugs. Do-it-yourself can get to be a habit. Even my pal Colby, the amateur electrician, eventually found the nerve to try again.

Most of us are capable of doing far more than we ever attempt. We don't trust ourselves to do it right, we listen too much to the self-interested claptrap of the specialists who want to be paid to do it for us, and we give up the effort when the first trial run doesn't come out as a letter-perfect copy of the commercial version. We end up being specialists ourselves as we gradually give up the idea of doing all those other things we're capable of.

As Robert Heinlein wrote, "A human being should be able to change a diaper, plan an invasion, butcher a hog, conn a ship, design a building, write a sonnet, balance accounts, build a wall, set a bone, comfort the dying, take orders, give orders, cooperate, act alone, solve equations, analyze a new problem, pitch manure, program a computer, cook a tasty meal, fight efficiently, die gallantly. Specialization is for insects."*

*from *Time Enough for Love: The Lives of Lazarus Long,* Robert Heinlein. The Putnam Publishing Group, New York.

9

Cheap Tips

If a visiting Martian were asked to pick the most inexpensive place to live in all of North America, a Saskatchewan farm would be a likely choice. Relatively cheap domestic oil, free health care, an abundance of fertile land, the most extensive co-operative system on the continent; and eating expenses, of course, should never be a problem on the farm - particularly in Saskatchewan where the nearest McBurger temptation might be a hundred miles away.

So much for the insight of Martians. A 1986 government survey shows that Saskatchewan farm families spent more than $4000 a year on food, even as farm incomes fell to under $12,000 a year. In rural areas all across Canada, farm families spent more on food than non-farm families! That can only be utter carelessness at the cash register. There are cheaper ways to eat, and cheaper ways to live.

I would say that knowing where to buy is less important than knowing not to buy at all. Scratching around for bargains can be a pain in the neck. It's easier to decide that you don't really want the thing after all. It's easier to decide to wait for the cheaper, lusher, vine-ripened summer tomato than it is to scour the market for a bargain tomato in January.

Nevertheless, the time does come when there really is no choice but to pull out the wallet and pay. How and where you perform that fiscal amputation is what distinguishes a conserver from a Saskatchewan farmer. How and where to spend is what this chapter is all about.

I won't even attempt to make an exhaustive list of all the ways in which the cost of living can be cut. I haven't found all the ways myself. Nor can tips like these be applied in a prescriptive way. Every market and situation is different. Saving money, however, is a result of a careful *approach* to spending. The examples listed here are intended to illustrate an approach to spending problems - not a solution to every problem.

FOOD

The obvious way to eat like a king for little or no cost is to raise it yourself. And that doesn't require a farm and a tractor either. Fruit and vegetables can be grown in the smallest city plot. Even an apartment balcony can grow most of a family's salads. Sprouts and mushrooms can be raised in a basement or closet. Rabbits, pigeons and poultry can be kept almost anywhere (though in some cities you may have to give names to these "pets" and have leashes handy if the zoning inspector calls). No growing space at all? Try renting a garden plot outside the city and tending it on weekends. In our area, a 25' X 50' ploughed and fertilized plot can be rented for $30 a season.

What's the worth of the output? Well, that depends on whether you grow truffles or wheat; but consider the products of our own small plot. This 50' X 75' patch produces the entire year round supply of vegetables for a family of four, with enough left over in the summer glut to send friends and visitors away with all they can carry. Another plot, 50' square, provides most of the feed to produce 600 pounds of pork each year. That's all we can eat and enough excess to pay the expenses. All together, in a space little bigger than a suburban lawn, we grow all of our own vegetables, meat, milk and eggs. Most of our fruit is home grown as well; and a short walk away nature provides the makings for all the jams, wine and syrups we can use. We do need cash for coffee, tea, flour and sugar, but most of the rest comes free.

Anybody growing grass in the back yard can't be serious about the cost of food. Get a good gardening book and discover what a *real* tomato tastes like. Saving a small fortune besides is a bonus.

If you have no access to the earth and sun, buying food may be inevitable. Spending a fortune at it is not inevitable:

1. Some shoppers save money by making use of discount coupons and refund offers. We don't often bother with these ourselves because most of them seem to be discounts on junk food, snacks, and convenience foods that we wouldn't buy at any price. However, if your tastes run to coffee whiteners and sugar snacks, they are cheaper with the coupons than without.

2. Shop for specials and loss-leaders. These are sometimes priced at or below the supermarket's cost...just to get you in the store where you'll buy all the non-specials too. Don't. Stock up on the specials when the price is right and don't be tempted by the more expensive stuff beside it.

3. Generic products and store brands are consistently cheaper than the advertised brands you recognize from television. Even the basics. It's amazing that plain old packages of butter that have "creamy" or "farm fresh" printed on the wrapper are always more expensive than the identical ones labeled "plain old butter".

4. Food co-ops and "no-frills" stores are sometimes (not always) cheaper than the ones with Muzak and uniformed bag boys.

5. Always shop with a list prepared at home. Impulse buying is expensive. In fact, some stores have found they can improve their profits by providing larger shopping carts. Impulse buyers keep going until the cart is full, and a bigger cart keeps them going longer. Stop when you've finished your list.

6. Buy in bulk. If you can't freeze or store a year's supply of a super bargain, get several families together and share the bounty. With several families sharing the work and investment, it may be worthwhile to branch out: take turns driving out to the country for a trunkload of potatoes, windfall apples, or a neighborhood steer.

7. Use farmer's markets. The food is fresher (and often cheaper) than the packaged stuff in the supermarket. If the price isn't right you can dicker.

8. Make the fullest use of leftovers. When Liz can't take any more meat off a bone, it goes in the pot with some beans or any other left-over bits and pieces. The pot goes on top of the furnace, and spends the day bubbling quietly away. By evening it's ambrosia. What the people can't eat, the pigs happily clean up.

9. Look for big discounts on seconds: bruised fruit, day-old bread, dented tins, and torn labels.

10. Check out the cheaper cuts of meat. The most expensive turkeys, for example, are those injected with butter or oil. Get a plain one and do the job yourself (with an inexpensive syringe

from the drug store). Better still, get an even cheaper utility turkey...that's an expensive one with a broken wing or a tear in the skin. Save a bundle and entertain Thanksgiving guests by explaining how your prize was injured.

11. Buy in season. Unless you live in Florida or California, having lettuce and tomato salad in February is for the birds (who can fly down there and get it fresh). Bean sprouts, shredded cabbage, raisins, currents, cress, carrots, celery, apples, or any of the more easily stored winter foods make interesting substitutes in salad. If you absolutely must have Southern produce in a winter salad, do it the cheap way: get green tomatoes in the fall (gardeners are happy to give them away at the first sign of frost), wrap them in newspaper and store them on a dry, cool shelf. They'll ripen slowly and still be good in January, when supermarket tomatoes are fifty cents apiece. And grow the lettuce in a flower box that can be brought indoors when weather gets severe (though I've used an axe to chop a perfectly good head of lettuce out of the ice in December). Having a diet with a seasonal rhythm of its own is more than just a money saver. Nothing tastes so fine as the first crisp apple of fall, or strawberries in May. That pleasure is greatly diluted when taste buds are jaded by eleven months of cardboard imitations brought to you by California Chemical and Teamster...

12. Your stomach will thank you for buying in season, but your wallet will be doubly grateful if you buy the very cheapest produce at the *end* of the season and store it for the future. Late fall potatoes, summer beans, winter fruits in the South, ...prices are at their best when there is a spoilable glut and growers face the cost of storing or shipping any unsold produce.

13. You can save the grower one more cost and get food even cheaper by picking your own. Since labor costs began to climb in the last ten years, more and more market gardens are switching to the "pick-your-own" system. Even the hardier vegetables, like potatoes, are being sold this way around major cities.

14. Whenever possible, eliminate the middlemen and buy direct. Get fruits and vegetables at the farm gate or from home gardeners. Even if they are not "commercial", most back yard gardens produce a glut of something in every season. Sports fishermen and hunters often lose interest in their catches after the photos are taken. Ask - these sellers rarely put up a sign.

15. If you live in an area where food is produced or processed, the commercial wastes are often free for the asking. Fruit and

vegetable packers discard perfectly good food on cosmetic grounds: crooked carrots, lumpy apples, etc. I've watched Florida packers bulldoze aside piles of beans simply because they fell off the trucks. Smaller slaughter houses often give away soup bones and dog food just to get rid of it.

16. Wild foods should not be dismissed, even in urban areas. You'll need a first rate guide to be absolutely sure of what you're picking, but the fare can be far more exotic than the stereotyped image of dandelion greens and blackberries. Just this spring a local newspaper columnist wrote of being tempted by a four ounce tin of morels (fancy mushrooms), imported from France and "discovered" in a gourmet shop 200 miles away. The price - $29 and change for the tiny can - deterred him. That week our eight year old staggered home with a two gallon pail full of fresh morels...picked less than a mile from the journalist's home! Fried with wild leeks and followed by bowls of succulent wild strawberries with lashings of maple syrup, we gorged on free food that only an orthodontist could afford to buy.

17. The greatest savings don't come from coupons or red letter specials, but from basic changes in your eating habits. Avoid nutritionless snacks and expensive convenience foods. Drink more water rather than bottled drinks. Make more meals from scratch; and that can be as simple as scrunching up your own dry bread crumbs to shake on chicken, or using your own leftovers to "help" the hamburger (at $2.00 a pound it shouldn't need any help!). Substitute cheaper protein for expensive red meat by using more poultry, eggs, fish, pork, and beans.

Heaven forbid you should ever be reduced to the theatre caper, but voluntary penury does not mean you have to quit eating, or even quit eating well. Apply the usual principles of doing it yourself, bypassing middlemen, buying when things are cheap to store for the lean times, seeking out alternative sources, and not scoffing at the freebies. That approach won't do for those addicted to microwave trays, McBurgers and beef, but more discriminating shoppers can eat better for less.

The theatre caper? Well...there was a year when a few enterprising fellows (whose budgets rarely covered meals, much less theatre tickets) discovered that the box office closed at the second intermission. They saw the third act of every new show in town and ate royally at the opening night parties that followed. The cost? A borrowed suit and an appetite for salmon and mousse.

CLOTHING

Like most consumer items, clothing costs are more easily trimmed by simplifying needs than by finding bargain sources. As usual, though, we will try to do both.

Now, make a quick inventory of the complete contents of your closet and drawers. Add everything in those boxes under the bed, suitcases, attic trunks, and Goodwill bags. Every bit of clothing you own. How many suits, shirts, skirts, sweaters, shorts, shoes, sandals...? Of all that, how many items have you worn more than three times in the last year? Take those off the list. How many items are worn out beyond repair? Take those off the list. What's the value of all that's left? All the clothes you bought but didn't really need? If you want to save money on clothing, *first quit buying what you don't need.*

A conserver wardrobe is basic. It's warm, durable, simple (to survive the vagaries of fashion), and neutral in color (to match anything else you might add to it). If you want to be noticed in a crowd, shave your head or get a tattoo - impressing with your clothes is expensive.

A conserver wardrobe is also deliberately small. Just enough to get down to your last clean set of everything by washday. Everything gets worn regularly and thus gets worn out before moulding at the bottom of the drawer or being left totally behind by the evolution of fashion. It's also easier to plan replacements in a small wardrobe. When socks go on sale, I know exactly how many pairs I'll need in the next twelve months. I know that my only pair of shoes will need laces soon, and then should last for at least three more years (for a total of 12 years of service). I doubt if I'll be able to find another pair like them for $6, but I've got three years to look.

When you've established a minimum, basic wardrobe, you can maintain it inexpensively if you:

1. Start with the most durable quality goods, even if you have to pay a little more. Wool, cotton, and leather generally outlast the cheaper synthetics. Well-made clothes have heavy seams and reinforcement at stress points. Don't assume, though, that the highest price buys quality. Fourteen ounce denim is 14 ounce denim,

186

whether you pay $20 on sale or $60 for the fashionable ones with a logo on the bum.

2. Wear them out - completely! Then repair them and wear them out again. Twenty-four years ago I bought my one and only sports jacket - a heavy, hand-woven, all-wool, Harris tweed. Set me back $20! After twenty-four years of regular wear, it has earned its second lining, and with a few leather patches it will last another twenty-four years. Shirts are worn until the elbows go. Then they become short sleeve shirts. Long trousers become shorts. When clothes are worn beyond repair they become work clothes, and finally, rags.

3. Imperfect clothes, or "seconds", are often first-rate value. The imperfections don't always affect the real quality of the garmet. It may be a misaligned print pattern, a color fade, or a stitch overrun. Look for quality brand seconds at discount stores and factory outlets.

4. Factory stores offer discounts of up to 50% over regular retail outlets. Better still, it's a good place to find seconds.

5. Wait for sales on end-of-season clearances and out-of-fashion bargain tables. Back-to-school sales are good times to buy casual wear. Winter clothing is cheapest in spring.

6. The cheapest source of quality clothing has to be a handy set of non-conserver friends with a closet full of clothing that is out of style, out of favor, or out of room for an expanding midriff. It would be bold to ask, but when word gets out that you won't be offended by the offer. Well...it would be a shame to throw out those perfectly good trousers just because the waistline has shrunk.

7. If you don't get the closet discards, chances are the rummage sale will. Look for them there. It will cost you some change, but the quality's the same.

8. Making clothes from scratch is a relatively popular effort, but not always as financially rewarding as it ought to be. The catch is the price of materials. But that's only a problem if you buy new material. Old clothing, drapes, or linens, which can be had for pennies at auctions and rummage sales, can be recycled to make "new" clothing. Sewing skills are equally useful in repairing existing clothes.

9. Children's clothing should never be a problem. They keep growing. Awash in North American affluence, there are always more hand-me-downs than hand-me-downees.

How easy is it? I buy most of my clothing new. I'm not that aware of appearances, but have never been accused of either elegance or shabbiness, so I imagine that I look sort of normal. Buying enough new clothing, footwear, and outerwear to keep me warm, comfortable, and sort of normal looking, costs less than $75 a year. I never considered that to be remarkable, or even unusual, until a student told me she spent $4000 a year on clothes. And she just looked...sort of normal.

FURNITURE AND APPLIANCES

Before settling down to work today I took a bag of garbage to the neighborhood pick-up point; one of those large metal bins that the garbage truck comes by to empty each week. I left our bag, but - as usual - came home with more than I left. Among today's gleanings were:

- ✔ outdoor chaise lounge with cushion
- ✔ patio table
- ✔ lamp (brass and milk glass) with shade
- ✔ wall light fixture
- ✔ antique wooden chair
- ✔ pine shutters
- ✔ two kitchen shelves
- ✔ four cupboard doors with hardware
- ✔ stainless steel breadbox
- ✔ aluminum stepladder

I had to replace one bolt in the ladder, and put a new bulb in the lamp. Apart from that, it was all in perfect condition - not even slightly soiled. All but the chair is new enough to take retail values straight from this year's catalogues. Total value, about $250.

Today's haul was, admittedly, an unusually good one. The chaise lounge, for instance. There hasn't been any good lawn furniture thrown out since we got the two chairs last year. We've had to wait a year for the lounge. And the table arrived just in time -the old picnic table (a telephone cable spool) was beginning to look a

188

little decrepit. The lamp, too, was sorely needed in my daughter's room. For the past year she has had to borrow my son's pewter lamp (of course it didn't look like pewter, all covered in green paint as it was...little wonder it was thrown out).

With a little patience, conservers should never need to buy furniture, as long as the Joneses keep buying the good stuff and throwing it out before wearing it out.

If you must buy furniture, shop second-hand sources, avoid any hint of the antique trade, and dicker. One good source that's often overlooked is asking at small hotels and boarding houses. They replace their furnishings regularly, and small shoddy places often discard older, better quality furniture. That's how we got an antique chest of drawers for $4.

Appliances are a little harder to come by. Their mechanical bits are prone to fail. If you're handy enough to fix them, you can pick up small appliances (kettles, toasters, irons, radios) for a dollar or two at auctions and rummage sales. Try them out on the spot if you want to be certain it works.

It's harder to be sure about the big appliances. If the kitchen range has a dead burner, you can't be sure if it's a $15 element or a $50 wiring job needed to get it going again. One way is to buy privately, through acquaintances or the classified ads, and take the time to ask all the necessary questions or poke around until you find out *why* the thing is being sold, and exactly *what* might be wrong with it.

When buying new seems the safest course, go about it slowly and carefully:

1. Use consumer guides to find which brands are most functional and durable.
2. Ask a repairman about the strengths and weaknesses of different brands.
3. Remember that the simplest models are not only cheaper, but have fewer parts that can fail. The more gadgets it has, the higher will be the cost of maintenance.
4. Remember that the cheapest model is not always the greatest bargain. It's the cost per year (including energy and maintenance costs) over the expected life of the appliance, that you should try to minimize.
5. When you know exactly *what* you want, wait until the price is right.

6. Clearance sales (after Christmas or Mother's Day for example) are good occasions to find lower prices.

7. Discount stores and mail order distributors can often undercut prices in regular stores. Knowing exactly what you want, it's easy enough to pick up the phone and compare prices all over town.

8. The Joneses worry about the appearance of appliances. They won't take anything that's marred. If your only concerns are function and durability, scratch and dent sales offer terrific savings.

TRAVEL

In the halcyon days of low-priced energy and high-priced dollars, bargain travel was a breeze. Europe on five dollars a day was a matter of simple meals and choosing the right hotels. Cheap travel is still possible, but it takes a lot more sacrifice and ingenuity to do it with dollars these days.

Getting there commercially depends on where "there" is. See a travel agent to get the latest on competitive fares, low season discounts, stand-by rules, charter savings, rail passes, and other internationally advertised bargain schemes. A travel agent will give you the latest rules and rates for nothing. His profit, however, is a percentage of the ticket price. The carrier pays the agent. Don't, therefore, expect the agent to be full of helpful advice on how to get there for nothing. It's not as easy as buying a ticket, but many conservers have used these alternatives:

1. Working passage on a ship. Commercial ships are tough to crack - a maritime card, union membership, a long wait, and a contract to complete the round trip voyage may be necessary. I've heard more success stories from those who hang around yacht harbors, checking notice boards and making friends until they find a private yacht in need of crew.

2. Walking holidays. It's undoubtedly slower, but you can see more sights and meet more people than you can at 35,000 feet. Take a tent, or rest your feet in inexpensive hostels.

3. All the rewards of walking with less effort and more speed? Take a bicycle tour. Even we older types can cover 50 to 100 miles a day with a little luggage on the back, and the boring stretches can be beaten by hopping a train - many lines will let the bike on free as baggage.

4. If a tent's not your style, use hostels, pensions, or bed and breakfast places. Outside the major cities, prices are quite reasonable. Check with the national tourist office of the country to which you're travelling for price brochures and booking information. Then make the arrangements yourself...the agencies prefer the big hotels.

5. Drive someone else's car. When the Joneses fly off to Miami for the winter, they hire car delivery firms to get the family car there too. The delivery firms get cheapie travelers to do the driving. Look for the ads in the classifieds of the nearest big-city paper.

6. Get a job. I know, I know, that's what you're trying to get away from. But some jobs entail being sent abroad. It usually takes a trade or special skill to land a foreign contract.

7. Working holidays are common fare around the British Commonwealth and in much of Europe. The idea is to pick a spot, get yourself there, then find a job - any job - to pay living expenses and to find out how the other half lives. Write ahead to be certain that work permits are not a problem, and to get some advance leads on the temporary job market. If language or credentials are barriers to practicing your own occupation abroad, you can always pick fruit, cut cane, or wash dishes in any language.

8. Meet people. Be nice to foreign visitors wherever you encounter them. Such meetings are prone to end in the swapping of addresses. Many folks have traveled the world by "dropping in" on such acquaintances.

9. Join an organization that swaps addresses for you. Most universities have a foreign students' club where contacts can be made.

10. Swap houses. If you're traveling someplace to stay awhile, make advance arrangements to trade houses with someone who lives there. (The Vacation Exchange Club can be reached at 12006 111 Ave., Youngtown AZ (602) 972-2186)

11. Know what to take. Embassies or large libraries can provide newspapers from the places to which you're headed. Read the ads and find out what's expensive there. That's what you should take. To be duty free, such "imports" are supposed to be for personal use (that's why there is a limit on quantities). But personal use can include gifts...like gifts to innkeepers, who might wish to return the gesture in some way.

12. Students and pensioners qualify for all manner of reductions on fares, museum passes, entertainments, and other assorted tickets. You'll need an ID card to prove your status (though if the

language gap is wide enough, a driver's license or library card works just as well).

13. Go native. The Hilton, Kodak, Sunflight, Club Med, Intourist, English-spoken-here vacation is for thumb suckers and the elderly rich (the richly elders go native). Take one small suitcase, local buses, a short walk down the hall to the can, and a wide, wide detour around anything with an American Express or Diner's Club sticker in the window.

Our North American obsession with tidy toilets and turnpike familiar fare leads to the spending of vast unnecessaries to duplicate our cultural environment half-way around the world. Anybody who insists on a McBurger in Paris or a shower in Japan could have saved the airfare and sent away for the souvenirs by parcel post.

My all-time favorite train ride (not for scenery but for the lesson learned) was on the Trans-Siberian railroad. Booking ahead, we faced a choice between:

"hard class"...Not recommended for more than commuting distance. Seats can be wooden - and hard!

"soft class"...Cushioned seats, a dining car, and sleeping berths. The native way to go.

"deluxe class"...The usual tourist choice.

At that time, deluxe fares were 50% higher than "soft". For no other reason, we immediately chose the soft class. It was a pleasant surprise. Coaches were modern and clean, meals were sumptuous, and our travelling companions delightful. We shared the compartment with a mother and child from Vladivostok. In the rest of the car were soldiers on leave, holidaying workers, and a friendly conductress who kept the tea pot humming. It was a linear party; and, as the only non-Soviets aboard, we were treated like welcome guests.

We were amazed then, at sundry stops, to overhear bitter complaints in a familiar language about lousy accomodations, suspected "bugs", and even pancakes. "You know, PANCAKES!" he shouted, making a six inch circle on his plate with a fingertip, "Like little black Sambo-ski". Mystified, the waitress served him a steaming bowl of soup with a whole chicken breast swimming in cream. The pancake man refused it.

Piqued, we vowed to see how the other half lived, and at the first opportunity slipped into the "deluxe" coach at the end of the

"You know, PANCAKES - like little black Sambo-ski."

train. It was truly a tsarist relic, a joke on cultural pretensions, a neat little touché of irony that only a Russian could devise. The "deluxe" coach was exactly that...in 1917. Fifty years later the Rubenesque seats were oozing stuffing onto the floor, the French flocked paper was peeling off the walls, and all the twiddly bits of Victorian decor were mouldering in the dark stuffy exclusivity of class. Whether or not there were "bugs" in the walls, there were certainly plenty of bugs. There wasn't a native in sight.

Much later, safe on the other side of the iron curtain, we were swapping Siberia stories with fellow travelers. "The worst thing about traveling in Russia," the lady lamented, "is that they never let you actually meet the ordinary people." She heartily agreed when I added that the pancakes are terrible too. Thank God for Howard Johnson's.

It isn't necessary to go exotic distances, either, to avoid the expensive tourist traps. One set of sun-kissed isles is so close to Ho-Jo land that shivering northerners threaten to sink it every winter. Pink and white bellies squeeze in between the casinos and souvenir stands that line the beach. What the travel agents don't tell northerners is that they can get a list of *all* accomodations by writing to the island government. Picking the cheapest rooms in the book - at a village too small to be seen on the map - we ended up right on the beach, under the coconut palms with miles and miles of clean empty beach in either direction. The innkeeper was so surprised to see a family of five outsiders that far from the casinos that he moved into the room we had reserved and insisted we take over his house. Oh, yes...there was one other outsider there - an anthropologist studying the natives. He, of course, had us beaten - he was being paid to be there.

10

Caesar's Due

Being a financial anarchist is fun. Like the Marx brothers snipping off the world's necktie, I enjoy walking into the stock broker's office with holes in my pants, writing personal notes to bureaucrats on the tax return, and disputing the gas company's right to round off the bill to the nearest penny. Twentieth century Luddites break conventions for the fun of it - because they're there.

It began as high camp, but the resultant lesson was clear enough the day the Yippies "raided" the New York Stock Exchange. Led by Jerry Rubin and Abbie Hoffman, the costume freaks wheedled their way up to the visitors' gallery and began tossing cash over the rail. Wheee...!! Millions of dollars of trading went by the boards as the stock wizards stopped their dealing to scramble after the one dollar bills wafting down from above. The traders were already down on their knees, scrabbling for bits of paper, before they realized they had just had their ties snipped off.

To a certain extent, we can isolate ourselves from the serio-comic farce of a glutted consumer economy absorbed in its own importance. We can walk right by the pre-packaged bread crumbs and the pet rocks. We can refuse to have a telephone and let the TV stay broken when we realize that nobody misses it. We can even walk away from jobs and say to hell with all that. But that's a desertion, not a revolution. Caesar lives, and the necktie economy keeps right on rollin' along - with us or without us. Even Jerry Rubin is wearing a tie and working at a desk on Wall Street now.

Sooner or later there are points at which we have to co-exist. We don't have to get right down on our knees and fight over bits of paper, but there are some arrangements we have to make with normal society, whether we like it or not. The object of this chapter is to plan those arrangements to keep them as simple, as cheap, and as hassle-free as possible.

WHAT TO DO 'TIL THE TAX MAN COMES

The surest way to save money on income tax is to lower your income. Facile perhaps, but it works. Married couples in the United States aren't even required to file a tax return on incomes of less than $9,550 (1990). Basic personal tax credits for a Canadian couple add up to a tax threshold of $11,300. Anyone who can't live on less than that just hasn't been paying attention. Add on other credits and deductions for children, certain forms of income, allowable expenses, and it's clear that although taxes may be complex, they certainly are not onerous for low income families.

In Chapter Four we dealt briefly with tax opportunities that arise *before* you leave your job. The general approach is to invest the maximum amounts in deferred tax shelters, often associated with retirement plans. The rules can get complicated, but the essence is to put money into the shelters now (when you are in a high tax bracket), and take the money out after retirement (when you will be in a lower bracket). You will eventually have to subject these funds to taxation, but at a much lower - or zero - rate. It's a form of income averaging.

The variety and complexity of different tax plans keep thousands of lawyers and accountants busy. It would be futile to attempt a useful detailing of different plans here. In any event, the rules and payoffs change so often that every investor should do some up-to-the-minute research of his own before investing a cent. Here's how.

Deferred tax investments of various types are offered through the company pension plan. Check first with your personnel office. Remember, though, that your employer may assume that you will be staying in harness until the age of 65, and a company plan may prevent you from cashing in a deferred tax investment until you reach a certain age.

Whether or not you're worried about starting rumors of your imminent departure in the personnel office, dig up some details on non-company plans as well. Generally speaking, banks, brokerage houses, and "near banks" (trust companies, credit unions, savings and loan) all have investment plans to sell and will provide free information on them. As a potential early retiree, you will primarily be interested in these five characteristics:

1. *The degree to which the investment is tax deductible.* Some, like the U.S. Keogh plans, or the RRSP's in Canada, are 100% tax deductible. If you put $1000 into the plan, you subtract $1000 from total income before calculating the tax. In the 35% tax bracket, that's a $350 payoff. Other investment plans allow partial tax write-offs under different rules: oil depletion allowances, real estate depreciation, capital gains versus dividend income. Some, particularly the 100% deductible pension plans, have upper limits on how much can be deducted in total. You can invest more, but only the portion within the limits is 100% deductible. For any plan considered, find out the percentage of the investment that can be deducted, the allowable limits, and the actual tax advantage - using your own tax bracket.

2. *Redemption rules.* The usual assumption of the pension plans is that the investment will remain untouched until the worker retires at a normal age. That's why the Keogh plans and the IRA's don't normally allow withdrawals from the investment until disability or the age of 59 1/2 is reached. "Premature distribution", or cashing in early, is penalized by including the withdrawal in your gross income and taxing it by 10%. Even with the penalty the tax break may be worthwhile. A U.S. worker in the 35% tax bracket, putting $1500 a year into an IRA for four years, saves $2100 in taxes. In his first year without an income, he withdraws $6000 and pays a $600 penalty tax. He's still ahead on taxes.

Canadian RRSP's have no lower age limits, and the only penalty is the normal tax bite at the time of cashing in. Again, the normal bite is much smaller in the lower brackets. Other tax deferred investments have their own redemption rules. Real estate investments for instance, defer taxes by deducting depreciation as a cost. When the investment is ultimately sold or redeemed the profit is calculated as the difference between the sale price and the *depreciated* cost of the investment. So the paper cost is also counted as a paper profit and is taxed later as a capital gain. The age of the investor is irrelevant. Find out the tax penalties for cashing in each plan under your own particular circumstances.

3. *Loading charges.* Many tax-inspired investments add administrative or sales charges either at the time the investment is made (front-end load), or at the time you cash in. Always ask about charges and include them in any comparison of different plans. Don't automatically assume that a "no-load" investment is a better deal, however. Administrative costs may simply be asborbed by paying out lower dividends.

4. *Risk.* All investments carry some element of risk. If you are investing primarily to defer taxes, don't overlook the risk of the investment itself in your enthusiasm to reduce what's due to Caesar. Oil and gas ventures, for example, are very attractive for the tax breaks they offer. With initial deductions, depletion allowances, and capital gains breaks, investors can hope to make a bundle with a very minimal tax bite. They can also make empty holes in the ground. Other plans offer more modest dreams, but with some greater guarantee of performance.

5. *Income performance.* The income potential of an investment can sometimes be predicted by its past performance and an estimate of the effects of future developments. If you want to invest in rental property for instance, recent rents, capital appreciation, zoning changes, and predicted developments in the neighborhood being considered might all be useful in calculating the expected income from the investment. Term savings and institutional investments sometimes "guarantee" income performance for the future.

With full information on tax and redemption rules, charges, risk, and income, you should be well equipped to judge which tax deferral plan is best suited to your own plans and circumstances.

AFTER THE SALARY'S GONE

Unfortunately, your days of dealing with the "revenooers" don't automatically end with the paycheck. Presumably you've set something aside, like a deferred tax investment, to soften the blows of penury; and cashing it in means paying taxes on it. Then, too, there's always the possibility that the Tahitian nudes will start selling, or the basement inventions actually start to work, and retirement begins to get profitable. In that event, tax hassles and costs may depend to a large extent on what you choose to call yourself and what form your income takes.

"I found a tax loophole today. I quit my job."

When the tax man asks your occupation, it's not idle curiosity. A salaried employee, small businessman, commission salesman, farmer, the self-employed, and the unemployed are all taxed under different rules. There are rules by which your category ought to be determined, but with the small scale enterprises contemplated here, the official distinctions get a little fuzzy.

If your income is going to be big enough to tax, there are definite advantages in finding a category that allows you to deduct *costs* from gross income, with the aim of reducing the remaining taxable income to zero. The self-employed, including those who operate farms or businesses, generally have the greatest range of opportunities to deduct all manner of costs from income. A business operated from the home may deduct a share of the house expenses, for example. Farmers may deduct fence repairs, depreciation on buildings, and in some circumstances can get rebates on property taxes, and exemptions on gasoline and sales taxes.

If you are a former office worker who has just dropped out to raise your own food on a small scale farm and make pottery in the barn, the decision to call yourself: "not employed", "farmer (sort of)", or "self-employed potter (mostly unpaid)", may be a matter of choice. If you qualify to fit more than one category* you will have to decide which title suits you best by considering just how much income you expect to have, and thus how many deductions you can make use of. On a small farm, for instance, if your gross income is expected to be so low that you may need only a few thousand dollars in deductions to cut taxes to zero, there's little point in fussing with the qualifications for farmer status, as long as the needed deductions can be scraped up from personal deductions or other easier routes. There's little to be gained by taking deductions beyond what you need to pay no tax. The exception is if you expect to return to high income levels in future years and are in a category where certain losses can be "saved" to offset future profits.

The other purpose for choosing your official "occupation" carefully is the possibility of putting earnings into tax-free forms. A business can use its profits to buy equipment, expand inventories, or anything else that may qualify as a cost. That use of earnings is tax free. If the proprietor takes a "salary" from his business, it's taxed at the full rate - even if he intends to save it and reinvest it in the business. Even ordinary taxpayers can convert some of their earnings to tax-free forms. Interest on some state and municipal bonds is exempt in the United States. Canadians pay less tax on capital gains than on earned income. From the tax perspective, the worst possible way to earn an income is to work for it.

---

*To be a "farmer", for instance, you will have to sell a given value of farm products each year. It's not hard to do. Many an overpaid professional has bought and sold a small herd of cattle - without ever seeing them - for the sole purpose of being able to call himself a farmer, and claim a list of deductions.

In the lower income brackets, where there isn't much tax to save by calling yourself one thing or another, you may still wish to choose your official occupation carefully. Businesses and the self-employed are required to report earnings quarterly and make voluntary pre-payments. If you think the once-a-year tax form is a frustrating hassle just to prove you don't owe them anything, wait 'til you're stuck with the job every three months. Worse still, at that point receipts and a more formal set of books become essential. Unless you're really serious about a business, or really happen to be making money at it, it's easier to be "not employed", but honest enough to report the odd dollar that comes in as "other income".

Most ordinary, no-longer-have-a-paycheck retirees are content to be out of the income tax game. Paying less is a middle-class frustration that no longer bothers the voluntary poor. Getting some back is a different matter.

A CREDIT BEATS A DEDUCTION

At the very best, taking advantage of all possible deductions can reduce your taxable income to zero. You owe nothing. More deductions will still leave you owing nothing. The only way to come out ahead is through tax *credits*. Most U.S. credits can only be subtracted from the tax total. If you don't incur taxes, you can't take any credits. The earned income credit, however, was made to order for low income survivors. Unlike other credits, the earned income credit is counted as a *payment* and can be taken as a refund, even if you pay no taxes. Full instructions are with the form 1040. In a simple case of a married couple with one child and an income of $10,750, no tax is payable but the earned income credit comes back as a $953 refund check.

Similarly, in Canada, provincial tax credits, federal child tax credits and sales tax credits can come back as refunds even if you pay no income tax. Other credits, listed on the back page of the tax form, are only useful for reducing the amount of tax owed.

YOU CAN DO IT

A final warning: nobody said tax law was simple. The possibilities and rules continue to sprout like dandelions in spring.

The complexities expand almost as fast as the tax preparation firms that offer to find the loopholes for you. In 1979, 40% of U.S. taxpayers hired commercial services to prepare their returns. Nevertheless, there are two very good reasons why you should consider doing it yourself. In the first place, even if you use a tax consultant, you will still have to do the hardest part yourself; and secondly, you're better equipped for the job than any tax firm could be.

A tax firm can only know as much about your finances as you tell them. You have the information, and the consultant has a blank form to be filled in. He can't *give* you any credits or deductions that you don't tell him about. The forms are free at the post office and all the credits and deductions are listed. Reading the form line by line, you'll trip over every credit and deduction. The guide will tell you whether you qualify. Start at the beginning and follow it through step by step. You'll be ahead by at least the amount of the consultant's fee.

U.S. taxpayers have an additional concern. In 1980 the Internal Revenue Service began enforcing negligence-penalty provisions enacted by Congress in 1976. The effect is to pressure accountants into correcting any errors or questionable items on a return that might otherwise result in lower taxes. The taxpayer can't help but wonder if the hired accountant is on his side, or on the side of the IRS.

The hardest part of the tax job is the preparation - sorting out the twelve months collection of receipts, check stubs, and records. Once those are in order, it's mostly a matter of filling in the blanks. And the tax preparation firms won't do that hard part for you. You've still got to amass your own documentation. Once you've gone that far, you might as well fill in the blanks yourself.

INSURANCE: WHAT IF SOMETHING GOES WRONG?

Insurance, like taxes, is another of those middle-class bugaboos which the voluntary poor can by-and-large do without. Not all insurance is expendable in every-man-for-himself land; but by looking through a different prism, we can easily see which ones are. The prism, the acid test for insurance needs, are the simple questions:

What have I got to lose?
Can it be replaced with money?

Curiously, it often seems that those with the least to lose are the most concerned with insurance policies. It must have something to do with living on the margin of a wealthy economy. When one's financial life is spartan, even a very small loss may mean disaster. In material terms, there isn't much room between the conserver lifestyle and what the wealthy around us would consider destitute. Depending on the perspective, life on the edge can be the most secure, or the most insecure spot on the continent. It is insecure for those who consider they're just an accident away from ruin; it's secure for those who know they have little to lose anyway, so what the hell.

Things are bound to go wrong in every family. Houses burn, accidents happen, illness strikes, and sooner or later most of us die. Fate besets us. We can't stop it, so we cushion the blow by arranging to receive sums of money whenever bad luck happens. Never mind the fact that it was our own money to start with. It still seems a curious custom when most such losses have little to do with money.

Arsonists might disagree, but the people I've known who have watched their houses burn have always seemed less concerned with the financial loss than with the things that cannot be replaced at any price: the family pet, the photo album, the kids' first paintings, grandpa's moustache cup. The most macabre of all is school accident insurance. Those check-a-box policies that the kids bring home from some corporate friend of the school board. So much for loss of an eye, twice as much if you lose two, $11,500 for an arm...but how do you tell a kid to forget the arm, we have $11,500 to make up for it? What's the point? The money is irrelevant in such circumstances. A cash windfall is not to be sneezed at, but there can't be any pleasure in it when it's the price of someone else's tragedy.

Life Insurance: You Bet Your Life

When a company wagers that you'll live to be old, it's called life insurance. If you grow old, you lose. If you die young, you win. Make sense? Sometimes it does. Let's apply the acid test.

What have you got to lose...besides your life? The standard rationale is that your death will also cause a financial loss for the surviving members of the family. This may be true if you are the main source of income for dependents; but if your survivors are capable of providing for themselves, then nothing is lost, monetarily, that can't be regained. A single person, without dependents, has no reason to insure his life. Life insurance, for a childless couple, implies that the spouse is not capable of earning an independent living.

Let's assume, though, that you are the sole wage earner with no financial reserves and a load of incompetent dependents. Chances are, in that position, you won't be interested in surviving without salary anyway. But never mind, perhaps you misread the title and were looking for guidance on how to have a salary without surviving.

A salary without surviving is only useful as long as your dependents remain dependent. When the children are grown, there's no reason to remain insured other than to insult your spouse's competence. There's nothing to lose by *not* being insured - except your very presence, and that can't be replaced with money. Can it? In the meantime, if and while the family needs to replace your salary, how does one choose insurance?

There are two basic types of life insurance: *whole life* (sometimes called permanent), and *term* insurance. The jargon is clear enough. Whole life policies are in force until you die. Whether you die at 97 or 27, your dependents will be equally well looked after. A term policy, on the other hand, only pays off survivors for a given period. If you buy a 20 year term policy at the age of 30, your survivors only benefit if you have the foresight to die before you reach the age of 50. After that, they're on their own. Most parents hope the kids will be on their own after 20 years in any event. That, in itself, is reason enough to choose term policies over whole life policies. The fact that term policies are considerably cheaper enhances the preference.

When insurance agents begin to suspect that you might be the type to prefer an independent streak in your grown-up children, or that you have every confidence your spouse could manage just fine without you, that's when the "guilt pitch" is dropped in favor of the "investment advantage" of whole life policies. Whole life policies, you see, earn a sort of dividend. They *grow in value* as the salesmen say, whereas those cheap little term policies just sit there at the chosen level, insuring your income powers. The problem with the investment pitch is that it's based on a common ignorance of the powers of compound interest. Investing the same premimums at the bank, and compounding it over the years, will show more profit than whole life policies. If the salesman's figures sound impressive, just ask him what the effective *annual* interest rate amounts to. If it's more than your savings account earns, it's time to switch your account to another bank.

Some argument is made for the borrowing capacity of a whole life policy. It's true that policy holders can borrow against these policies at very attractive rates. The rates should be attractive - after all, *it's your own money*. Had you put the premiums in the bank, you could "borrow" against that for nothing...just by withdrawing the funds anytime you wish.

Death has several consequences for families. Among them are personal loss (against which any policy is irrelevant), and loss of essential earnings (which can be compensated with survivors benefits and death benefits from Social Security or the CPP, personal investments, or as a last resort, term insurance policies). Judge insurance schemes as you would any other investment - strictly on investment criteria: *risk, return, growth, tax advantages, and redemption features*. Love and guilt and family responsibilities have nothing to do with the quality of investments. Make that distinction clearly before considering any insurance policy.

How do we cope? Well, when needs are so reduced that a salary becomes unnecessary, then it is also unnecessary to insure against the loss of the salaried. Death and finances are unrelated.

The cost of dying need not be a problem. If the family income is guaranteed either by term insurance, personal investments, low cost of living habits, or the survivors' own earning capacities, then the tragedies of early death do not have to be financial ones. The other costs are a matter of making the usual conserver decisions. There are cardboard coffins and rental coffins. Cremation saves the cost of plots, markers and coffins. You can die for free by donating your body to a medical school or to a hospital for its usable parts. Make arrangements ahead of time. Too disrespectful? Unloving? Perhaps to some, but think about it this way. If love and respect can be given through the medium of money, then why give it to the undertaker who has earned neither your love nor your respect? Spend your money and your love on the living, while they can still enjoy it.

Health Insurance: In Sickness and In Health

Dying may be cheap, but getting better isn't. As long as doctors and dentists assume that an hour of their time is worth a week of mine, sickness is a considerable risk. And hospitals are even worse. Not even doctors and dentists can afford to pay their own hospital bills.

How can low income survivors protect meagre resources from ruinous medical costs? Insurance is one possibility. 85% of Americans carry some form of hospital insurance. Almost 100% of Canadians are covered by public hospital and medical insurance. In Canada, coverage is free in most provinces, and there are special arrangements for low income families in the provinces that do levy charges. Americans of working age are stuck with the costs of private insurance. The usual rules apply: shop around, and don't buy more than you need.

The best solution is to stay healthy...and that's not being flippant. Individuals have a surprising degree of control over the state of their own health, and thus over the cost of their medical care. A recent government study concluded that individual habits and lifestyles accounted for a major part of health problems and costs. These "diseases of choice" that spring from careless driving, heavy drinking and smoking, junk food diets, obesity, stressful lifestyles, and other self-imposed risks can all be controlled by choosing between healthy and unhealthy practices. "About half the burden of illness is psychological in origin" the report claimed; and for the physically ill, "Diseases of the cardio-vascular system were by far the principal cause of hospitalization..." Accidents were second.

The report went on to note that "self-imposed risks and the environment are the principal or important underlying factors in each of the five major causes of death between age one and age seventy..." The five major killers were: motor vehicle accidents, heart disease, all other accidents, respiratory diseases including lung cancer, and suicide.

Accidents and ill health can strike anywhere of course. Healthy lifestyles won't ensure the end of medical bills, just as an apple a day won't really keep the doctor away (even when properly aimed). But, statistically, a sedentary smoker-drinker-worrier who refuses to wear a seat belt is guaranteed to die younger and more expensively than he would if he chose healthier habits.

Knowing we can reduce the risks of catastrophic medical bills, but can never really guarantee good health, there's comfort in having back-up insurance for major problems. There's greater comfort in knowing that we're less likely to need professional health care. Health conscious survivors who do not have access to public health plans can tailor their insurance to the possibility of catastrophe, and work on reducing the need for uninsured minor maintenance by taking better care of themselves. In practice, that means: brushing and flossing instead of sending the dentist to Las Vegas, taking a cold to bed instead of to the doctor (who can't cure it anyway), or treating your nerves to a day of rest instead of Valium.

Auto Insurance

Doctors aren't the only financial calamity around. Lawyers can be worse. Thus driving can be a financial risk as well as a physical one. Fending off posible disaster with insurance policies is a major part of the cost of transportation.

Auto insurance, like health costs, can be greatly affected by the decisions you make. An inexpensive car is also cheaper to insure. A good driving record reduces costs. Some companies offer special low rates to non-smokers and non-drinkers. The fastest way to save money, though, is to cut out whole chunks of coverage.

Remember that the greatest risk, the possible calamity, would be a lawsuit to recover the damages you might cause. Insurance to meet that possibility is called "liability" insurance. That part is almost indispensible. In some jurisdictions it is mandatory. You can save on the liability coverage by maintaining a good driving record, and by limiting the maximum coverage. The safe driving record speaks for itself. The extent of coverage is a matter of some dispute. Insurance agents, and some lawyers, advise carrying big liability packages - in the vicinity of the highest awards being given by the courts. That's fine for those who can afford it. Those who cannot may not need it anyway. Gauge the risk by looking at your assets (remember the acid test - what have you got to lose?). The more you have to lose, the more careful you should be to insure it. The less you have, the less it costs to defend it.

Insuring against damage to your own vehicle is called "collision" insurance. Combined with coverage against theft, injury, fire, brimstone and marauding Visigoths, it's called "comprehensive" coverage. Again, the most significant question is - what have you got to lose? This time, instead of looking at your assets, look at your car. If it fell under a steamroller tomorrow, how much compensation would the old clunker warrant? Remember that repair costs won't be covered beyond the depreciated value of the vehicle. Also remember that if the accident is your fault, you pay the first $100 (or whatever the deductible portion is) and a claim for the rest will boost your future insurance rates. If the accident is the other guy's fault, you can be compensated through his liability coverage whether or not you have your own collision insurance. Comprehensive coverage seems to be designed for the person who has an expensive new luxury car and who never has to claim on the policy. It was not designed for the person who drives a middle-aged economy model and is inclined to accept a dent here and there as a part of the decor. A lady who drives a car just like that finally accepted my argument that a single insurance premium would cover all the damage her car could suffer without being sent to the junkyard. Her last defense was the theft coverage. "I need my car. What if somebody should steal it?" It was a cruel thing to do, but I asked her to look at the car again and pretend she was a car thief. Knowing the penalty was the same, would she steal her own car or the new Corvette beside it? "I see what you mean," she relented. It suited her own needs just fine, but no self-respecting Visigoth would touch it.

Still in doubt? Look at it this way. Insurance companies profit by the statistical certainty that the average driver, in his lifetime, will pay more in premimums than he will collect through claims. If you are an average driver with an average car, you can put the equivalent of the insurance premimum into a bank account or private investment. You can have an average number of accidents, pay for them yourself, and still be ahead by the margin of the insurance company's profit. With a cheaper car and better than average safety habits, you can make even more than the company. In fact, you *are* an insurance company - with a single client. By all means insure against the total calamity of a big liability claim, but the rest you can do yourself.

Risking the Family Jewels
Fire, storm damage, theft, and all manner of financial threats beset the family property. What have you got to lose? For most

homeowners, the family home is more than they can afford to lose. If it's mortgaged, the lender will likely insist on the property being insured. Make a list of all assets and consider their vulnerability to loss. The house can burn. The land cannot. Tools can be stolen. The house is usually left behind. Are vandals and Visigoths a problem where you live? Is it a hurricane zone? Earthquake prone? Strike off everything (like land) that's relatively invulnerable, everything (like Auntie's ugly heirloom jewelry) that you wouldn't particularly *want* to replace, and everything (like the wedding rings) that *couldn't* be replaced. The rest should be things that would have to be replaced at a high cost. Consider insuring those things with a homeowner's policy. The rest? If you or your money wouldn't replace it, there's no advantage to insuring it.

Like other aspects of conserver living, however, the most secure household is not the one with the most insurance, but the one with the most modest possessions, the one with the least to lose. The less you have, the less you have to worry about...and the less it costs to protect it.

Our most expensive theft was a lawnmower. It was relatively new, but no great loss since it never worked right from the start. In fact, I accepted the theft with a surprising measure of relief mixed in with the resignation. I began to understand how grandfather felt about his Kaiser (the Edsel of its day). He used to park it with the keys left in and fervently hope it would be stolen. When someone suggested the price of gas might be deterring prospective thieves, he took to leaving a dollar on the seat as get-away money. Anyway, the lawnmower was gone and easily forgotten...until the following spring when the police showed up with it. Not only was the loss replaced, but an obviously frustrated thief - with greater skills than mine - had repaired all its faults.

PENSIONS: WAITING FOR THE GOLD WATCH

My favorite retirement story (and I heard it twice so it must be true) was the gentleman who stayed on in faithful service until the company finally pensioned him off with a gold plated watch and a modest stipend. They had the usual little ceremony in the tea room just before five o'clock. The assistant manager attended (the manager was too busy, but sent his best regards) and cracked a few jokes at the expense of our faithful servant before telling everybody what a great old guy he really was and how the company would find it hard to get along without him and how this little gift was just a token of the high regard in which he was held. Our faithful servant's young replacement, chomping at the bit for six months past, and already making more than O.F.S., cried "Speech! Speech!", and all eyes fixed on dewy-eyed O.F.S. The hush was expectant. Even the sales staff held their glasses at half mast out of respect, and turned the hub-bub down to a whisper. "I'm not much at making speeches," he croaked (and the secretaries dabbed their eyes), "so I'll just say 'thanks for everything' and I know you'll all understand how I feel about you." And with that he held up the new watch for all to see, waved, and strode out the door - a jaunty sprig of mistletoe pinned to the end of his coat tail.

I'm always surprised at the number of people who quietly confide their disenchantment with working life, the dodos they have to work with, or the meaningless nature of the daily chore. More surprising is their reluctance to kiss it all goodbye in favor of some more satisfying task. The usual excuse is the pension - waiting for the gold watch. Even those with the confidence to support themselves today, worry about ensuring an income for their later years. The promise of a pension is one of the strongest ties to the nine-to-five labor force.

The Company Pension

There are thousands of variations. The usual form takes a contribution from each employee's paycheck (usually a fixed percentage of salary), adds a contribution from the employer, and places both contributions into a special pension fund. The pension fund is invested where some interest can be earned. When the employee retires, he begins to receive regular payments from the fund. The size of the payment is based on the number of years of service, and on the employee's salary. The higher the salary and the longer you work, the greater will be the total of your contributions over the years, and the higher will be your pension.

A fair and tidy scenario, but not entirely foolproof. No one can guarantee the future. Here's what can go wrong:

1. The pension fund's *raison d'entre* is security. Therefore the fund is nearly always invested in the safest, long-term investments

around; and the penalty for being conservative is in earning the lowest interest rates around. Pension funds grow notoriously slowly. If he could get his hands on the employer's contribution, the average employee could invest his own pension funds much more profitably.

2. Employers can, and do, go out of business with alarming disregard for niceties like pension rights and severance pay. If you're hanging around just for the pension, you'd better be confident that the company is going to stick around too.

3. Some employers have a nasty habit of firing or laying off older workers just before they qualify for full pension rights or early withdrawal rights. What are your own rights to withdraw pension funds should you be laid off tomorrow?

4. The most serious flaw in the security of pensions is also the most certain - inflation! Some pensions are indexed to the cost of living. That is, pension payments are regularly raised to keep up with inflation. Most pensions are not indexed, however, and that is what makes them virtually useless for long term security.

A friend of mine (let's call him Joe) was 55 last year. He and his wife worked out a detailed budget, and concluded that they needed $20,000 to spend in a year. Joe's take-home pay will cover that nicely. They have a little money in the bank, and a pension plan that will give them two-thirds of Joe's salary when he retires in ten more years. He expects some raises between now and then, and was feeling quite secure about his future. I asked him if he had figured out the effects of inflation on the family budget. No, he hadn't, but he was confident that things wouldn't get any worse, and inflation would likely drop down to about 5% and stay there (Joe's an incurable optimist).

So we took his $20,000 budget and inflated it by a mere 5% a year between now and retirement, ten years away. "At 65, Joe, you are going to need $32,578 a year - just to maintain your present standard of living." He was a little shocked, but not too worried, since he expected his salary to keep pace with inflation. He hoped to be bringing home $45,000 a year by then, and a two-thirds pension would provide $30,000 a year for life. It sounded like plenty, until we figured that he might live for another twenty years after retirement. At age 85, his modest standard of living will require an income of $86,438 - and his pension will still be paying him $30,000! And that's only if the company doesn't fold, Joe doesn't get laid off, he keeps getting raises, and inflation stays down at the 5% level. Some security!

Check your own situation in the following table. Estimate your present cost of living and find the appropriate column. Then make a guess as to how much longer you expect to live. Follow the column down to your own life expectancy and see what you will need to maintain your present standard of living then. Thus, if you are 35 now and spending $20,000 a year, you will need $140,800 a year at the age of 75.

INFLATION TABLE (at 5% per year)

Life Expectancy	Present Annual Salary ($)			
Years	15,000	20,000	25,000	30,000
5	19,144	25,526	31,907	38,288
10	24,433	32,578	40,722	48,867
15	31,183	41,578	51,973	62,368
20	39,799	53,066	66,332	79,599
30	64,828	86,438	108,049	129,659
40	105,600	140,800	176,000	211,200

If inflation returns to 10% instead of the current 5%, the future gets bleaker even faster. At 10% inflation, a $20,000 budget would swell to $905,194 in forty years.

The obvious question is, can your pension plan compensate for the effects of inflation? If it can't, is it worth hanging on to a job just for the hope of a pension? Is there an inflation-proof way to provide for the future? The first two questions, only you can answer. Inflation-proof pensions? Perhaps.

A WAY OF LIFE TO BEAT THE COST OF LIVING

It isn't really a pension, but in many cases it's far more effective than pensions. Inflation is hardest on those who spend the most. You can drastically reduce its long term effects by improving spending habits in a marginal way now. Take Joe's case for example. In thirty years, remember, it will require $86,438 to support his lifestyle. His pension will provide $30,000 (leaving him with a $56,438 deficit). Now let's assume that he loses his senses and throws caution to the wind. He quits the job, gives up the pension, and moves to a cheap little place out of the city. With lower taxes, a vegetable garden, and no more parking fees, they might manage to trim $5,000 off the budget.

That's barely a dent in his anticipated deficit, but look what it does to the effects of inflation: With his new, slimmed-down $15,000 lifestyle, the five percent inflation has a smaller base on which to build. After thirty years his needs will take $64,828 a year to satisfy. Even if he saved nothing and earned nothing, his deficit would still be little more than the deficit he was headed for with a salary, a pension and a more expensive lifestyle.

Do-It-Yourself Pensions

It is possible to set up your own pension plan in a way that may offset inflationary effects. Directly or indirectly, company pensions are financed by employee contributions. Part of it comes straight off your paycheck, and part of it comes from company profits (which your labor helps to produce). You're buying the pension, but you just don't have any control over it. If you want to control a pension - make it grow as fast as the cost of living - you will have to set up your own fund. Subject to certain rules and limits, *contributions* to your private pension fund can be tax free, and you can invest it in a way that suits you. If you're a worrier, you can pick the same kind of low interest securities that the company funds are buried in. Gamblers can put their funds into riskier, high-yield investments. Or, you can tie your pension fund directly to the cost of living.

One way is to distribute investments into fields where you may be most vulnerable to price increases. Are you a renter worried about the cost of apartments in thirty years? Buy the building. Invest in real estate, property management firms, or holding companies. If rentals do go sky high, the profits on your pension fund investments will rise with them. The future price of food bothers you? Invest in the food industry. Your losses in the supermarket will be recouped in the dividend checks. Scared by soaring medical costs? Hospital and drug stocks are soaring just as fast as the costs.

Economists call that *hedging*. Gamblers, investors and farmers do it all the time. Simply put, it's an offsetting transaction that guarantees the investor cannot lose. A bookie can calmly accept a million dollar bet that the National League will win the World Series...and not lose a wink of sleep over the outcome. His hedge is to take an offsetting bet that the American League will win. No matter who wins the series, the bookie collects a million and pays out a million (minus a handling charge of course).

Inflation fighters protect themselves by investing in fields where soaring costs will provide an offsetting profit. Motorists who bought oil stocks have been immune to the pain of higher gasoline prices. What they lose at the pumps, they gain on the stock market.

My own pension plan? A young hardwood forest. A few acres of maple, ash, hickory and beech. It's mostly young stock now, but - by the time we're too infirm to do whatever it is we're doing now - the trees will be worth enough to keep us rocking merrily around the hearth. In the meantime, they get bigger and more valuable every year; pay an interim dividend of winter fuel, spring syrup, and summer building supplies. The price of lumber and fuel inflates along with everything else. There's always a chance that fire and pestilence could cashier the pension prematurely, but that risk is no greater than the company pension disappearing to Rio or into bankruptcy. The future can never be 100% assured, but an inflationary future doesn't seem quite so scary with a pension that grows all by itself.

The Peoples' Pension

The Cadillac of pensions is the indexed model. Payments increase with the cost of living. That's peachy for the person who has one, but there's some argument as to whether society can afford to be that generous. Consequently, few North American workers have access to indexed pensions. For most of us, the only thing that approximates self-inflating pensions are the government models: Social Security in the United States and the Canada Pension Plan.

The catch, for our purposes, is that both these plans require that the would-be retiree be a bona fide, contributing worker. No problem with that. Fair's fair. However, most workers who can now contemplate some form of unsalaried existence have probably already contributed to the public plan during the years of formal, normal work. What portion of that can be salvaged at 65?

The Social Security system is similar to the Pension Plan in Canada in that qualification depends on having had some minimum attachment to the regular work force. Self-employed persons can also contribute. Generally speaking, benefits are available to those retiring at 65 (62 with lower benefits) provided you have contributed for ten years during your career. Survivors and the disabled usually need fewer work credits to qualify for special benefits. The size of the retirement benefit is based on your record of earnings, and is indexed to the cost of living. Social Security has an additional advantage for those with a history of low earnings - under some circumstances, there is a Supplemental Security Income that can provide a larger pension than earnings would normally warrant.

The Canada Pension Plan pays a retirement benefit based on a percentage of pensionable earnings over the period of contributions. In other words, the longer you work, and the higher your salary, the higher will be the pension. If you earn a small income, or work only sporadically, the pension will be reduced accordingly. If your income comes from rentals or investments, or if earned income is less than $3000 (the 1991 exemption), then you aren't required to make any contribution - and neither will you earn any pension credit for that year. If you are self-employed, and earning over $3000, you contribute at a higher rate (4.6%). You don't have to stay in the plan continuously. Moving in and out depends on the level and nature of your earnings. And at the age of 65, your whole work history sets the level of the retirement benefit. After that, it's adjusted each year for cost of living increases.

Canadians who have earned too little to qualify for a maximum CPP pension can fall back on the two universal pension schemes that are not related to earnings. The basic Old Age Security pension, combined with the Guaranteed Income Supplement, are available at the age of 65 regardless of how spotty your work history may be. So Canadians who leave the regular work force early may still receive (at 65) pensions from OAS, GIS, and probably a smaller amount from CPP as well.

Both Social Security and the CPP require contributions in order to maintain coverage. It is very tempting, therefore, to give first priority to a pauper budget and drop out of the contributory plans, hoping that OAS, GIS, trees, or whatever will suffice at 65. There is a strong argument, however, for remaining qualified...if only at the minimum level. Check with your local Social Security or CPP office to see what it would take to keep your own qualification up. It may be no more than a temporary job every few years, or an occasional burst of self-employment. Minimum qualification may not provide much of a retirement pension (remember it's set according to your average earnings), but it does have these advantages.

 ✔ The pension, however small, is tied to inflation and will grow.

 ✔ In addition to retirement benefits, both plans give benefits to widows, widowers, orphans, and the disabled.

 ✔ Not all benefits are earnings related. Death benefits, and the CPP orphan's allowance, for example, pay a standard amount regardless of how little the contributor earned.

 ✔ Social Security qualifiers receive free hospital and low-cost medical coverage under Medicare.

 ✔ Survivors' benefits, under both plans, are a form of "life insurance" for families. It may be cheaper to qualify for this coverage through occasional contributory work than to pay for commercial insurance policies.

LIVING FOR CAESAR

It's a circular logic, self-perpetuating, all-ensnaring - the one-eyed notion that one must work to pay the high cost of living, when in fact that high cost of living is, in great measure, composed of the costs of earning and maintaining high incomes. Like the cart horse who can't give up the wagon because he needs it to carry all the grease and wheels and spare parts the wagon requires, the

216

modern worker feels obliged to cling to the highest salary he can get in order to support a network of insurance policies, pension plans, and government programs that might protect him against the loss of his high salary.

The greatest security is not in having the most, but in needing the least. A simple lifestyle, with a bare-bones budget, is not only cheap in itself, it's also cheap to protect.

11

What Do You Do For a Living?
(and other difficult questions)

Strangers are the worst. People who have worked beside us long enough know better than to ask. It's the well-meaning strangers, attempting innocent small talk, who become most vexing to this sort of life. "And what do you do?" they ask, with a brittle little smile which says that any answer longer than a single sentence would severely try the listener's patience. If there's an exit handy I can answer cricket player, or sheriff, or pope. The usual response is "How interesting". And the inquisitor goes back to the canapés.

Others, whose interest is more genuine, warrant some more truthful explanation. I've tried them all, and none really fit. "Independently wealthy", "independently poor", "domestic economist", "self-employed peasant", all have a measure of truth, but they all begin to sound like smart-assed ways to say that we do nothing at all - and that is certainly *not* the truth.

ARE YOU WORKING?

The last time someone asked me that I answered (truthfully), "Yes, I'm building a house."

"Where?"

"At home. We're building a house for ourselves."

"Oh, I see. You're not really *working* then...?"

In fact, we were working 70 to 80 hours a week creating something useful from stone and timber. In twenty years of various paid labors, I had never worked so hard or accomplished anything so concrete and lasting as that. But in his eyes, and by any economist's definition, it wasn't really work because it wasn't performed in the marketplace. Unlike "real" construction, there was no earning and precious little spending going on. If you don't get paid, it can't be work.

We could dismiss such cock-eyed views as a semantic quibble, if it weren't for the fact that this society places the mantle of virtue only on work of the official, paid variety. The rest of us are said to be "housepersons", "unemployed", "dropouts", even "parasites". Regardless of how we may spend our time, if we aren't actually selling ourselves in the marketplace, the implicit question is; "Can you justify doing 'nothing'?" The semantics of the thing, in fact, create a pressure to work only at those things which consumers are said to demand, whether or not it is rational, sensible, useful work. Thus, the man who is paid to package "pet rocks" for sale is *working* and is accepted as a useful member of society. The man who pays him, and accepts the profit, is a businessman and is seen to be even more virtuous than the worker. The man who takes the rocks and builds himself a house, however, is doing *nothing* in the economist's eyes. If he isn't paid for his labor, then he's unemployed and is subject to conservative scorn and liberal rehabilitations.

Now if I were to go over and build a neighbor's house, while he came here to build mine, I could pay him and he could pay me and we would both be officially *working*. We would have to settle the question of pay, of course. Since we each want the same type of house, I should charge him what he charges me. As long as the price is the same for each, society should accept the deal as fair and praise us both for seeing the light at last and becoming contributing members in good standing in the ranks of the gainfully employed.

So if I gave him a dollar, and he gave me a dollar, everybody would be happy. Right? Well...not really. That would mean that we would both be officially poor - poorly paid and living in cheap housing. Even worse, our one dollar wages would be too low for the government to tax. And our feeble effort would make no perceptible contribution at all to the growth of the Gross National Product. We would officially be giving little more than stagnation to the economy.

Better all around if we agreed to give each other a million dollars for the mutual building effort (by check of course). Now society would honor us as wealthy and successful men. We might even be appointed to boards of directors and government commissions. Our homes would be considered valuable real estate instead of worthless one dollar hovels. The GNP would jump by two million dollars and politicians would rejoice that the economy was recovering. They would also send us each a tax bill for half a million or more. Best of all, we could finally retire to our homes without the need to work at all...having justified ourselves in society's eyes as successful gentlemen of independent means.

Please note that in that entire farce no mention is made of what the houses might really be like. They could be palaces or mud huts. The economist is totally indifferent to quality. If we trade our labor for a million dollars, the economists add two million to the GNP. If we trade for a dollar, we're only worth a dollar. If we each give up the farce and go home to build our own houses, then neither of us is working, and our official worth to society is zero. In actual fact, *what we produce is totally irrelevant. Only the price is counted.*

DOWN WITH THE GNP!

To the economist, a $4.95 pet rock has the same value as a $4.95 dose of polio vaccine. Two pet rocks would be twice as valuable as a single polio shot; and, if society were forced to choose between them, the economist would insist on the pet rocks. The vaccine, at half the value, would be dismissed as an "uneconomic" alternative. It sounds absurd when reduced to that limit; and yet society, led by economists and GNP-worshipping politicians, consistently chooses the profits of quantity over the costs of quality.

Consider the arguments over the use of coal to generate electricity. National planners dismiss solar energy as "uneconomic" and accept coal as the more economic alternative. But how do they decide what is economic and what isn't? Coal burning fouls the air with sulfur compounds that turn to acid in the rain. The air, however, is *free*. That is, air is not metered and controlled in the marketplace. Nobody makes a profit from it. Therefore, say the planners, polluting the air is not to be counted as part of the cost of burning coal. Nor do they count the cost of ruining forests and crops with the fallout - since the forests and crops belong to someone else. If the utility company doesn't have to pay the cost, then the cost does not exist. It could very well be that even if we considered all of the human costs as *real* and gave them dollar values, coal might still be cheaper than the uneconomic alternatives; but that is not the point. The point is that economics is only *one* of the measures of man, and a very inadequate one at that.

Drive through the commercial zones that serve as fast food arteries for every North American suburb and start adding up the multi-billion dollar cost of superfluous baubles. Drive-in burgers, topless bowling, Bar-B-Q, go-cart, thick shake, mini golf, donutty, X-rated, pinball smash-em, blinking, glittering, hollow-brained, pimply, masturbating, overweight, gum-chewing, pornographic glut of commerce that makes up...ta da...GNP!! The Wealth of Nations! The continent could become a coast-to-coast carnival midway and the economists would rejoice at our riches, the politicians would take proud credit for the economic growth. The skies might ooze with acid rain, and the farms that once produced the burgers might be paved, but the economy would be booming. What's good for the GNP is good for the country. The invisible hand of the marketplace knows best. Or does it?

As always, it comes back to choices. I like an occasional burger myself, and I can accept that another might legitimately spend his money on topless bowling, and dismiss the cost of smokestack filters to stop the acid rain as uneconomic. Enforcing my values on the economy is no more acceptable than dictating that we must all chew gum or squeal our tires in the parking lot of the McPimple Burger. That's the price of freedom. But that freedom also implies the right to quit spending, the right to quit earning, the right to be "uneconomic", the right to produce what we value, and to ignore what the marketplace values. Repeat after me:

"There is no shame in choosing to consume less, rather than more."

"There is no shame in choosing to grow vegetables for nothing, rather than bowling for dollars."

"There is no shame in producing art that never sells, rather than kiddie porn that does."

"There is no shame in subtracting from the GNP."

A lady actually told me once, that she was worried about leaving her job. She didn't need the money. She didn't think her job was either interesting or important. She wanted to make time for the things that she did consider important, but those things were not attached to a salary. "How can I justify not working?" she asked. "Does that make me a parasite?" I asked her to ignore salaries for a moment and consider whether society would be better served by what she proposed to do with her retirement, or would it be better served by having another publicist, another civil servant, another hamburger stand, another game show host, another roller derby queen, or another anything else that economists value by their salary rather than by their product. If the product was worthwhile in *human* terms, then to hell with the money. That alone never justified anything. She admitted then that her job was perhaps more parasitical than her retirement. She left her job. No one else has filled it. Society never noticed the difference. The GNP dropped by $20,000 a year and the world was actually better off.

WHAT IF EVERYBODY DID IT?

In the first place, everybody won't. The inventors of capitalism knew what they were doing when they selected greed and envy as the fundamental motivating forces of the system. Only sex is a more potent human impulse, and it's not entirely free of greed and envy either. A preference for consuming less must always be about as popular as celibacy.

Secondly, even if the *doctrine of less* does become more popular, it's the shallow end of the economic pool that empties first. With less money to spend, we didn't give up food, clothing, books, music, health care and the things that really matter. We did, however, quit paying for French wine, credit, life insurance, restaurant lunches, and silly gifts like pet rocks and navel brushes. I daresay half the working population of North America could quit their jobs and the important parts of the economy would keep right on producing food, clothing, health care, and so on. There might be fewer topless bowling emporiums and pet rock salesmen as the shrunken economy sets spending priorities more carefully, but the civilized world wouldn't end. It might even be improved.

Finally, there's the Second Law of Thermodynamics (It's not the final one of course. There are a third and fourth, but the second law is the only one that matters to our economic future.). The Second Law of Thermodynamics shows that many processes are irreversible. Envisage, for example, a locomotive with a head of steam, parked beside an icy pond. The steam in the engine has a great capacity for potential work - pulling trains, pumping out the pond, whatever. Now, if the locomotive ends up in the pond, the total energy in the system remains unchanged. The steam cools off and the pond heats up. But the system has lost the capacity to perform work. The steam is a dribble of tepid water that couldn't pull the train if it tried...not even with the help of the slightly warmer pond. And nothing can reverse the heat transfer and make it work again without the addition of new, outside energy to heat it up to steam again.

What's that got to do with the economic future? In a word, everything. It means that every industrial conversion we make changes some part of the earth's resource to a less useful state. The plastic box around the pet rock has spent the potential of the oil that made it - forever. That loss is universal, eternal, and irreversible. Every bauble and bit of garbage that makes up the world's GNP is a permanent debit against the future. While we go around frantically pushing locomotives into ponds, the economists count them and add the activity to the GNP. The politicians cheer the pushers on, since a higher GNP is the measure of their success. No one asks if that's the best use to make of locomotives. And those of us who decline the chance to participate in the great mass defiance of the Second Law, thank you very much, are treated as virtual traitors to the capitalist cause...not doing our bit for the GNP.

The Second Law is so important that Lord Snow has called it the scientific equivalent of Shakespeare in explaining the human condition. It was the Second Law that convinced me to stop pushing locomotives, but what if everybody in North America did it? What if everybody began consuming less, deliberately damping the economy? The consumer diet - the material fast? Would the Western world really collapse under the stress of moderation?

DOES THE CONSERVER HAVE A PLACE IN THE CAPITALIST ECONOMY?

Given the Second Law and a finite world, the most disturbing aspect of capitalism has to be its essential reliance on growth. According to theory, a capitalist economy must grow to remain healthy, even if the growth itself will ultimately prove malignant. Crudely put, the rationale for growth goes something like this·

Assume we have a simple economy that consists entirely of the production and consumption of gizmos. We consume 100 gizmos a year, and those hundred are produced by ten machines. One machine wears out each year, so the economy must include another factory which turns out one gizmo-making machine per year. The total GNP will be: 100 gizmos plus 1 gizmo machine (replacement).

Now there's a war or a baby boom to start the economy growing, and consumption increases by 10% to 110 gizmos a year. But we only have enough machines to produce 100, so the gizmo machine factory has to *double* its output to cope with a mere ten percent increase in gizmo consumption. Now they must make the usual replacement machine, plus another machine to cope with the growth.

The following year consumption remains stable at 110 gizmos, and the gizmo machine factory goes back to making the single replacement machine required - one gizmo machine instead of last year's two. So stable consumption causes a 50% slump in the machine industry.

The traditional answer to that dilemma has been to encourage continual growth. The overall capitalist economy is stable only when consumption continues to grow. That's why economists cry "recession" even when the economy is producing and consuming more than ever before in the history of the world.

When resources were plentiful and energy was cheap, continual growth was accepted as an adequate short-term solution. Somewhere along the line it got to be a religion and neither OPEC nor Club of Rome calculations* have managed to dissuade western politicians from accelerating down the road to disaster. Accelerating consumption, fed by natural greed and envy, and officially encouraged by the slavish pursuit of an ever-expanding GNP, is a powerful force to thwart. What, then, can one man do?

Until an economic messiah comes along to forever cast GNP out of the temple, the best we can do is conduct our lives conscious of the Second Law and the limits of growth. That means living like conservers, reducing consumption, producing for permanence -even at the expense of short-term profit, putting aside competitive earning and competitive spending in favor of less material measures of satisfaction.

Capitalism is founded on greed and envy. That's not a pejorative slur. It's an accepted part of the creed that the economy performs most efficiently when each man takes as much as he can

*These calculations involved computer models to predict *when,* not if the earth's supply of commonly required resources would disappear at present rates of consumption.

get and gives as little as he must. Each man striving competitively to have more than those around him is supposed to fuel the engine of progress. Greed and envy, far from being vices, are necessary virtues for material success. What, then, is the place of the conserver - who eschews material success? Is a conserver a traitor to the cause?

The obvious answer is that only a few can win in any competition. In the competition for material success there must be losers as well as winners - otherwise, it wouldn't be any fun for the winners, having no one to look down on. So, as long as there have to be losers, it might as well be those of us who aren't that interested in the game in the first place. We're not only part of the system, we're as essential to it as those on top. You can't have mountains without valleys, and you can't enjoy wealth without a few of us down here eating pigeons, getting our furniture from the rich man's junk, and making wine from the sour grapes.

In a more serious vein, it may take a conserver streak in all of us to preserve enough of the earth's energy and resources for our grandchildren to live half as well as we have. Under an ethic where each man takes as much as he can get, those of us who refuse to take more than we need are a small but unapologetic brake on the wasteful excess of consumption. Like a governor on a runaway engine, far from being disloyal to the system, we may in fact be helping to save it from itself.

BUT ISN'T IT UNECONOMIC?

This question is usually directed at what we do rather than what we refuse to do.

Isn't raising your own food uneconomical?
Wouldn't corn be a more profitable crop than trees?
Wouldn't a mobile home be more economical than stone?
Wouldn't a tractor till the garden faster than a pig?

The answer to every such challenge has to be "yes" - as long as you accept the one-sided system of accounting that ignores quality, counts no input or output whose value is not controlled in the marketplace, and takes no responsibility for the future. Under that

225

blinkered view of economics - yes, we're uneconomic.

Let's take those one at a time. Quality first (and the term here includes permanence as well as taste). Yes, despite the fact that stone is free and aluminum siding costly, the time it takes to move the heavy stones around may well make them uneconomical. But stone makes a better house, a more permanent house, an errant baseball will not dent it. There is, however, no provision in modern accounts for quality - only quantity. Just as well the efficiency experts were not involved in the decorating of the Sistine Chapel. I can hear them now, clipboards in hand, peering up at Michaelangelo on the scaffold above..."Mike! Hey Mike! I'm tellin' ya that paint would go on twice as fast with a roller!"

How do you count what's "free"? The marketplace doesn't put a price on good health or even on life itself; and if health and nutrition are ignored, then yes, I suppose raising your own food could be uneconomical. The home grown stuff, however, is free of added sugar, coloring and unpronounceable chemicals that get blamed for everything from cavities to miscarriages. The security of knowing it would never give cancer to a lab rat isn't worth a dime to an economist. If you dismiss that fact, and the terrific taste (which is also free and therefore considered irrelevant), then it would definitely be more economical to spend our gardening time earning a salary and leave nutrition in the hands of Dupont, Kraftco, and wetback labor.

Finally, the accepted ways of deciding what is and what is not economic take no responsibility for the future. Farmers continue to grow corn on shallow topsoil, knowing that the soil itself will be permanently lost or damaged. *This year's* profit counts. Logging companies clear cut vast tracts of forest, stripping the best and leaving the most genericly inferior species to propagate future forests. Profits are calculated on this year's costs.

Even under the current idiocy of ignoring all costs that can't be measured in dollars, many essential activities persist despite their "uneconomic" character. Farming for instance. At the end of 1986 the average Canadian farmer had $374,206 invested on the business end of his 572 acres. The net return. .$16,718. That's a return of less than 5% at a time when banks were getting 13% on prime rate loans. The economic thing for farmers to do would be to forget about raising food and go into the lending business instead. That would be a human disaster, but sound economics according to the official wisdom.

226

Under the circumstances, I've never felt either foolish or guilty for behaving "uneconomically".

WHAT DOES IT FEEL LIKE TO BE POOR?

Having never considered ourselves poor, the question always seems to be misdirected; and yet folks who have more money than us invariably wonder. Perhaps a better question would be: how do we manage to feel so rich with so little money?

The difference between feeling rich and feeling poor has little to do with how much is consumed, but a great deal to do with how it's consumed. Ironically, it's deprivation, more than anything else, that seems to enhance the appreciation of material things. The surest way to appreciate anything is a bit of self-denial. *The material fast.*

One night last summer, we sat down to a particularly sumptuous family meal. The centerpiece was a platter-sized rainbow trout, garnished with cherry tomatoes and salad things. There was hot buttered corn on the cob, peas and tiny green beans, kohlrabi and cucumber - everything taken from the garden less than thirty minutes before the meal. There was a loaf of bread still hot from the oven, a bottle of chilled white wine, and fresh raspberries and cream for dessert. The highlight of the meal? The choicest morsel at the feast?...A few lowly potatoes! Steamed in their skins and served whole, without even so much as a lick of butter and salt to tart them up. We're not addicted to potatoes, and two days later they were just a part of the culinary furniture again - no more remarkable than the butter on the bread. What made them so special in the midst of all that mouth watering fare? The winter stock of old potatoes ran out in the spring. For four months we did not taste a single potato, and this special treat was the very first batch of new summer potatoes. Tasty enough at any time, but with appreciation honed by a four month potato "fast", it seemed like the richest food at the table.

Strangely enough, even economists accept this view of wealth as a relative feeling. "Diminishing marginal utility" is one term used to describe the concept. In plain English, that means that a hungry man's first steak is of very great value to him. The second one served is slightly less useful, and the one-hundredth steak at the meal earns nowhere near the appreciation that the first one did. At some point beyond saturation, the arrival of still more steaks can get to be an absolute nuisance. It sounds so obvious when stated like that, and yet eyebrows still arc incredulously when I say that it's easier to feel material satisfaction (wealth) by limiting consumption than by extending it. The material glutton has reduced all of his marginal pleasures to zero. He dines on nothing but the one-hundredth steak and never knows the joys of the first one. How many rich men can enjoy a potato?

MAN AS PEACOCK - AND FRIGHTENED PEACOCK

Consumption is not all there is to wealth of course. There is also the display of wealth, and the security it purports to bring, that compel some men to material success. The display of wealth can be even more important than its consumption. It's what Western man has chosen as the basis of his hierarchy. The conserver has the choice of finding satisfaction at the bottom of the hierarchy, or refusing to participate in the peacock game - displaying something else besides wealth as the measure of his worth.

The urge to display is insidious, partly because it can be hard to recognize. We pretend to shop for quality and satisfaction when the more honest criterion is the social status of the acquisition. Houses, clothes, cars, even holiday destinations are as often chosen for their display value as they are for their intrinsic values.

Once upon a time we considered living on a boat. The initial impetus was pure conserver thinking: life aboard dispensed with the most expensive part of landlubber housing, the need to occupy real estate. Also boats were cheaper than houses. In the course of this research we made connections with a yacht broker - a genuine teak and mahogany, absinth on the poop deck, how are things in Ibiza, yacht broker. It took awhile, but we eventually realized that getting mail from our yacht broker (and better still making mention of the fact) was a lot more fun than the thought of actually living on the water. We kept the broker going for two more years after realizing that he did as much for the sheen on our tail feathers as any old boat could do, and it only cost an occasional stamp.

Preening is part of the impetus for material success. Security, however, is the essence of that drive. For many materially driven men, there can be no such thing as having *enough*. The goal is to have more than his peers, and more again to protect that status from any possible incursions against the wealth. *Enough* means having enough to withstand the loss of income, inflation, old age, recession, black plague and infidels without losing his number one status. Enough never comes, so materially driven man can never stop. And the more he has, the more he has to protect.

I know a man who, at twenty, planned his life so he could retire at forty. The initial plan was to take the highest paying jobs he could find, regardless of whether they were interesting or satisfying. He intended to spend as little as possible, maximize his savings, and invest them. The investment dividends would eventually provide a liveable income for early retirement. Gradually the goal changed so that the dividends would have to do more than simply provide for family needs; now it was thought necessary to replace current earnings (which were much higher than needs). Then, as that goal was reached, it was raised again to accomodate the possible effects of future inflation. Each level of success is not recognized as a greater security, but as a new responsibility - the more he accumulates, the more he has to protect by accumulating even more wealth. His fortieth birthday is long past now, and retirement (and the plans for working at the jobs he was really interested in) is still a distant dream.

THE TRAGEDY OF MATERIAL MAN

The drive for material success is fundamentally based on aggressive competition and material acquisition. But true satisfaction is impossible under those rules. Material man compares himself to his peers - who always have more than he does. When material man exercises his greed and envy with greater skill, he achieves even more material success...and compares himself to a new set of peers. His new peers, again, have more than he does. Although you may be working overtime to keep up with the Joneses, the Joneses don't compare themselves to you and feel rich. They compare themselves to the Rockefellers and feel poor. Only at the very pinnacle of material success can greed and envy be satisfied. But even there - especially there - at the very top of the money heap, success is incapable of buying peace. For it's never enough to win - the winner must forever defend his spoils from all of the envious strivers beneath him.

The tragedy of material man is his inability to ever say "enough". When material needs are established only in relation to what others have, irrespective of what little is really needed to be warm and well fed, then needs can never be satisfied. Conservers don't come from any higher spiritual plane, free from greed and envy. They have merely reached the point of admitting that they really don't need more *things*. *They have reached the point of "enough"*.

WHAT KIND OF PEOPLE WOULD DO SUCH A THING?

Greed and envy are powerful forces, not easily restrained. What is it then that is powerful enough to pull us in another direction? To say that material ambition is a futile, or even a silly competition - akin to running the bulls in Pamplona or squealing tires at the McPimple Burger - is simply not enough. What else, besides disillusionment, causes people to pin mistletoe to their coat tails and walk out the door to do something else?

Each man is driven by his own little engine (or "different drummer" in Thoreau's more poetic world), and these suppositions may only be valid for one, but it seems to be that those who have walked away from salaries and survived have had two characteristics in common: strong personal goals, and a sense of their own mortality.

Personal goals, for a lucky few, can be pursued entirely through paid employment. At some point, however, those who set out to achieve something else in the world feel the constraints of the employer's rules, the employer's interests, the employer's inarguable right to direct the work towards *his* own goals. Breaking away successfully invariably involves positive rather than negative motives. Leaving a job to devote full time and energy to other goals works. Leaving a job only because the job is a bore, leads too often to another boring job.

The only problem with a regular job is that it can begin to get in the way of more important things. Sooner or later, people with those strong personal goals find that evenings and weekends just aren't enough. The choice is to hang onto the job and hope it gets better, or follow the path that interests you, regardless of what - if anything - it pays. Some meet more success by leaving jobs than by keeping them. Babe Ruth could have stuck it out as a bartender, and Howard Cosell was once a lawyer. Albert Einstein was a clerk, Golda Meir a schoolteacher. Quitters all. Others of us may never attain that much by leaving vocations for avocations. All we can manage is the joy and satisfaction of trying.

Doing what's important - and damn the pay - smacks of youthful rebellion. It's as likely, however, to strike in middle age. In the first place, it takes years of salaried toil (and perhaps an early taste of material success) to fully realize that that kind of success is not always everything it promised to be. It's hard to abandon financial security without first having had some, and seen that it is not enough. More importantly, the young so rarely have a sense of their own mortality. At twenty-five there seems to be plenty of time ahead to have a career for money, a second career later for interest, a family, leisure, travel - anything is possible. At thirty-five, or forty-five, death seems to be possible - even probable. All the unfilled dreams begin to niggle at the back of your sleep. All the things you were going to do with your life. All the important things, are still waiting for the time to do them, and the future isn't somewhere over the horizon anymore. It's here and now...or never.

WHY BOTHER?

The tragedy of the industrial age has been the overwhelming dominance of consumption as the measure of man. Even work - each man's art, creation, contribution to the world - has come to be measured not by its quality or human worth, but by its commercial value. *What is it worth in trade for consumable goods?* I am what I am paid. I am what I consume. I spend, therefore I am. Like so many swine, we've allowed the economists to define us and rank us by our basest animal instinct - our appetites.

It's a small act. Each conserver's individual declaration of independence from Mammon's frenetic hierarchy of consumer envy and material ambition is not a world-shaking trend. It's not even a socially responsible act in the eyes of many. They are the ones who cannot believe that work can be done for a spiritual purpose. To them, the material measure is the *only* one. If you don't get paid, it isn't work.

Surviving without a salary is not the denial of work's importance. Quite the contrary. It is the celebration of work - real work -as a human act whose value is intrinsic, irrespective of its value in the consumer market. We do our work in our own small way, not because Mammon pays us, but because it makes us human.